Citizenship across Borders

Citizenship across Borders

The Political Transnationalism of *El Migrante*

Michael Peter Smith and **Matt Bakker**

Cornell University Press *Ithaca and London*

First published 2008 by Cornell University Press
First printing, Cornell Paperbacks, 2008

Printed in the United States of America

Library of Congress Cataloging-in-Publication Data

Smith, Michael P.
    Citizenship across borders : the political transnationalism of el migrante / Michael Peter Smith and Matt Bakker.
        p. cm.
    Includes bibliographical references and index.
    ISBN 978-0-8014-4608-5 (cloth : alk. paper) —
    ISBN 978-08014-7390-6 (pbk. : alk. paper)
    1. Transnationalism—Political aspects—United States.   2. Transnationalism—Political aspects—Mexico.   3. Immigrants—United States—Political activity.   4. Mexican Americans—Politics and government.   5. Citizenship—United States.   6. Citizenship—Mexico.   7. United States—Emigration and immigration—Political aspects.   8. Mexico—Emigration and immigration—Political aspects.   I. Bakker, Matt, 1971–   II. Title.
    JV6477.S65 2008
    323.6'3—dc22   2007028872

Cornell University Press strives to use environmentally responsible suppliers and materials to the fullest extent possible in the publishing of its books. Such materials include vegetable-based, low-VOC inks and acid-free papers that are recycled, totally chlorine-free, or partly composed of nonwood fibers. For further information, visit our website at www.cornellpress.cornell.edu.

Cloth printing   10   9   8   7   6   5   4   3   2   1
Paperback printing   10   9   8   7   6   5   4   3   2   1

Contents

Part 4

The Two Faces of Transnational Citizenship

Acknowledgments

This book has been seven years in the making. It would not have been possible without the willingness of our interview subjects to tell us their stories of transnational political engagement. We especially wish to thank the main protagonists of our five case studies, migrant political activists Ángel Calderón, Andrés Bermúdez Viramontes, Guadalupe Gómez, Efraín Jiménez, Martha Jiménez, and Manuel de la Cruz. We also wish to thank the *jerezano* activist Raymundo Carrillo and each of the other migrants, Mexican government officials, and other interview subjects who shared their time and perspectives with us.

Over the course of this project we have amassed many debts to friends and colleagues, both near and far. At times these intellectual networks seemed to stretch as far as those of the transnational migrants we studied. Closest to home, and doubtless our most compelling debt is owed to our colleague Fred Block, of the sociology department at the University of California, Davis, who provided generous critical comments and support throughout the *longue durée* of our project. Luis Guarnizo and Ming-cheng Lo, also members of the intellectual community at Davis, provided very helpful comments on selected parts of the book. Louis DeSipio, a political scientist at the University of California, Irvine, provided us with insightful comments and suggestions in two rounds of reviews of our manuscript. Greta Gilbertson of the Department of Sociology and Anthropology at Fordham University also provided a helpful review of the manuscript.

As the manuscript was being developed, portions of it were previewed in various venues, professional conferences, and journals. These earlier efforts benefited from the incisive comments of colleagues from Britain, Mexico, Canada, Hong Kong, Germany, Spain, Denmark, and the United States.

Steven Vertovec invited Michael Smith to spend a portion of his sabbatical in 2005 as a Visiting Scholar at the Centre on Migration, Policy, and Society at the University of Oxford, providing the opportunity to write and present research that was a precursor to parts of this book. While there, Smith received helpful commentary from many migration researchers. He especially benefited from his many thought-provoking exchanges on transnational politics in the receiving context with Davide Peró, now at the University of Nottingham.

That same year Alan Smart of the University of Calgary invited Smith to be the featured speaker at an interlocutor session of the Society for Urban, National, Transnational/Global Anthropology at a conference in Santa Fe where the theoretical reflections on contextualizing dual identities and loyalties deployed in this book were first explored. Useful critical commentaries on these ideas were offered by anthropologists Gordon Mathews of the Chinese University of Hong Kong, Nina Glick Schiller of the University of New Hampshire and the Max Planck Institute of Social Anthropology, and Robert Rotenberg of DePaul University.

Matt Bakker received similarly helpful comments on portions of this manuscript from numerous transnational scholars at the Segundo Coloquio Internacional sobre Migración y Desarrollo held in Morelos, Mexico, in 2006. Especially useful were the comments of Luin Goldring of York University, Miguel Moctezuma of the Universidad Autónoma de Zacatecas, Eva Østergaard-Nielsen of the Universitat Autónoma de Barcelona, and Ninna Nyberg Sørensen, who is now at the Programa Regional de Dinamarca para Centroamérica in Guatemala. Our analysis of the transnational politics of the Tomato King benefited from the anonymous journal reviews done for *Global Networks* and *Migraciones Internacionales*, for which we would like to thank Alisdair Rogers at Oxford and Rafael Alarcón of the Colegio de la Frontera Norte.

At critical junctures over the years, this book has benefited from the research support provided by a number of indispensable research associates and colleagues. Postgraduate researcher Gustavo Galindo provided valuable field research assistance during the Guanajuato stage of the research. This portion of the research also benefited from a collaborative ethnographic interview conducted by Remedios Gómez Arnau from the Centro de Investigaciones sobre América del Norte at the Universidad Nacional Autónoma de México. Our research in Zacatecas benefited from the critical assessments offered over the years by Zacatecan development scholars Raúl Delgado Wise, Rodolfo García Zamora, and Miguel Moctezuma Longoria. In the final stages of our book, we have been grateful to Leticia Jáuregui Casanueva, a community development graduate student at the University of California, Davis, for her extensive and invaluable editorial and research assistance. Peggy Hauselt timely prepared the four maps included in the text. Our thanks are also extended to Peter Wissoker, our editor at Cornell University Press, for his support and editorial management of this project and to Susan Specter and Karen Hwa at the Press for all the work they have done to help bring this book into being. Katy Meigs improved the final manuscript through her excellent copyediting.

We would like to thank UC MEXUS (University of California Institute for Mexico and the United States) for the generous financial support they provided for field research conducted in California and Guanajuato (2000–2002) and California and Zacatecas (2004–5). Although most of this book is newly published, some chapters have drawn on portions of our previously published work that have been substantially revised for this book. We are grateful to the editors and publishers for permission to use selected materials from our research that appeared in the following journals: Matt Bakker and Michael Peter Smith, "*El Rey del Tomate*: Migrant Political Transnationalism and Democratization in Mexico," *Migraciones Internacionales* 4 (2003): 59–83; Michael Peter Smith, "Transnationalism, the State, and the Extraterritorial Citizen," *Politics and Society* 31, no. 4 (December 2003): 467–502; "The Social Construction of Transnational Citizenship," *Journal of International Law and Policy* (Spring 2003): 105–25; "Transnationalism and Citizenship," in *Approaching Transnationalisms*, ed. Brenda Yeoh, Michael W. Charney, and T. C. Kiong (Boston: Kluwer Academic, 2003): 15–38; "Power in Place/Places of Power: Contextualizing Transnational Research," *City and Society* 17, no. 1 (2005): 5–34; "From Context to Text and Back Again: The Uses of Transnational Urbanism," *City and Society* 17, no. 1 (2005): 81–92; "The Two Faces of Transnational Citizenship," *Ethnic and Racial Studies* (forthcoming); and Michael Peter Smith and Matt Bakker, "The Transnational Politics of the Tomato King: Meaning and Impact," *Global Networks* 5, no. 2 (2005): 129–47.

In closing, Matt Bakker would like to express his sincere gratitude to all the members of his family. Their enduring support even through the rockiest of times have made his intellectual formation possible. Above all, he thanks María Luisa, Braulio, and Caramelo, *presentes en la ausencia*, whose love and energy see no borders.

Michael Smith dedicates this book, with love, to his wife Pat. She has given him the time to write and the courage to endure. Her artistic vision and photographer's eye have contributed greatly to our field research. For all of this, and for so much more, he is eternally grateful.

Acronyms

CDPME	Coalición por los Derechos Políticos de los Mexicanos en el Exterior (Coalition for the Political Rights of Mexicans Abroad)
CHDC	California Human Development Corporation
CHIRLA	Coalition for Humane Immigrant Rights of Los Angeles
CIC	Centro Interuniversitario del Conocimiento (Interuniversity Knowledge Center)
CISAN	Centro de Investigaciones sobre América del Norte (Center for North American Studies)
COESPO	Consejo Estatal de Población de Guanajuato (Guanajuato State Population Council)
DACGE	Dirección de Atención a Comunidades Guanajuatenses en el Extranjero (Program for Attending to Guanajuatense Communities Abroad)
FCZ	Frente Cívico Zacatecano (Zacatecan Civic Front)
FCZSC	Federación de Clubes Zacatecanos del Sur de California (Zacatecan Federation of Hometown Associations of Southern California)
G8	Group of Eight
HTA(s)	Hometown Association(s)
IADB	Inter-American Development Bank
IFE	Instituto Federal Electoral (Federal Electoral Institute)
IME	Instituto de Mexicanos en el Exterior (Institute of Mexicans Abroad)
IMF	International Monetary Fund
INEGI	Instituto Nacional de Estadística, Geografía e Informática (National Institute of Geography, Statistics and Information)
INS	Immigration and Naturalization Service

MALDEF	Mexican American Legal Defense and Education Fund
MIF	Multilateral Investment Fund
NAFTA	North American Free Trade Agreement
NALEO	National Association of Latino Elected and Appointed Officials
OEAMs	Oficinas Estatales de Atención a Migrantes (State Offices for Attending to Migrants)
OPME	Oficina Presidencial de Atención a Migrantes en el Exterior (Presidential Office for Mexicans Living Abroad)
P4P	Partnership for Prosperity
PAN	Partido Acción Nacional (National Action Party)
PCME	El Programa para las Comunidades Mexicanas en el Exterior (Program for Mexican Communities Abroad)
PRD	Partido de la Revolución Democrática (Party of the Democratic Revolution)
PRI	Partido Revolucionario Institucional (Revolutionary Institutional Party)
SEDESOL	Secretaría de Desarrollo Social (Secretariat of Social Development)
TRIFE	Tribunal Electoral del Poder Judicial de la Federación (Federal Electoral Tribunal)
UAZ	Universidad Autónoma de Zacatecas (Autonomous University of Zacatecas)
UC MEXUS	University of California Institute for Mexico and the United States
UNAM	Universidad Nacional Autónoma de México (National Autonomous University of Mexico)

PART 1

||||||||||||||||||||||||||||||||||||||||||||||||||||||||||||||||||||||||||||||||||||||||||||||||||||||||||||||||||||

Setting the Stage

1 The Politics of Transnational Citizenship

> Perhaps the primary cultural consequence of transnational dias-
> pora life is that it necessarily stretches the idea of national belong-
> ing by disengaging it from its presumed territorial and linguistic
> imperative, de-centering it in relation to any putative "core" values
> or marks of greater or lesser "authenticity."
>
> JUAN FLORES, "The Diaspora Strikes Back:
> Reflections on Cultural Remittances"

Discourses on the rights, entitlements, and obligations of citizenship have
changed dramatically in the past two decades as a result of the increasingly
transnational character of global migration flows, cultural networks, and
sociopolitical practices. The once taken-for-granted correspondence between citizenship, nation, and state has been called into question as new
forms of grassroots citizenship have taken on an increasingly transterritorial character. Resident noncitizens now routinely live and work in transnational cities throughout the world, while maintaining social and political
networks that link them to people and places in their countries and communities of origin.

At the same time, the rise of supranational institutional networks that
promote the neoliberal globalization project and the spread of international agencies that promote the discourse on human rights also challenge
received notions of state sovereignty and the rights associated with national
citizenship. Thus, for example, some scholars (e.g., Soysal 1994; Held 1991)
now depict the activities of international human rights agencies and the development of supranational authority structures such as the European
Union as signs of a new international order premised on the creation of
plural authority and "transnational citizenship." What sense can we make
of these developments? What do they mean for the future of the nation-
state? What prospects do they hold for the future of localities that become

interconnected across borders by political practices and networks that span national borders?

Contextualizing Transnational Research

In this book we draw extensively on five years of community-based ethnography on the practices of U.S.-Mexican transnational citizenship, while expanding the space of "community" to encompass the multiple cross-border locations in which our ethnographic subjects are orchestrating their political lives transnationally. How can we appropriately contextualize this sort of global or transnational ethnography (see Burawoy et al. 2000; M. P. Smith 2001) when the principal metatheories used to frame ethnographic narratives in terms of "structured wholes" have lost intellectual purchase? We take as a starting point the call made by the anthropologist George Marcus to find new ways of "imagining the whole" in a period when the grand narratives of systems theorists have lost their capacity to inform our understandings of how the world works (Marcus 1989, 7–30). In an essay by that same name Marcus called for the development of an ethnography of *places* and their interconnections rather than a place-focused ethnography of single locales. He argues that "an ethnography of complex connections, itself, becomes the means of producing a narrative that is both micro and macro, and neither one particularly" (1989, 24). The shift from place to places, simultaneously and complexly interconnected by intended and unintended consequences, Marcus argues, requires three methodological moves: (1) the use of multilocale ethnography, (2) attention to networks of complex connections and to their simultaneous, reciprocal effects, and (3) an effort to contextualize the connections studied in terms of the sorts of "wider wholes" in which the connections and their effects are taking place.

In this book we seek to gain contextual clarity by combining the qualitative richness of transnational ethnography with political-economic and institutional analysis of neoliberal globalization and state restructuring processes across the U.S.-Mexican border. In conceptualizing the "wider wholes" that might best inform our ethnographic account of U.S.-Mexican political transnationalism, we have identified four distinct types of context that must be kept in mind. Each affects the opportunities and constraints experienced by our ethnographic subjects. These four contexts reciprocally affect each other. They help to situate our ethnographic subjects and mediate their transnational practices in the multiple, interconnected places in which the actors we have interviewed are orchestrating their lives.

1. The *political-economic context*, now called neoliberal globalization, creates conditions necessitating, facilitating, or impeding migration

and return migration across the two-thousand-mile-long U.S.-Mexican border.

2. The *historical context* germane to the study of migrant political transnationalism includes the historical development of interstate relations between the United States and Mexico, the changing contexts of reception and exit at different historical periods, and the changing state-policy frameworks that have affected the practices of transnational migration and citizenship inclusion and exclusion across the Mexico-U.S. border.

3. The *sociocultural context* also is a key element in the formation and continuity of migration patterns over time and from place to place. The historical particularities of migrant recruitment, migration histories, migratory narratives, and changing gender and class relations all affect the character and geography of transnational migration between the United States and Mexico, determining who migrates, where they come from, and where they go. These sociocultural forces have affected the social structures of community formation on both sides of the border as well as in the transnational social spaces where new modes of political activism across borders are being enacted.

4. The prevailing *institutional context* sets up opportunities and barriers that our ethnographic subjects must accommodate to or resist, as they attempt to politically construct new spaces for practicing citizenship across borders. This institutional context includes: (1) the legal framework of permissions and constraints governing access to citizenship and dual citizenship rights in both countries; (2) the prevailing political cultures surrounding those institutional arrangements; (3) the practices of established political institutions, including political parties, interest groups, and local and regional states in both countries, and the effects of these institutional practices on political incorporation and exclusion; and (4) the rise of new grassroots political formations such as transnational social movements and migrant hometown associations (HTAs) that have become politicized in the face of state-sponsored neoliberal governmentality.

In the extended case studies that form the basis of our book, the interactions of Mexican migrant transnational activists, their hometown and home-state associations, and their electoral candidates with state-centered agencies of national, regional, and local governments are situated in a particular political-economic context of neoliberal governmentality. The North American neoliberal project has produced a historically contradictory form of U.S.-Mexican economic integration in which expanded capital mobility fueled by the North American Free Trade Agreement (NAFTA) has been accompanied by increased militarization of the U.S.-Mexican border—now punctuated by the planned construction of a several-hundred-mile-long border fence—that attempts to symbolically and materially restrict the mobility of Mexican migrants despite the continuing economic demand for their labor across the international divide.

The increasingly obvious contradictions of these state policies are circumscribed within a post-9/11 geopolitical terrain characterized by a single-minded preoccupation with transnational terrorism. In this context of changed political reality in the United States, the present possibilities for resolving this contradiction appear limited to alternative versions of highly restrictive guest-worker schemes. The limitations of such proposals are only too obvious to migrants and their advocates who complain that most guest-worker programs would delink Mexican migration from the normal routes to U.S. citizenship, trapping migrants in a permanent nonimmigrant status with little or no political rights.

Political changes within Mexico must also be contextualized historically, socioculturally, and institutionally. On the one hand, the Mexican state's neoliberal turn has ushered in an elaborate consolidation of state policies toward migrants. This has been designed largely to co-opt migrants into supporting the state's neoliberal policy priorities. On the other hand, the neoliberal turn has also been accompanied by a certain degree of democratization of the Mexican political system, which was previously characterized by a highly authoritarian form of corporatism dominated by a single party-state. As party politics in Mexico have become more open and competitive, new opportunities have been created for grassroots participation of all sorts, including that of transnational migrant activists and their associations as interest group claimants, electoral activists, and candidates.

The hometown associations established by Mexican migrants have taken advantage of the emergence of these new political spaces. These HTAs were not originally created for political purposes. In fact, self-organized migrant HTAs, which date back at least to the 1950s, initially served sociocultural purposes, reinforcing social ties and creating a sense of translocal community solidarity. Some explicitly eschewed political engagement in either Mexico or the United States. The HTAs' apolitical stance toward the Mexican political arena was prompted by some leaders' deep mistrust of the corporatist political culture of Mexico and a desire to avoid cooptation by the Partido Revolucionario Institucional (PRI, Revolutionary Institutional Party) state apparatus. Their reluctance to become engaged in U.S. politics was in part a result of concerns that such engagement might jeopardize their tax-exempt status as nonprofit organizations (Zabin and Escala Rabadán 1998).

Up until the last two decades, HTAs relied largely on voluntary donations and fundraising activities among their *paisanos* in the United States to carry out a range of philanthropic activities for the betterment of their communities of origin. These included emergency assistance after natural disasters, sending money to needy families, constructing sports and recreation facilities, renovating churches and public plazas, and contributing to public works projects such as building roads, health clinics, and school facilities (see Mestries 1998). These philanthropic activities, which were organized by HTA leaders, not only generated resources for community betterment projects but helped to bring a much larger pool of paisanos together, reactivating the sources of their cultural identity and strengthening their claims to community membership in the localities they had left behind (González Gutiérrez 1995; Mestries 1998; see also R. Smith 1998, 2005; Rivera-Salgado 1999; and Fitzgerald 2000).

Beginning in the 1980s the PRI-dominated Mexican state took notice of the effects these migrant organizations were having on community betterment in their home communities and of the inroads that opposition political parties were making on the U.S. side of the border. It thus began to develop the coherent set of migrant reincorporation policies that we detail in chapter 2. A key dimension of these policies focused squarely on HTAs, promoting their expansion, consolidating them into larger state-level federations, and channeling them into transnational public-private partnerships. This was not a one-way flow of state-directed initiatives. Pressures from migrant organizations were also a key element in the changing political opportunity structure and the new forms of state-migrant relations that emerged over the last two decades.

By the late 1980s, Mexican HTAs had overcome their reluctance to enter the political arena. This was particularly obvious among migrant leaders from Greater Los Angeles who had formed a federation of HTAs from the state of Zacatecas. These migrant leaders took advantage of a new opportunity for collaboration between their federation and the Zacatecan state government to pressure the PRI governor, Genaro Borrego (1986–92), who had sought improved ties with the migrants, to promote federal legislation attentive to the human and social rights of migrants and their families. This political stance adopted by the Zacatecan migrant leaders led to a significant legislative victory, namely the formation of the Paisano Program, which strengthened the migrant leaders' sense of political efficacy and encouraged the Zacatecan federation leaders to become further engaged in transnational politics in Zacatecas. This enhanced sense of political efficacy, combined with the everyday problems and barriers to social mobility encountered by Mexican migrants in the United States, have prompted them to also become increasingly engaged in political life on the U.S. side of the border. In short, the migrant activists at the heart of our extended case studies have helped to usher in a new social space of transnational political engagement.

The Polemics of Resurgent Nationalism and Incipient Postnationalism

These new modes of transnational political practice have provoked a lively debate throughout the social sciences on how these cross-border political currents are affecting our taken-for-granted categories of citizenship, national identity, and cultural belonging. In light of heightened political, economic, and cultural interconnectivity across national borders, some have suggested that the political boundaries of the nation-state are being disrupted and a new epoch in the history of national identity formation is coming into being. The growing prevalence of dual-citizenship arrangements and the rise of international norms of personhood are seen by some as weakening the capacity of receiving nations to orient the lives, loyalties, and identities of such categories of newcomers as transnational migrants and guest workers. A considerable amount of scholarly writing has tended to address this issue in fairly black-and-white terms. For example, Benedict Anderson (1994, 1998), author of the classic work on "imagined communities" (Anderson 1983), has warned of the dangers he sees in the activities of transnational political activists who practice a kind of unaccountable "long-distance nationalism." Anderson's pessimistic reading is shaped by his selective use of evidence, such as highlighting the case of those Croatians who lived in Bosnia and in the United States but helped finance and bring to power the Croatian nationalist Franjo Tudjman as Yugoslavia dissolved. At the same time, Anderson studiously avoids any discussion of transnational social networks whose practices have helped to open up previously one-party-dominant states, as with the political role played by U.S.-based Mexican migrants in changing the political culture of contemporary Mexico.

In a somewhat different vein, in her book *Limits of Citizenship*, Yasemin Soysal (1994) tries to make the case that the prerogatives of national citizenship are being undermined by the global diffusion of widely held international norms of personhood and by the construction of a "postnational" European citizenship. Although this argument about the "unbounding" of national citizenship is different from Anderson's skeptical view, Soysal, like Anderson, advances her argument by selectively presenting evidence. She sees such postnational norms as operating to extend economic and political rights to guest workers in Europe, while ignoring or overlooking the exclusions and racialized imaginary around which a common European identity is being constructed.

These two discourses differ sharply in emphasis. Anderson recognizes the extraterritorial exercise of *national* citizenship, which he views with great skepticism. Soysal celebrates the *transcendence* of national citizenship by the emergence of a postnational legal and normative order. Despite their differences in substance and tone, both Soysal and Anderson frame their arguments in a way that creates the impression that an entirely new global structural dynamic is inexorably changing the world. For Anderson this structural dynamic is the spread of new communication and transportation technologies that are facilitating long-distance nationalism; for Soysal it is the emergent international human rights regime on a global scale that has ushered in a postnational political order. In both instances global forces drive local outcomes, with territorially based national identity formation losing ground to globalizing tendencies.

This discourse on the impact of globalizing trends on national identity formation also permeates the literature on transnational migration and its effects. Key texts in this literature have posited a world in which the transnational or postnational identities assumed by migrants to advanced postindustrial societies are diminishing the capacity of the latter to assimilate the former, both culturally and politically. This claim has too often been deployed at a theoretical, if not polemical, level, detached from empirical research into the political practices of transnational migrants and their experiences with dual citizenship. Two prominent cases are political scientist Samuel Huntington and anthropologist Arjun Appadurai. The former decries what he calls a growing trend toward the nonassimilation of U.S. immigrants, particularly migrants from Mexico, and calls for a resurgent nationalism to restore American patriotism and civic virtue. The latter celebrates what he posits as a similar trend, underlining the putatively liberating experience of "postnationality" by third-world migrants. Though these thinkers share little else in common, they both ignore a growing body of empirical work on the actual practices of dual citizenship and the capacities of transnational migrants to simultaneously become politically engaged citizens of their new countries while maintaining enduring transnational socioeconomic and political ties (see, for example, Østergaard-Nielsen 2003a, 2003b; M. P. Smith 2003b; Guarnizo, Portes, and Haller 2003; Levitt 2004; Levitt and Glick Schiller 2004).

In the most controversial part of his recent book, *Who Are We?* (2004b), derived from his polemical essay "The Hispanic Challenge" (2004a), Huntington represents Mexican migration as a special case of nonassimilation to "the American Creed," a series of civic virtues derived, in his view, from America's Anglo-Protestant cultural heritage. The story arc of *Who Are We?*

is punctuated by numerous lists of causes and effects of the decline of U.S. national identity, ranging from the perverse effects of the cosmopolitan identities and globalizing vision promoted by U.S. elite groups to the "other-nationalism" exhibited by a group of Mexican migrants who waved Mexican flags while watching a Confederation of North, Central American, and Caribbean Football Gold Cup soccer match between the United States and Mexico in Los Angeles in 1998 (2004b, 5). The book contains so many lists of perceived subnational, transnational, and "other-national" threats to the development of patriotic American identities that one reviewer has described it as "a 400-page PowerPoint presentation." (Kakutani 2004, B36)

Be that as it may, in his discussion of Mexican migration, in both works Huntington (2004a, 33–36; 2004b, 221–30) posits a list of six attributes of what he calls "the Mexican problem" of cultural isolation and nonassimilation. These attributes are: (1) the contiguity of the two-thousand-mile land border between Mexico and the United States; (2) the spatial concentration of Mexican migrants in the Southwest, particularly in southern California; (3) the large scale of Mexican migration; (4) a "persistent" Mexican migration, uninterrupted by war, economic change, or restrictive legislation; (5) their "historical presence," a shorthand marker for his unsupported claim that today's Mexican migrants "can and do make . . . a historical claim to American territory" in the Southwest because of their deep-seated memories of the U.S. annexation of this region following the Mexican-American War (2004b, 229); and (6) the "illegality" of contemporary Mexican migrants.

Out of these attributes Huntington constructs a narrative in which Mexican immigration poses unique challenges to U.S. national identity. He claims that "Cultural America" is under siege by a massive "illegal demographic invasion" by Mexicans that is comparable to a military invasion (2004b, 12, 318). He calls on his fellow Americans to resist the cultural "bifurcation" posed by this "invasion." He even claims that the bilingualism and biculturalism of Mexican immigrants, which many see as signs of successful integration into a multicultural society, are indicators of the retention of the Spanish language across immigrant generations and thus barriers to socialization into the Anglo-Protestant creed. The bedrock creed, in turn, is defined in terms of mastery of the English language, Protestant religiosity, and commitment to the rule of law and to "dissenting" Protestant values of "individualism and the work ethic" (2004b, 62–69).

Huntington is critical of contemporary immigrants in general, whom he labels "ampersands" who maintain "dual loyalties and dual citizenships" (2004b, 204–13). But he reserves his wrath for Mexicans. He constructs today's Mexican migrants as unitary, undifferentiated subjects who have failed to assimilate because of "their" low educational and economic "activity," their "creeping bilingualism" (2004b, 319), and their spatial concentration and cultural isolation in southwestern and southern California ethnic enclaves that he views, again without evidence, as constituting endogenous cultural communities (see 2004b, 230–47).

Aside from the two-thousand-mile-long land border and the scale of Mexican migration, the entire set of assumptions on which Huntington's argument rests has been vigorously contested by social science researchers and by other public intellectuals who have reviewed his book (see, for example, Massey 2004; Kakutani 2004; Menand 2004; Wolfe 2004). These works and others have offered clear empirical evidence that (1) Mexican migration is now widely dispersed throughout the United States rather than solely concentrated in one geographic region (Massey 2004); (2) Mexican migrants, past and present, have been subject to restrictive legislation (Menand 2004; Massey 2004) and the virtual militarization of the U.S.-Mexican border (Nevins 2002); (3) current migrants come from all levels of Mexican society rather than only from poor, uneducated peasant backgrounds (Guarnizo, 1998; M. P. Smith 2001); and (4) their putative "illegality" is clearly a juridical artifact of immigration laws, which assign to Mexico the same twenty-thousand legal entries to the United States as granted to such countries as Belgium (Menand 2004)—but which has been all too easily conflated in political discourse with a cultural attribute of "criminality." Moreover, this illegality has regularly been transformed into "legality" by offering "amnesty" in response to political pressures and periodic shifts in the economics of labor demand (De Genova 2002). As for the supposed lack of commitment by Mexican migrants to the work ethic, this claim is so derisory as to require no rebuttal. All one has to do is look at the large groups of day laborers congregating to find work on street corners and near Home Depot stores throughout the nation every day to see how absurd it is to treat the work ethic as an exclusive feature of an Anglo-Protestant value system.

As for Huntington's fears about dual loyalty and dual citizenship, abundant research on the relationship between transnationalism and assimilation in migration studies makes clear that the two are not mutually contradictory social processes. For many Mexican migrants there simply is no tension. Their immigration experience constitutes a relatively straightforward trajectory of intergenerational incorporation, a shift to English speaking, and upward social mobility, in short, a trajectory of assimilation without transnationalism (e.g., see Alba and Nee 2003). But for many others, where the tension does exist, including the Mexican migrants we are studying, their cultural and political incorporation into the practices of citizenship in the United States has occurred simultaneously with their maintenance of robust social, economic, and political ties to their country and place of origin (M. P. Smith 2003b, 2005a, 2005b; Bakker and Smith 2003; see also Guarnizo, Portes, and Haller 2003; Levitt and Glick Schiller 2004). In sum, the overwhelming weight of the evidence is that neither transnationalism nor Mexican migration are threats to U.S. civic republicanism.

If Samuel Huntington's voice from the nationalist Right were the only voice predicting the declining significance of U.S. national identity formation in an increasingly transnational world, there might be less need to confront the discourse on declining assimilation with additional empirical evidence. But other voices, inflected with a postcolonial sensibility, have also entered this debate. Perhaps the most prominent member of this group is Arjun Appadurai (1990, 1991, 1996). In his book *Modernity at Large*, particularly in the chapter "Patriotism and Its Futures," Appadurai argues that because of their continuing connections to their homelands— through transnational media images produced by cultural voices in their countries of origin—transnational migrants to the United States and other core countries are unlikely to acquire a sense of loyalty to their new abode.

Appadurai uses the concept "trans-locality" as part of this larger argument, conceiving it as a potentially constitutive element of "locality," understood as the grounded "neighborhood" sites of traditional ethnographic inquiry (1996, 192). For Appadurai, translocalities are "virtual" neighborhoods that emerge at the articulation of media and mobility. They are "imagined" communities of ethnonational identity formation that "implode" into real immigrant ethnic enclaves, becoming agents in the production of a felt sense of locality *unmoored* from the pull of the nation-state in which the enclaves are located.

Appadurai interchangeably uses expressions such as "virtual neighborhoods," "displaced public spheres," "counter-hegemonic imagined worlds," and "translocal communities," investing these imaginings of identity with the capacity to generate new "postnational identities" and "diasporic communities" that have become freed from "the linguistic imaginary of the territorial state" (1996, 166). His understanding of postnationalism tends to apply only to the waning power of receiving states such as the United States to gain the loyalty of transnational migrants to the host society. He characterizes translocal communities in the United States as being "*doubly loyal* to their nations of origin *and thus ambivalent* about their loyalties to America" (1996, 172, emphasis added).

With his singular focus on the role of global mass media in shaping identities, Appadurai fails to address the actual political practices of transnational migrants. Similarly, Huntington ignores empirical evidence about the political participation of Mexican migrants in U.S. politics, concocting his argument for their supposed lack of patriotism and civic engagement from a handful of anecdotes and stacking abstract assumption after assumption into a dubious house of cards. Our multisited fieldwork on political transnationalism on both sides of the U.S.-Mexican border directly contradicts both Huntington's assertion of nonengagement by Mexican migrants in the political life of their adopted country and Appadurai's claims of double loyalty to homelands. We have found that Mexican migrants are extensively and actively engaged in politics in both the United States and Mexico. The migrants we have interviewed do indeed express ambivalence, but theirs is an ambivalence about their experiences on both sides of the U.S.-Mexican border. Rather than being *doubly loyal* to their nation of origin, the politically engaged migrants we have studied express a kind of dual allegiance to both countries that is conditional and contingent.

The Discourse on Dual Citizenship in Transnational Studies

Our approach to transnational citizenship under conditions of neoliberal globalization differs sharply from the nationalist warnings of Huntington and Anderson and the postnationalist celebrations of Appadurai and Soysal. We insist on the need to carefully historicize the relationship between transnationalism and citizenship—that is, to map the contingency and agency underlying the changing practices of states, migrants, and transnational political and institutional networks vis-à-vis questions of citizenship. In our view this is best done by paying close attention to the political dynamics that form and reproduce social networks, which are linked to historically specific political projects that extend the practices of citizenship across borders. This kind of work is beginning to be done, and often done well, within the confines of a large body of emerging multisited field research in transnational studies.

At the present moment, the term *transnationalism* is all the rage. In some circles, the *transnational* has displaced the *global* as the ruling sign of our times. More widely, it has become a leading modifier characterizing institutions, networks, and social practices that span geographical and political borders. The meteoric rise of transnational studies has produced a substantial but uneven research literature. This has led a number of the leading theorists of transnationalism to propose delimiting the concept (Itzigsohn et al. 1999; Portes, Guarnizo, and Landolt 1999), substantially modifying it (Waldinger and Fitzgerald 2004), or even abandoning it altogether in favor of more limited concepts such as "transnational life" (R. Smith 2001) or "transnational living" (Guarnizo 2003).

Although we accept some of the critiques leveled against the indiscriminate application of *transnationalism*, we do not agree that either the concept or the research field should be abandoned. To the contrary, we plan to enrich its conceptualization by further extending the transnational into the realm of the political, an area of scholarship in which it has recently begun to be applied in fruitful ways. Much of the literature in economic sociology tends to approach the subject of transnationalism under neoliberal globalization by focusing on the macroeconomic driving forces of global migration (Sassen 1988) or the microeconomic practices of "immigrant entrepreneurs," sometimes represented as "grassroots forces" whose entrepreneurial practices are said to create "transnational communities" engaged in resistance to the hegemonic logic of global capitalism (Portes 1996a, 1996b). Reacting against the largely economic logic underlying these approaches, some anthropologists and cultural studies scholars working in the field of transnational studies have contributed to our understanding of how the local affects the global, in particular how the everyday practices of ordinary people "from below" produce cultural meanings that sustain transnational networks and make possible enduring translocal ties (Ong and Nonini 1997; Mahler 1998; Schein 1998a, 1998b; Ong 1999). Yet these scholars have not generally made politics the central focus of their analysis of transnational practices and processes. Their emphasis has been on economic logic versus cultural meaning as driving forces of transnational migration or on the interplay of culture and economy in the making of transnational subjects.

Starting from the pioneering efforts by Nina Glick Schiller and her associates, who analyze the role of the state in reincorporating transnational migrants into state-centered efforts to construct a "deterritorialized nationhood" (Basch, Glick Schiller, and Szanton Blanc 1994), political transnationalism has emerged as a growing dimension of transnational studies. These efforts have included a series of extended case studies on migrant hometown associations and their practices (Imaz 2006; Caglar 2006; Moctezuma Longoria 2005; Rivera-Salgado, Bada, and Escala Rabadán 2005; Lanly and Valenzuela Varela 2004; Rivera-Salgado and Escala Rabadán 2004; Bada 2003); comparative analyses of diaspora or "homeland" politics (Landolt and Goldring 2006; Østergaard-Nielsen 2003a, 2003b; Itzigsohn 2000); and efforts by sociologists to quantify transnational political practices (Guarnizo, Portes, and Haller 2003). In this book we seek to further develop this field of political transnationalism. Our book focuses on key political spaces where the practices of citizenship across national borders are being constructed. Grounded in extended case studies of U.S.-Mexican political transnationalism, we show that transnational political spaces have become unavoidable meeting grounds where plurilocal economic and cultural relations have become politicized. Put differently, we argue that, in any particular time and place, multiscalar political institutions, agencies, understandings, and practices necessarily mediate macroeconomic conditions and microlevel cultural practices.

Pathways to Political Transnationalism

Political analysis has entered the field of transnational studies through four principal pathways. The first is through the discourses of international relations scholars on the emergence of "global civil society." Second, extended case studies have documented the emergence of politically salient transnational networks, coalitions, and social movements. Third, recent approaches to political transnationalism that rely on quantitative research methods have begun to examine the connections between migrant transnational politics in countries of origin and immigrant incorporation and ethnic politics in the United States. Finally, and most germane to our research, extended case studies of transnational migration and the social networks enabling it have developed new conceptualizations of the practice of citizenship across borders, including migrant membership in a transnational public sphere and new vocabularies of the "substantive" (Goldring 2002) or "extraterritorial" (Fitzgerald 2000; M. P. Smith 2003a, 2003b) citizen.

The first of these approaches tends to focus on the agency of global-level institutional actors and their norms and practices. Such actors include international governmental, nongovernmental, and emerging supranational organizations that seek to disseminate universal discourses involving such issues as human rights, peace and international security, and environmental interdependence. The shared "global consciousness" (Olesen 2005) that these universalizing discourses both promote and reflect is said to be the foundation for a "global civil society" in the making (see Lipschutz 1992; Wapner 1995; Falk 1999; Kaldor 2003; for a strong critique of this discourse, see Drainville 1998). This global civil society literature also devotes considerable attention to the rise of regional political formations such as the European Union. Nation-states have vested these supranational institutions with important policy-setting or decision-making authority. These new institutions are seen as key to the development and codification of universal, or at least "postnational," norms of human rights and personhood (Soysal 1994). While focusing on the emergence and impacts of new transnational norms and institutional actors, the global civil society literature tends to downplay or ignore many of the microscale practices and mesolevel political institutions and processes that mediate and often shape the dynamics of top-down forms of transnational political agency.

The second of these approaches takes a different tack by focusing precisely on the agency of one kind of mesolevel actor, namely the new transnational social movements such as the human rights movement that includes such organizations as Amnesty International that seek to modify the practices of renegade states by invoking universal norms such as gender equality or indigenous rights. (For case studies see Cohen and Rai 2000.) The work of Margaret Keck and Kathryn Sikkink (1998) on "transnational advocacy networks" laid the foundation for this field and has been elaborated on and extended by subsequent scholarship (see, for example, Tarrow 1998, 2005; Evans 2000; Khagram, Riker, and Sikkink 2002b; Fox 2003; and Piper and Uhlin 2003). Although this attention to mesolevel actors is a welcome complement to the more globalist approach of international relations scholars, the transnational social movements literature also tends to locate political agency at the level of supranational actors, such as the social movements themselves and the alliances they form with dominant "northern" states and international institutions. Subnational actors such as local grassroots forces in peripheral societies are seen as responding to the political opportunities afforded them by the initiatives of these macro- and mesolevel actors in the global North. Seldom do these studies highlight the initiative of grassroots social actors in the global South (see M. P. Smith 1994 and Bob 2005 for important exceptions).

The third pathway has focused on the connection between transnational politics in sending countries in Latin America and Latino ethnic politics in the United States. Much of the research in this area has drawn on quantitative survey methods in which the individual level of analysis and the factors influencing an individual migrant's propensity to engage in U.S. civic and political life are given precedence.

For some political scientists, transnational politics and Latino politics in the United States constitute "alternate social universes" (Jones-Correa 2005). This view sharply distinguishes between transnational forms of organization and ethnic organizations among Mexican migrants. For example, although Michael Jones-Correa (2005) recognizes a limited number of areas of collaboration across these otherwise divided "organization layers," such as immigrants' rights, he sees Latino ethnic organizations as focusing on mobilizing migrants as U.S. citizens and voters, whereas transnational organizations such as HTAs concentrate on creating and strengthening homeland ties.

In a similar binary formulation, Louis DeSipio (2006) distinguishes sharply between modes of political engagement by "citizen Latinos" and "immigrant Latinos." The former have experienced a "relative decline in organizational life" at the level of grassroots community politics, as existing Latino organizations concentrate increasingly on electoral politics in wider political arenas. In contrast, the transnational organizations of "immigrant Latinos" maintain a more traditional organizing focus on hometown community politics because, as noncitizens, these organizations' members are precluded from direct participation in U.S. electoral politics. One problem with these types of binary formulations is that they provide little space for analyzing the political identities and practices of "immigrant Latinos" who happen to be naturalized citizens. The transnational activists we profile in this book fall largely into this latter group.

In fairness to those writing at the intersection of political transnationalism and U.S. ethnic politics, many of the same scholars who construct this kind of binary as a theoretical distinction nonetheless treat the overlap and interconnectivity between these two modes of politics as empirical questions. Jones-Correa (2005), for example, has found that on particular issues, such as immigration reform and immigrants' rights, national Latino advocacy groups and migrant hometown associations "are largely on the same page" (Jones-Correa 2005, 12). In fact, DeSipio et al. (2003) found that "migrants who were engaged in transnational political activities, and particularly transnational organizational activities, were more likely to be members of U.S. civic organizations and to participate in U.S. electoral activities than were those migrants who were not engaged transnationally" (DeSipio et al. 2003, 25). Thus, at the empirical level at least, this literature leaves open a space for the possibility of a politics of simultaneous engagement and does not view transnational and ethnic politics as necessarily separate and incompatible universes.

Much of the research literature on Latino ethnic politics nonetheless tends to assume that over time and across generations political transnationalism will weaken as migrants and their descendants shift from a homeland-oriented politics to a receiving-society politics, for example, from a concern for the human rights of migrants to a civil rights discourse of citizenship (see Jones-Correa 2005). This approach leaves little analytical space for considering the emergence of a new social space of transnational citizenship in which there is considerable overlap between putatively separate categories of subject positionality. Our approach abandons any teleological logic of a shift from "migrant" to "immigrant," first-generation "home country politics" to second-generation "U.S. ethnic politics," producing a sequential movement from "Mexican" to "immigrant" to "Latino" ethnic politics. Our research reveals far more fluidity in the practice and construction of transnational citizenship than this formulation, which, in the end, mirrors the logic of assimilation theory, which maintains that people's experiences in the "core" eventually trump their ties to "peripheral" social formations. Our view is therefore more consistent with the findings of research by political sociologists who have found that "incorporation and transnational participation are concurrent and intertwined social processes" (Itzigsohn and Giorguli-Saucedo 2005, 915; see also Guarnizo, Portes, and Haller 2003).

The fourth perspective, largely found in anthropological and sociological case studies of global migration, centers on the actual cross-border political practices engendered by transnational migration. This approach has been the most ethnographically grounded, and therefore the most grassroots agency–oriented approach to transnational politics. Important studies in this literature have focused on the politics of translocal community development (Goldring 1996, 1998; R. Smith 1998; Moctezuma Longoria 2003a; M. P. Smith 2003b); the politics of transnational voting rights and dual citizenship (Guarnizo 1998; Martínez Saldaña 2003a, 2003b; Calderón Chelius 2003; Badillo Moreno 2004); and the extraterritorial extension of homeland political parties (Glick Schiller and Fouron 1998; Levitt 2001b; Østergaard-Neilsen 2003a, 2003b; M. P. Smith 2003a). Because our work builds on this ethnographic sensibility, we further elaborate on this perspective as a prelude to presenting our own approach to the politics of transnational citizenship.

These studies of migrant political transnationalism have been framed within a wider debate on whether globalization "from above" and transnational migration "from below" are severely restricting, if not erasing, the sovereignty of the nation-state (see, e.g., Guarnizo and Smith 1998). These debates hinge on the extent to which global capitalism, the state, civil society, or attributes of the migrants themselves are key driving forces in the extraterritorial conduct of migrant politics. First-wave discourses on economic globalization tended to envisage the nation-state as losing ground as the major shaper of the economic fortunes and political identities of its citizens. Reacting against the economistic logic underlying this "hyper-globalist" approach (Held, McGrew, Goldblatt, and Perraton 1999), transnational scholars generally acknowledge that transnational practices are unavoidably anchored in—while also transcending—the institutional and geographical boundaries of the nation-state (Kearney 1991, 1995a, 1995b).

Several researchers in transnational studies have usefully detailed the practices of state-level institutions that are said to structure and make possible transnational politics (Itzigsohn 2000; Østergaard-Nielsen 2003a, 2003b; R. Smith 2003a, 2003b). Robert Smith, for instance, has rightly criticized what he terms the "globalist" and "hard transnationalist" perspectives for attributing causality to global capitalism and global structures while overlooking "the role of an active state in creating transnational public spheres" (R. Smith 2003b, 301). Although Smith devotes considerable attention to a nuanced discussion of the political practices of migrants, their networks, and their organizations, the underlying driving force in his framework nonetheless remains the state and its political and developmental strategies and maneuvers aimed at its (re)positioning within the world system. In his framework, migrant civil society is represented as "semi-autonomous" and largely determined by the state's "channeling" of the political opportunity structure, state policies of transnational political reincorporation, and the state's capacity to extend recognition and resources to particular migrant organizations.

Following from this logic, the differences in membership practices and claims making in Smith's comparative study of migrants from the Mexican states of Zacatecas and Oaxaca are traced to "different ways each is embedded within relevant local, national and global institutions and conditions" (R. Smith 2003b, 311). Smith's "instituted process framework" tends to overvalorize the role of the state in shaping and conditioning the agency of migrants. Although we wholeheartedly endorse Smith's critiques of the "globalist" and "hard transnationalist" perspectives, we remain concerned that his framework can too easily be read as a complete inversion of the global capitalism versus nation-state binary. Although Smith's overall body of work offers a more nuanced perspective on the state-migrant interplay, the focus in his "instituted process framework" on the embeddedness of people in social structures loses sight of the role that migrants' practices might play in altering the "institutions and conditions" in which they are implicated.

This framework epitomizes a major limitation that faces many of the ethnographically rich studies of migrants' homeland political transnationalism—their tendency to privilege a particular level of analysis and overemphasize the agency of the actors operating at that privileged level of analysis. In some cases, as in Robert Smith's stress on the continuing importance of the state in transnational life, state-level actors are given theoretical primacy. In other instances, as in studies of Mexican HTAs, research has largely focused on the local scale and has shed important light on migrants' hometown ties and the politics of translocality (see, e.g., R. Smith 2005; Moctezuma Longoria 2003a; Fitzgerald 2000). We find limitations in both of these approaches. The first is overly deterministic, leaving little room for local and translocal level actors to act back upon the state; the second is excessively voluntarist, paying insufficient attention to actors and processes operating at extralocal scales that condition HTAs' agency and influence local and translocal political life. The trick is to study the interplay of multiple actors and structures operating at different spatial scales and the outcomes of this coproduced reality.

In our book we seek to transcend the limitations of these earlier, primarily uniscalar perspectives. We enter the debates on political transnationalism from a clearly agency-oriented perspective that contextualizes the local and transnational practices of migrants within relevant historical, political-economic, and institutional contexts, without assuming that those contexts can be invoked to explain outcomes. Rather than presenting these contexts as determinative structures we conceive of them as factors that situate the acting subjects that form transnational networks and mediate their practices without determining them. Furthermore, these new forms of transnational agency "from below" as well as "from in-between" have become crucial driving forces in the remaking of citizenship across borders.

The politics of constructing and contesting citizenship across the U.S.-Mexican border is the central focus of this book. In our agency-oriented approach we try to shed new light on the *interplay* of social actors operating at multiple scales in the political construction of transnational citizens. Without neglecting global context, our approach focuses on the transnational politics of incorporation, accommodation, and resistance initiated by grassroots actors at various local, translocal, national, and cross-border scales. These practices do not operate in a vacuum or a world of pure voluntary action. Rather they are embedded in a web of opportunities and constraints operating in the context of economic globalization and at the institutional level of the state. The political opportunity structures most important in shaping transnational citizenship across the U.S.-Mexican border are Mexican and U.S. national, regional, and municipal governments and their institutions, agencies, understandings, and practices. The emergent state–civil society interplay is producing a transnational public sphere across the U.S.-Mexico border. This new public sphere is a new space of political possibility existing alongside more traditional, nation-state-centered public spheres that are the taken-for-granted arenas for the practice of citizenship. This new transnational political space emerges as myriad state and nonstate actors seek to reposition or "re-place" themselves in the wider political-economic setting of neoliberal globalization. To envision this new political space and make sense of its meaning requires us to enter the domain of transnational ethnography.

The Sites of Transnational Ethnography

As politics in Mexico has become more open and competitive, new spaces have opened up for grassroots participation of all sorts, including cross-border political participation. This book is a qualitative study of the people, places, and interconnections constituting the new transnational spaces where political rights are being fought for and transnational citizenship is being constructed. We have chosen to focus on the transnational political engagement of migrants from the Mexican sending states of Zacatecas and Guanajuato. We made this choice for several important reasons.

Zacatecas has the longest history of state-migrant relations and the most fully institutionalized network of hometown associations and federations devoted to economic and community development in migrants' communities of origin. The relationship between the Zacatecan state government and these migrant organizations began in the mid-1980s as a limited-scale collaborative matching-grant program between migrants and the PRI-controlled government to improve the infrastructure in sending communities. Under the Partido de la Revolución Democrática (PRD, Party of the Democratic Revolution) administrations of Governors Ricardo Monreal and Amalia García this state-migrant "partnership" has expanded into a highly visible and fully institutionalized program promoting both infrastructural improvements and productive investment. This arrangement has become a model for other Mexican states and other migrant-sending countries across the globe. Political transnationalism in Zacatecas has moved beyond the mode of substantive citizenship expressed by this partnership to encompass more formal/legal modes of transnational citizenship. Migrant-initiated legislative reforms have created a legitimate place for Zacatecan migrants in state and local electoral politics. The Zacatecan case is also notable because migrant associations from that state, which were initially created to participate in diasporic politics in Zacatecas, have begun to engage more fully in political issues, targets, and campaigns that are part of Latino and immigrant politics in the United States.

Guanajuato was chosen because, like Zacatecas, it has historically been among the leading states in sending migrants to the United States. Also like Zacatecas, its state policies during the Panista (for the Partido de Acción Nacional, or PAN) governments of Vicente Fox and his successor have been exceptionally oriented toward reintegrating migrants into the state's economic development. Perhaps even more than Zacatecas, the relatively conservative panista regimes in Guanajuato have inscribed *guanajuatense* migrants as heroes whose sacrifice and continuing contribution is a necessary element in the future political and economic development of the state. Consistent with the valorization of entrepreneurship that is at the core of panista political ideology, Guanajuato developed one of the earliest and certainly the most comprehensive campaigns to capture the monetary resources of migrants by getting them to invest in a state-coordinated network of maquiladora factories in migrant-sending localities throughout Guanajuato. Ironically, while using a neoliberal-tinged discourse of entrepreneurship to attract investors, the state has sought to manage these investors through the technical assistance and loan guarantees it provided them and by organizing these migrants into a state-sponsored network of hometown associations known as the Casas Guanajuato. Finally, these two states were chosen because they afforded potentially fruitful political comparisons of both state-led versus migrant-led transnational practices (Goldring 2002) and the nature and effects of the migrant-oriented policy initiatives of the left-of-center PRD state of Zacatecas and the right-of-center PAN state of Guanajuato.

In conducting our extended case studies of migrant political transnationalism in Guanajuato, Zacatecas, and California we have used a form of ethnography that has come to be known as transnational or global ethnography (for details, see M. P. Smith 1999, 2001; Burawoy et al. 2000; and the appendix to this book). Although the types of ethnographic materials gathered for our book are often used in addressing microlevel theoretical issues, it is worth stating at the outset that we have larger ambitions. This project follows a theoretically informed, extended–case method in seeking to link microlevel observations and interview data to the larger transnational and global forces, connections, and imaginations that connect the global to the local in the everyday lives of our interview subjects (Burawoy et al. 2000).

The ethnographic subjects drawn together in this book are particularly amenable to this transnational ethnographic endeavor. These migrant leaders and activists are not only continually engaged as individuals in the practice and imagining of transnational living but they are also some of the globe's most prominent transnational migrant activists. The border-crossing connections the migrant leaders create as they engage in a multiplicity of social and political networks, ranging from the translocalities formed between their villages of origin and cities in northern and southern California, to the corridors of power in Sacramento or Washington, D.C., to the cosmopolitan globe-trotting circuits of the international political and financial elite, provide an intriguing glimpse into the possibilities and challenges of this age of globalization.

To complete this study we have therefore had to expand the space of community-based ethnography to encompass the multiple spaces across borders in which our ethnographic subjects are orchestrating their transnational lives. Numerous ethnographic interviews and extended conversations were conducted with the key informants whose lives are at the center of the stories we tell. These deep ethnographies were supplemented by additional interviews with migrants, elite interviews with Mexican state and local public officials and political party activists, and participant observation and informal interviewing at state-sponsored gatherings, electoral campaign rallies, and related transnational political events. The ethnographies and related extended–case study materials on which this book is based were gathered between 2000 and 2005 in multiple locations in California, including Napa, San Jose, Los Angeles, Santa Ana, and other cities, as well as in the capital cities and numerous other localities in the Mexican states of Guanajuato and Zacatecas.

In addition to the ethnographies and elite interviews at the center of our project, we have tried to make sense of the qualitative narratives of our subjects by considering them alongside a wide range of documentary and archival research materials, including government policy documents, campaign propaganda, and judicial decisions, as well as other visual materials such as magazines and policy videos that promote transnational community development policies and television documentaries reporting on the interconnections of transnational migration in California and rural Mexico. In sum, our transnational ethnographic method draws on a wealth of interrelated cultural materials including deep ethnography, participant observation, elite interviews with Mexican public officials, historically contextualized political-economic and documentary analysis, and the analysis of myriad cultural and political artifacts. The ethnographic, historical, archival, and documentary methods we have used in our research are fully detailed in the appendix to this book.

Looking Forward

Part 1 encompasses the first two chapters of our book. In the first chapter we have situated our political ethnography theoretically within key discourses on nationalism, postnationalism, and transnationalism and contextualized the ethnographic data of our study. In chapter 2, we detail the historical construction of *el migrante* in the discourses and practices of the neoliberal Mexican state. We trace the efforts of Mexican state policymakers in the past two decades to institutionalize a policy offensive directed at reincorporating the migrant as part of state-centered efforts to develop Mexico. This strategy accepts many of the key premises of neoliberalism and conceives of the Mexican migrant as an integral part of the "Mexican global nation." As a result of policy initiatives spanning the Mexican presidential administrations of Carlos Salinas, Ernesto Zedillo, and Vicente Fox, migrants—once regarded as lost to the homeland and not entitled to Mexican citizenship rights—are now promoted as "extraterritorial citizens," whose contributions are beneficial to the newly transnationalized Mexican nation.

In the next five chapters of our book we offer a series of extended case studies of the political transnationalism of Mexican migrants. In so doing, we have had to constantly move back and forth between multiple spatial scales, from the local and translocal to the national and global, to understand the complex and ever-shifting dynamics of transnational migrant politics. In part 2 we show that community development politics in the transnational social spaces constructed by contemporary migrants range in spatial scale from translocal migrant networks all the way up to the institutional circuits of global development. At all scales, institutions of the Mexican state have become engaged in these transnational social processes. Policymakers at the regional and national levels in Mexico have entered into transnational "public-private partnerships" to promote a variety of community and economic development activities in the migrants' communities of origin. The two chapters in part 2 are extended case studies of community development politics in the traditional migrant-sending Mexican states of Guanajuato and Zacatecas.

In chapter 3, we show how the politics of transnational community development is playing out in the case of Mexican migrants in Napa, California who have forged links with their sending village of El Timbinal, Guanajuato. For the past twenty years these migrants have engaged in self-organized community development projects to improve their native village. In the mid-1990s, as a result of the state's overtures, the migrants from El Timbinal were persuaded to join a transnational public-private partnership designed to bring "productive investment," in the form of a textile maquiladora, to their hometown. Through this "partnership," elites of the PAN in Guanajuato sought to reconstitute the migrants as clients and funders of new neoliberal-state economic and social policy initiatives, as political subjects with "dual loyalty" but limited political autonomy. However, the PAN's effort did not go as the policy makers had planned and is now actively contested by the migrant hometown activists, whose views of transnational citizenship, translocal community, and party loyalty differ sharply from those of party elites. The migrants have begun to view the state initiatives as diverting their energies from true civil society and local development initiatives.

Chapter 4 moves beyond the politics of translocal community development. Here we trace the discourse on migrant social capital and its role in development from the level of the regional state up to the institutions of global governance. In this chapter we focus on the role of a federation of over fifty Zacatecan HTAs based in Los Angeles, California, in the economic and community development of the villages and municipalities supported by their member clubs. Zacatecas has had a longstanding history of successful state-migrant collaboration. By the late 1990's the Zacatecan "model" had captured the attention of national and international development policy makers. Many of the key agencies in the field of global development, from the World Bank and the International Monetary Fund (IMF) to leading foundations of the "donor community" such as the Rockefeller Foundation, have come to regard migrant remittances and social capital as key instruments of neoliberal development. As a result, the notion of "partnership" has been expanded from one involving migrants and the regional state to one involving migrants acting in collaboration with global, national, and regional actors, both public and private. In the Zacatecan case, the entrepreneurial vision of translocal community development that we found in the case of Guanajuato has been extended into a full-scale model of migration-driven global development. In chapter 4 we show how this wider model is playing out on the ground in Zacatecas and Los Angeles.

We have found a multiscalar gaze to be essential in considering the other modes of transnational politics, such as electoral coalition building and citizenship struggles discussed in parts 3 and 4 of our book. This back-and-forth movement allows us to map both the dynamics of transnational political coalition formation in Mexican politics addressed in part 3 and migrant political engagement in the U.S. receiving context analyzed in part 4.

In chapters 5 and 6, which make up part 3, we show that when studying transnational electoral politics one must look beyond the practices of translocal migrant networks to take into account state-centered actors and their policies in sending and receiving states, regions, and localities; non-migrating actors such as public intellectuals, social movement activists, and members of the existing political class in sending localities and regions; and actors from other Mexican and U.S. cities and states, who become more than passive spectators of the political "network of networks" being forged. We analyze the deployment by these actors of different and often conflicting conceptions of citizenship and dual citizenship.

In chapter 5 we present an analysis of the successful electoral dynamics of a prominent transnational mayoral candidate in the Zacatecan municipality of Jerez, Andrés Bermúdez, who has come to be known globally as the "Tomato King." In forging a winning transnational political coalition Bermúdez had to move well beyond gaining political support from translocal networks of circular migrants between his hometown of Jerez and his place of work and residence in the northern California city of Winters. His political ties to Mexican migrants were spatially far more dispersed, encompassing Zacatecan migrant association leaders in Los Angeles and southern California, as well as potential return migrant leaders from other U.S. and Mexican cities and states. The Tomato King's political strategy, discourse, and appeal was multistranded and highly mediated by global mass media, wider transnational political connections, and the constraints and opportunities offered by the Mexican legal system.

In chapter 6 we further expand our analytic focus by looking at the networks and campaigns that have successfully gained recognition for the political rights of el migrante at a variety of sites across Mexico. The chapter focuses on three nested sites for this expansion of the political rights of extraterritorial citizenship. At the federal level we explore the activities of the Coalición para los Derechos Políticos de los Mexicanos en el Exterior (CDPME, Coalition for the Political Rights of Mexicans Abroad), a transnational network of "right to vote" activists that, in 2005, after years of struggle, gained important electoral reforms that allow migrants to vote from abroad by mail ballot in Mexican presidential elections. Next, we move to the state political scale in Zacatecas. We detail the emergence of the Frente Cívico Zacatecano (FCZ, Zacatecan Civic Front) and examine the processes leading to its most important success to date, the passage of the Ley Migrante legislation in Zacatecas in 2004 that institutionalized "binational residency," enabled migrants to run for all public offices in the state except for governor, and set aside two seats in the twenty-eight-seat state legislature for migrant representatives. Finally, in chapter 6 we deploy deep ethnography to tell the story of two transnational activists, who parlayed their connections as leaders of the Federación de Clubes Zacatecanos del Sur de California (FCZSC, Federation of Zacatecan Hometown Associations of Southern California) into prominent roles in Zacatecan state politics. Manuel de la Cruz used these connections to become the first elected "migrant deputy" from the PRD in the Zacatecan Congress. Guadalupe Gómez used them to position himself as a possible future migrant candidate for governor of Zacatecas if migrant electoral rights are further extended.

The wider lens we have chosen to deploy in this book allows us not only to comprehend the construction of transnational political coalitions oriented toward Mexican political life but also to address the important but often overlooked second face of transnational citizenship, namely the political involvement of transnational migrant activists in the political spaces of the receiving society. This second face of transnational citizenship forms the basis of chapter 7, which moves the study of U.S.-Mexican political transnationalism back across the border. In this chapter we demonstrate how migrants are able to transfer to U.S. urban, state, and national politics the political and social capital that they have developed in their hometown networks and extend it into wider arenas of Latino and immigrant political empowerment in the United States.

In the final chapter of our book we revisit the nationalist and postnationalist theoretical frames introduced at the outset of our book in light of the ethnographic narratives contained in our five extended case studies. The rich instances of Mexican-U.S. transnational citizenship we have uncovered throughout the course of this book fundamentally challenge the jingoistic nationalist and utopian postnationalist representations of global migration and its impacts on national identities under neoliberal globalization. The five extended case studies reveal the new social spaces of transnational citizenship Mexican migrant activists are now creating across North America. Our studies trace out the full contours of these emerging social spaces, highlighting both their inclusions and their exclusions. The transnational modes of empowerment we have studied are clear signs of a new democratic opening but also entail exclusions on the basis of class, status, and gender. Thus, the construction of a radically democratic social space of transnational citizenship is still an unfinished project.

2 Reconstructing the Migrant in Mexican State-Policy Discourse

Historically, the Mexican state has deployed various discourses and policy initiatives to encourage the continuing allegiance of Mexican migrants to their *patria*. In this chapter we offer a detailed analysis of the remarkably consistent set of migrant reincorporation policies implemented by the previous three presidential administrations of Carlos Salinas, Ernesto Zedillo, and Vicente Fox. Through these policies, the Mexican state developed transnational means to mobilize "the local" in order "to integrate itself into the global arena" (Sherman 1999, 869).

Although we focus here on the policies of the contemporary period, the Mexican state's attempt to reincorporate migrants has a long history. From the very outset of the U.S. annexation of parts of Mexico in 1848 until well into the twentieth century, the Mexican state sought to maintain a relationship with its migrant population abroad through the activities of its consulates and through intermittent efforts to deploy revolutionary nationalist discourses to encourage migrants' continuing allegiance and return to the *patria*. Although the Mexican state pursued a variety of policies aimed at the country's migrants in the early decades of the twentieth century, those policies were fundamentally different from those of the contemporary period. In contrast to the policies of the last three decades, which have been designed to forge ongoing cultural, political, and economic connections across borders with Mexican migrants in the United States, the policies pursued in earlier decades, particularly during the 1920s and 1930s, attempted to police the borders of the nation, discourage emigration, and promote return to the homeland.

These policies expressed a highly territorialized view of the Mexican "nation" and the relationship between nation and state. They stand in sharp contrast to the more contemporary initiatives of the Mexican state to promote what Nina Glick Schiller and her associates (Basch, Glick Schiller, and Szanton Blanc 1994) have called "deterritorialized nation-building." The policy incentives underlying these earlier policies were both cultural and material. On the cultural side, for example, during the administration of Álvaro Obregón (1920–24) new consulates were established in U.S. cities with the express purpose of cultivating and maintaining a Mexican identity among those who had migrated. In this period, the consulate in Los Angeles, for example, created community-based charity organizations, such as the Comisiones Honoríficas and the Cruz Azul. Other "grassroots" organizations created by the consulate organized celebrations of Mexican holidays and created Spanish-language schools (Sherman 1999, 841–42). As a complement to these policies, the Obregón administration established the Department of Repatriation within the foreign ministry aimed at directly encouraging return (Ayón 2005).

Throughout the early decades of the twentieth century numerous federal and state initiatives sought to prevent further emigration to the United States. For example, as early as 1904 federal and state laws forbade municipal authorities from issuing travel documents to migrants bound for the United States. A 1926 migration law, approved under Obregón's successor, Plutarco Elías Calles, sought to restrict exit by authorizing federal officials to prevent workers from leaving Mexico unless they had contracts approved by municipal authorities in their home communities (Fitzgerald 2006, 267). Other state strategies designed to control emigration included propaganda campaigns, restrictive labor-recruiting laws, coercion at the border, document searches on U.S.-bound roads and trains, and, more positively, material incentives for return, such as subsidized train travel from the border to enable emigrants to return to their places of origin in the interior of Mexico (Sherman 1999; Fitzgerald 2006).

The objective of all the policies enacted by the Mexican federal government from the early 1900s through the 1930s was to repatriate migrants from the United States and discourage continued emigration. As David Fitzgerald (2006) has perceptively argued, these policies were rarely effective because of contradictory pressures emanating from both outside and within the state. Internationally, Mexican emigration policy did not always converge with U.S. policy objectives. The U.S. government often allowed or encouraged illegal migration, especially at times of labor shortages, such as that induced by World War I. The asymmetrical power relationship between the United States and Mexico left the latter with little choice but to acquiesce to the shifting turns in U.S. immigration policy, even when these directly conflicted with Mexican state-policy goals. For example, when Mexican labor power was no longer needed after World War I, the Mexican state, fearing U.S. deportation of Mexican nationals, preemptively financed selective repatriation of return migrants to avoid a humiliating confrontation with the coercive apparatus of the U.S. government (Fitzgerald 2006, 267).

Within the federal structure of the Mexican state, the interests of other levels of government also often conflicted with the nation-building policies of the national government, undermining the federal government's efforts to police the national border and stem the flow of migration to the United States. Many local governments, for instance, were unable to sustain their populations economically, and thus they often defied the dictates of federal authorities by encouraging out-migration, which they saw as an escape valve (Fitzgerald 2006, 260). Even within the federal bureaucracy the state was not a unitary subject. The period from 1926–29 and on through the mid-1930s was a period of political rebellion. Cristero rebels from the west-central Mexican states of Guanajuato, Zacatecas, Jalisco, and Michoácan sought to maintain the political influence of the Catholic Church and the relative political autonomy of these more peripheral regions by taking up arms against the centralizing ambitions of the federal state. This pitted the interest of the Interior Department in keeping Mexican citizens within the boundaries of the national territory against the interest of the army, which granted amnesty and safe passage out of the country to leading Cristero rebels when they turned in their arms and agreed to go into exile in the United States (Fitzgerald 2006, 268). The army also sought to frustrate the recruitment efforts of the rebel leaders by concentrating masses of peasants within particular municipalities in the west-central states, where their activities could be more easily monitored. This had a major unintended effect. Local governments with inadequate resources to cope with the basic survival needs of this population influx encouraged the peasants to leave by issuing them safe-conduct documents allowing them to pass through government checkpoints, move to northern border areas, and eventually to migrate across the border. Local elites also undermined the national state's emigration control efforts. In Arandas, Jalisco, for example, the local land-holding oligarchy encouraged emigration, going so far as to provide letters of recommendation and loans to prospective migrants in hopes of reducing the concentration of landless peasants who might challenge their interests under the federal government's emerging land reform program (Fitzgerald 2006, 269). It is estimated that nearly 340,000 Mexicans emigrated to the United States between 1926 and 1931, adding to the already substantial out-migration from Guanajuato, Zacatecas, Jalisco, and Michoácan, the states that then accounted for 60 percent of Mexican emigration to the United States (Fitzgerald 2006, 268).

As historical circumstances changed, the state's policies toward migrants shifted. The heightened labor demand in the United States following

U.S. entry into World War II prompted the Mexican state in 1942 to negotiate a binational labor recruitment arrangement known as the Bracero Program. The Mexican federal state's posture toward its migrants shifted from an explicit encouragement of return migration to one of legalizing, channeling, and controlling migration flows between Mexico and the United States. The Bracero Program lasted from 1942 until 1964, when it was unilaterally terminated by the United States. Because undocumented Mexican migration grew along with the continuing flow of authorized workers during the latter years of the program, the United States no longer found it necessary to support such a formal labor supply program. Initially, the Mexican state sought to persuade the United States to reestablish the Bracero Program, but by the mid-1970s it had become clear to the Mexican government that it was no longer in its own interest to do so. The rapidly increasing size of the Mexican population (from twenty million in 1940 to forty-eight million in 1970) had placed severe strains on the Mexican economy and on state services such as education. Thus, Mexican state policies toward migrants shifted once again. Instead of seeking to constrain or otherwise control emigration, in 1974 the Mexican government removed penalties for leaving without a contract and declared it was no longer interested in renewing the Bracero Program (Fitzgerald 2006, 278). This shift amounted to a kind of deregulation of emigration controls that has been characterized by Larry Manuel García y Griego as "a policy of having no policy" (1988, cited in Martínez Saldaña 1998). The result was simply to let migration happen as a household survival strategy in order to take pressure off the state to create jobs and provide schooling.

In the face of the economic and debt crisis of the 1980s, Mexican state policies toward migrants shifted once again. As Luis Guarnizo (1998, 57–63) has shown, various Mexican state agencies transformed the limited and ad hoc policies toward Mexican migrants that followed the termination of the Bracero Program into a systematic policy offensive designed to help manage the crisis, as well as to command the loyalty and attract the resources of migrants. Ruling elites of the presidential administrations of Carlos Salinas, Ernesto Zedillo, and Vicente Fox in Mexico have reshaped and institutionalized several of the policies and practices of earlier decades to instill new forms of loyalty and to secure a continuing flow of remittances from Mexican migrants. The emphasis in these policies has shifted from a territorial view of the nation, which encouraged return migration, to a deterritorialized view of national membership, which seeks to reincorporate Mexican emigrants as part of an emergent globalized Mexican nation while they remain working, accumulating resources, and even becoming citizens in the United States. This shift, in effect, has expanded the national imaginary by reenvisioning migrants as a part of the nation even while they are positioned beyond the territorial boundary of the state.

In the past two decades Mexican state agencies have therefore pursued a coherent framework for action that may be characterized as a transnationalization of the long-standing corporatist strategy of the PRI. No longer driven primarily by revolutionary nationalist impulses, this strategy is being shaped by emerging political and economic elite sectors in each of the major Mexican political parties that accept many of the key premises of neoliberal globalization. They have developed policies toward the Mexican diaspora in order to favorably reposition Mexico in the emergent international political economy and vis-à-vis the United States (see Guarnizo 1998, 60). The state's new strategy conceives of the Mexican diaspora as an integral part of what, under the administration of Carlos Salinas's PRI successor, Ernesto Zedillo, began to be officially called the "Mexican global nation" (see R. Smith 2003b, 309). This imagery, driven as it is by the importance of migrant remittances and political loyalty, was not lost on the PAN administration of Vicente Fox. The Fox government further institutionalized migrant reincorporation programs initiated under his PRI predecessors. As a result, through a series of policy and program initiatives spanning the three Mexican presidential administrations under study, migrants—once regarded as *pochos* (Americanized Mexicans), lost to the fatherland and not entitled to Mexican citizenship rights—were promoted as "extra-territorial citizens" who are beneficial to the transnational Mexican nation (for elaboration of this concept, see Fitzgerald 2000; M. P. Smith 2003a).

Reconstructing "El Migrante"

What was the origin of these new state-policy initiatives? Why did the state systematically consolidate its heretofore ad hoc migrant initiatives? What forms did this consolidation take? The first Mexican politician to seek to establish closer links with Mexican migrants in California was Genaro Borrego Estrada, the PRI governor of Zacatecas from 1986 to 1992. Borrego regularly visited members of Zacatecan migrant associations in Los Angeles and other southern California cities. Addressing the state's concerns that self-organized migrant hometown associations in cities where Zacatecan migrants were concentrated (e.g., Los Angeles and Chicago) lacked continuity, often dissolving once specific goals were met, Borrego formalized and institutionalized a federation of hometown associations in southern California in 1988. To promote the cooperation of migrants, he also initiated the state-financed Dos por Uno (2×1, Two for One) program of matching funds to channel migrant investments into infrastructure and social development projects that benefited their communities of origin. The 2×1 program was eventually signed into law in late 1992, under the governorship of Arturo Romo, Borrego's PRI successor.

In early 2001, Borrego, who is a federal senator of the PRI, was interviewed in Mexico City by Remedios Gómez Arnau of the Centro de Investigaciones sobre América del Norte (CISAN, Center for North American Studies) at the Universidad Nacional Autónoma de México (UNAM, National Autonomous University of Mexico) as part of an earlier binational collaborative study funded by UC MEXUS (University of California Institue for Mexico and the United States) that was a precursor to this book (see M. P. Smith 2003b). As described by Borrego, the institutionalization of the Organización de Zacatecanos Unidos (Organization of United Zacatecans) was initiated by the Zacatecan regional state to fulfill three enduring policy objectives: promoting greater collaboration among individual HTAs; creating a formal program to channel migrants' donations into community development projects in their communities of origin; and attracting migrants' investment in Zacatecas. In Borrego's words:

> I was the first governor of México who actively promoted direct meetings with the Mexican communities, in this case with Zacatecanos. We constituted the Organización de Zacatecanos Unidos to help them get organized because they had already established what they called "clubs," but these only represented a few of the municipalities in the state and it was necessary to have a meeting place and a common objective. So we established a federation, and in relation to the state we pursued five main objectives: first, [to promote] unity, communication and reciprocal help, that is, Zacatecan solidarity, in the United States; second, to act in defense of labor and human rights; third, to create the conditions where Zacatecans living abroad could help improve their communities of origin through formal programs channeling the financial resources they wished to donate to their communities. The fourth objective was to make investments in the state to create employment and in some way address the causes that forced them to migrate; and fifth, to give support and assistance when they [re]cross the border. Months or years later, I don't exactly recall, the *Paisano* Program emerged from the federal government after our initiative. I believe that the fact that I went over there broke a taboo. . . . After me, other governors followed, many from the different [Mexican] states that export human labor. (interview with Genaro Borrego Estrada, Mexico City, January 26, 2001)

Once Borrego's successful initiatives broke the taboo of Mexican state involvement in political relations with migrants on the U.S. side of the border, the PRI-dominated federal government initiated two related migrant-oriented programs in the early 1990s. The most far reaching of these was the Programa para las Comunidades Mexicanas en el Exterior (PCME, Program for Mexican Communities Abroad) instituted by President Carlos Salinas de Gortari in 1991. The PCME, initially run by the Ministry of Foreign Affairs, was charged with promoting the formation of migrant associations by state of origin and developing collaborative social and economic projects in Mexico with groups of transnational migrants. The program organized meetings of Mexican state and municipal authorities and industrial leaders with groups of Mexican migrants in the United States (Gómez Arnau and Trigueros 1999, 284). To promote a sense of "Mexicanness" across borders, it also distributed historical information and the work of painters, poets, writers, and musicians whose work was viewed as strengthening Mexican national identity (Goldring 1998, 171). The PCME program was created in part as a state-centered initiative and in part as a corporatist response by the PRI to demands by leaders of migrant associations in the United States (Gómez Arnau and Trigueros 1999, 284; Goldring 1998, 170). Complaints on both sides of the border by human rights organizations also provided a contextual opening for political actors in Mexico to build support among migrants for policies at least nominally targeted at improving their political rights. Out of these complex political dynamics, the PCME program emerged as a key policy instrument in the PRI's effort to politically construct an extraterritorialized sense of national belonging among the Mexican diaspora living in the United States.

The Regionalist Turn: Invoking Migrants' Local and Regional Ties

The PCME tried to build and reinforce a national identity among transnational migrants, many of whom had stronger local or regional identities and who often held the PRI, and corrupt politicians in general, responsible for their need to leave Mexico in the first place. For these reasons, even under the administration of the PRI it became clear to PRI political elites that the only effective way to build enduring bridges to migrants was to tap into the migrants' sedimented memories of their communities and regions of origin. Therefore, during the mid-1990s the PRI-dominated national government began to deploy a regionalist approach. The federal state decentralized the policy system for state-sponsored outreach to migrants. It authorized regional Oficinas Estatales de Atención a Migrantes (OEAMs, State Offices for Attending to Migrants) to achieve many of the objectives of the PCME initiative. Each of the twenty-three state-level offices established by the main migrant-sending states under this initiative stressed its unique regional connections to its paisanos living abroad. Regionalism thus became a key sociocultural and political structuring element of the Mexican state's transnational practices and discourses.

The multidimensional state-centric objectives of the OEAMs included: (1) promoting a closer relationship between state institutions and the states' native migrants abroad; (2) forming and consolidating migrant organizations in the United States; (3) providing an institutional framework for the involvement of migrants and their organizations in the development of their states and communities of origin; (4) improving the image of migrants in their respective sending states and disseminating the culture and history of the respective states among the migrant communities; (5) helping migrants obtain the permits and licenses necessary for infrastructure projects in their native communities; (6) helping relatives of migrants who depend on remittances but have not been receiving them; and (7) providing general support to the activities of the PCME (Gómez Arnau and Trigueros 1999).

Perhaps not surprisingly, the regionalism expressed through the OEAMs was welded on to ideological and programmatic differences found at the state level. This combination of regional and ideological differences led the various state governments to pursue distinct policies toward migrants. The main cleavage in these policies was between a neoliberal-tinged entrepreneurial emphasis and a social-philanthropic logic that was more compatible with traditional Mexican corporatist structures (Torres 2001; see also Moctezuma Longoria n.d.; Iskander 2005). In PAN-governed states, for example, political elites sought to encourage migrant investment in income- and employment-generating projects. These states have developed a number of investment schemes and incentives to induce migrant investment in their communities of origin. Such programs include Guanajuato's Mi Comunidad program, described in depth in chapter 3, and the FIDERAZA (Investment Trust Fund for Mexicans Abroad) program in Jalisco, which helped to finance productive investment through a contribution of one-quarter cent per dollar remitted through its affiliated Raza Express money-transfer corporation (García Zamora 2003; Lanly and Valenzuela 2004). The state's financial role in these programs was limited. In Guanajuato the state provided technical and marketing assistance to investors, whereas in Jalisco the state provided seed money for an investment fund but relied on contributions from remittance transactions for the fund's continued financing.

By contrast, in PRD- and PRI-governed states, political elites have tended to engineer programs more heavily geared toward the development of public goods in collaboration with what Miguel Moctezuma Longoria(2002a, 2003a, 2005) has termed "collective migrant" investors. These programs entail a more active role for the state. Relying less on the entrepreneurial drive of migrants, these state governments attempted to fortify and expand links with HTAs and other migrant associations and to use these connections to encourage migrant participation in co-investment programs. The Tres por Uno (3×1, Three for One) matching-grant program first developed in Zacatecas, which matches each dollar HTAs provide for community infrastructure projects (e.g., potable water systems, roads, church renovations, and recreational facilities) with a similar contribution from the municipal, state, and federal governments, is the most visible example of such communitarian projects.

The number of such migrant hometown and home-state organizations targeted by these state-level programs increased dramatically in U.S. cities throughout the 1990s. For example, by 2003 the number of Zacatecan HTAs across the United States had grown to 126, more than double the fifty-eight registered with Mexican consulates in 1996 (Escala Rabadán 2005, 89; Lanly and Valenzuela 2004, 15; Díaz de Cossío, Orozco, and González 1997, 311). The mid-1990s growth of Zacatecan HTAs in the Los Angeles area, while not as dramatic as the national trend, was also significant, from around forty in 1996 to fifty-three at the time of our study in 2004. This more measured growth in Los Angeles is largely due to the fact that Zacatecan HTAs had begun to flourish there earlier than in other U.S. cities and had already grown rapidly by 1996 from just six a decade earlier (Cano and Délano 2004).

This dramatic expansion of Mexican migrant associations in U.S. cities is the result of a number of interacting political developments. First, as mentioned above, a political offensive was launched by the PCME, in conjunction with the network of Mexican consulates in the United States, whose numbers were greatly expanded under the Salinas administration. Second, these efforts gained the support of a number of Mexican American interest groups and community organizations such the National Council of La Raza and the Mexican American Legal Defense and Education Fund (MALDEF), which supported the creation of the PCME and the Mexican state's efforts to improve relations with Mexican migrants and to improve their living conditions and social status in the United States (see Cano and Délano 2004, 20–21). Third, the growth of clubs further accelerated in the second half of the 1990s because of successful efforts by the OEAMs from the major migrant-sending states to form and consolidate migrant associations.

Representing the Migrant as an Agent of Neoliberal Modernization

Under Carlos Salinas's leadership, neoliberal "modernization" became the key ideological structuring element of Mexican political and economic development strategies. In this wider ideological context, transnational migrants were invited to contribute to the modernization of Mexico along with other Mexican citizens. To this end, in 1993, the PCME program began to work closely with Solidaridad Internacional, the transnational arm of the successful domestic National Solidarity Program (PRONASOL) instituted by Salinas. This transnational program, directed through the Secretaría de Desarrollo Social (SEDESOL, Secretariat of Social Development), initiated for the first time on a national level a public-private partnership in which migrant organizations cosponsored public infrastructure projects in their hometowns and villages (Goldring 2004; García-Acevedo 2003). In addition to burnishing Salinas's image as a member of a modernizing elite, this program also served his partisan political interests and that of his embattled PRI regime, following his questionable electoral victory over leftist presidential candidate Cuauhtémoc Cárdenas in the 1988 elections.

The significant mobilizations of migrants in the United States on behalf of Cárdenas's insurgent candidacy under the banner of the Frente Democrático Nacional, the precursor of the PRD, awoke the PRI-dominated Mexican state to the need to address migrant concerns, lest those concerns be transformed into a potent political opposition. The domestic Solidarity program (PRONASOL) and its international component, in collaboration with the PCME, were viewed by the neoliberal Mexican state as politically promising ways to both dampen electoral discontent and take credit for modernizing backward rural localities and regions of Mexico, while paying for these programs through financially "participatory" community and infrastructure-development schemes that off-loaded a significant portion of the infrastructure costs to migrants and other civil society groups (Dresser 1991). These programs were sold to both constituencies as forms of needed assistance to help transform "backward" villages into localities prepared to enter the "global village" and compete in the global economy. Cast in this ideological frame, the PCME and Solidarity programs can be interpreted as part of a larger strategy by the state to generate political support for Mexico's entrance into the North American Free Trade Agreement (NAFTA).

The symbolic impacts of the public infrastructure projects initiated under the PCME and Solidarity program's international and domestic components were multifaceted. The programs spoke to migrants as signs of the government's newfound commitment to community betterment through the modernization of their native communities. They spoke to potential foreign investors as signs of Mexico's commitment to creating the material conditions for first-world status. Finally, they sought to symbolize to migrants' families that the neoliberal future would not be much of a threat and might even bring modern urban conveniences, such as sewage systems and potable water, to the countryside. These efforts to create a space for the migrant in Mexican political development were driven as much by the PRI's interest in maintaining its long-standing control over the state apparatus as they were by its proclaimed objectives of reducing poverty, modernizing the countryside, and legitimating NAFTA.

Transnationalizing the Political Scale of the Mexican Nation

The PRI administration of the successor to Salinas, Ernesto Zedillo (1994–2000), continued and expanded earlier migrant reincorporation efforts by explicitly advocating the opening up of new political spaces for migrants. This new political imaginary was expressed in the Plan Nacional de Desarrollo 1995–2000:

> Priority will be given to the initiative entitled "The Mexican Nation," which will include a series of programs to strengthen the cultural ties and connections with Mexican communities and of people of Mexican origin abroad. . . . The Mexican nation extends beyond the territory contained within its borders. Therefore, an essential element of the Mexican Nation program will be to promote constitutional and other legal reforms so that Mexicans preserve their nationality, regardless of the citizenship or residency that they may have adopted. (President Ernesto Zedillo, Plan Nacional de Desarrollo 1995–2000; authors' translation)

This new formulation was explicitly linked in the Plan Nacional to efforts to establish a right to dual nationality for Mexican nationals living abroad. By 1997, the Mexican Congress acted on Zedillo's recommendations and approved a constitutional amendment making Mexican birthright nationality irrevocable and thus allowing dual nationality. The Congress also approved amendments to electoral regulations that removed obstacles to the extension of voting rights to Mexican citizens residing abroad—although these rights were not implemented until 2005.

It has been widely assumed that dual nationality reforms recognized individuals' *membership in the nation* but denied them the status of *citizenship in the state*. Thus, dual nationals, according to this logic, were offered some social and economic rights but denied the political rights to vote or hold office. Political developments in the last few years, however, including the examples discussed later in this book of the election of dual nationals Andrés Bermúdez and Manuel de la Cruz to public office in the state of Zacatecas, tend to refute such definitive assertions of the laws' limitations. Moreover, after intense lobbying by migrant leaders and associations, in

2005 the Mexican federal Congress granted absentee voting rights in presidential elections to Mexican nationals residing abroad. Although this law does not explicitly extend the right to vote to dual citizens, in fact, dual citizens were among those who registered to vote from abroad in the presidential election in 2006 (see Durán 2005), although the number of absentee voters was quite small because of the complex registration requirements. Overall, regardless of the intentions of Mexican state officials with respect to the scope and limits of dual citizenship in the mid-1990s, these more recent political developments have helped to establish an institutional and legal framework that make possible extraterritorial candidacies and voting rights.

Even though he trumpeted himself during the campaign as "the candidate of change," President Vicente Fox of the PAN retained the policy objectives and initiatives of his PRI predecessors. Discursively, Fox resolved this contradiction between his promise of wholesale change and the continuity of his policies by feigning ignorance of the reincorporation policies pursued by the previous two administrations, claiming:

> We are not indifferent to the massive emigration of Mexicans to the United States. On the contrary, Mexico's migration policy of the past—a policy that consisted of having no policy—ends today. . . . I will govern for all Mexicans. I will listen to the needs and I will respect the dreams of all those who share our Mexican heritage, here in Los Angeles and in Mexico. My objective is to establish a special connection with the Mexican origin communities in the United States, Mexican-American or Mexican, documented or undocumented, temporary or permanent, Democrat or Republican, Panista, Priísta, or Perredista. (Fox speaking to the Mexican American Legal Defense and Education Fund, Los Angeles, 2000)

Having labeled the migrant a national hero during his campaign, one of Fox's first moves in office was to create the Oficina Presidencial de Atención a Migrantes en el Exterior (OPME, Presidential Office for Mexicans Abroad) under his direct control and led by Juan Hernández, a guanajuatense-bred Mexican American. Under Hernández's watch, the OPME pursued a binational agenda, advocating in the United States on behalf of Mexican migrants—lobbying for undocumented migrants rights to driver's licenses and access to state-funded higher education in California, for example—and promoting migrant participation in state-led investment schemes in Mexico.

In April 2003, following a number of conflicts between Hernández and Foreign Affairs Minister Jorge Castañeda, Hernández was fired and the OPME was dissolved. These conflicts were occasioned because under

Hernández the OPME operated independently of the Mexican consular system. Moreover, Hernández tended to claim that his actions were aimed at addressing the failures of consular activities, such as when he touted his efforts to support Mexicans affected by the World Trade Center attacks of September 11, 2001 (Cano and Délano 2004; González Gutiérrez 2003; López Dóriga 2001). Shortly after its dissolution, the functions of the OPME and the PCME were consolidated into a new agency, the Instituto de Mexicanos en el Exterior (IME, Institute of Mexicans Abroad). The IME was returned to the Ministry of Foreign Affairs. It is charged with carrying out the policy dictates of another newly created body, the National Council for Mexican Communities Abroad. The National Council, which is governed by the president of Mexico, helps to coordinate the activities of fourteen federal agencies that deal with the migrant community.

The IME receives policy recommendations from still a third body, a consultative council made up of its corporatist clients and collaborators. These include 110 migrants or Mexican descendents, ten representatives of major U.S. Latino organizations, ten additional consultants, and thirty-two representatives of Mexican state governments. The IME pursues similar strategic objectives to those defined by earlier administrations. The new institute has focused much of its efforts on developing closer relations with local and regional U.S. government officials and Mexican-origin community leaders in the United States as a means of developing the Mexican government's much-coveted Mexican lobby within the United States. The consultative council, while not directly engaged in lobbying for Mexican interests in the U.S. polity at this time, may prove to be extremely fertile ground for cultivating future Mexico-friendly activists in the United States (Cano 2004).

The Turn to "Productive Investment"

In early 2002, the Fox administration expanded the social-philanthropic 3×1 program from the state of Zacatecas to the federal level. The newly federalized program emphasized funding both social infrastructure and productive projects (*Diario Oficial de la Federación*, March 5, 2003, 2), indicating that Fox's migrant policies would tend toward the entrepreneurial emphasis of the state of Guanajuato's policies over an approach emphasizing social philanthropy. This is one area where the Fox administration policies did represent change vis-à-vis the administration's Priísta predecessors. Fox moved beyond earlier public-private partnerships that encouraged migrants' participation in infrastructure development projects to promote migrant participation in a variety of productive investment schemes. These multiple programs share an unswerving neoliberal faith in the market as the ultimate guarantor of the material well-being for Mexico's poor.

Several of the Fox administration's programs were deployed in collaboration with neoliberal development institutions and fall under the umbrella of the stated intention of Presidents Fox and George Bush to create a transnational Partnership for Prosperity (P4P). For example, in one short-lived policy collaboration, the Inter-American Foundation initially committed to provide a $2 million grant to fund the Adopta una Comunidad program that sought migrant *padrinos* (sponsors) to make job-creating investments in ninety of the country's poorest microregions. In 2002 the Fox administration launched a more extensive project, the Invierte en México (Invest in Mexico) program, seeking to ensure that "savings, the product of remittances sent by our paisanos, be invested in the creation and strengthening of productive business and in development" (Imagen 2002). The program, funded by the Inter-American Development Bank and administered by the Mexican state's own development bank, Nacional Financiera, operates in five migrant-sending states and, according to its justifying rhetoric, "offers migrants the opportunity to . . . provide their family members back home financial independence and a dignified income by starting their own business."[1]

Even administration initiatives purportedly aimed at migrant protection, such as the promotion of a revamped *matrícula consular* (consular identification card), can be read as efforts to increase the amount of migrant remittances sent through formal channels and to steer them toward productive investment. By encouraging migrants to obtain the *matrícula* and by promoting its acceptance by local and state governments, the Fox government met dual objectives of generating a register of its migrants abroad and encouraging their incorporation into host societies (Cano 2004). U.S. local governments' acceptance of the *matrícula* as valid identification provides migrants with greater security against deportation, thus maintaining the remittance flow to Mexico, inasmuch as migrants who are able to present valid identification are less likely to be deported when detained by local officials for minor violations. A telling indicator of the role of remittances in driving the *matrícula* issue is the Mexican government's high-profile campaign to convince major banks to accept the document as an acceptable form of identification for opening new accounts. Fully consistent with the neoliberal "remittances to development" agenda being driven by states, development banks, and the international financial institutions (which we detail in chapter 4), this campaign seeks to channel

1. http://consejo.nafin.com/portal/page?_pageid=340,139311&_dad=portal&_schema= PORTAL

migrants into formal banking institutions, purportedly as a way to reach "financial democracy" (Terry and Wilson 2005), that is, the right to access the formal banking system and its financial services.

State Power and Migrant Agency

Whether led by Salinas, Zedillo, or Fox, the Mexican state's migrant reincorporation policies have remained remarkably consistent over the course of the last three *sexenios* (the six-year presidential term). The institutional structures that served to confront the legitimacy crises facing the PRI government in the late 1980s proved successful at that task. The legitimating objective that was the raison d'être of those institutions no longer plays such a crucial role in the present period of apparent party competition. Released from the need to sustain the crumbling regime, these institutions have quite effectively turned their corporatist structures toward the state's current project: the further entrenchment of the neoliberal model.

However, as the Mexican state has reached out aggressively to court Mexican migrants, it has created an interdependent relationship with the migrants that has opened up new political spaces for their agency. This interdependence needs to be kept in mind as we begin to sort out the effects of these far-reaching efforts by the state to reincorporate migrants into the state's neoliberal agenda. The estimated twenty-three million people of Mexican origin currently living in the United States now constitute about one-fifth of all Mexicans living in North America. The importance of economic remittances to the local, regional, and national economies of Mexico is clearly obvious to the dominant political class. The possibility of turning more migrant remittances from household reproduction to community development and productive investment is thus a hallmark of the state's policy initiatives. This is no small matter. In 2006, migrant remittances were estimated at $23 billion by the Banco de México (Banco de México 2007). The potential for organizing the pool of transnational Mexican migrants as a political force also has not been lost on any of the major Mexican political parties. Yet, as we shall see in subsequent chapters, the potential economic and political power of the migrants' remittance flows and their political voice have become clear to Mexican migrants as well as to political elites.

PART 2

||||||||||||||||||||||||||||||||||||||||||||||||||||||||||||||||||||||||||||||||||||||||||||||||||||||||||||||||||||||||||||||||||

*The Politics of Transnational
Community Development*

3 The Regional State and the Politics of Translocality

The Napa–El Timbinal Connection

Since the mid-1990s, political elites of the Partido Acción Nacional in Guanajuato have sought to reconstitute guanajuatense migrants to the United States as clients and funders of new state economic and social policy initiatives, as political subjects with "dual loyalty" but limited political autonomy. The translocal character of global migration networks created unique opportunities for Guanajuato's state government under Vicente Fox, who went from there to become president of Mexico, and his successor, Juan Carlos Romero Hicks, the leaders of the relatively conservative PAN in the state, to reconfigure the meanings of "nation," "region," and "citizen" in order to co-opt extraterritorial migrant groups into local and regional development projects designed by the state but financed by the migrants. Yet, the PAN's effort is now actively contested by migrant hometown leaders whose views of translocal community, partisan loyalty, and transnational citizenship differ sharply from those of party elites. They have begun to view the state initiatives as diverting their energies from true civil society and local development initiatives.

In this chapter we assess the character and consequences of particular discourses, policies, and practices that constitute a partisan political project to reincorporate transnational migrants into the panista regional state. We first focus on the changing representation by the state of el migrante, the elevation, indeed, the glorification of the migrant in guanajuatense public discourse. This transformation of the migrant from an outsider, disdainfully labeled a *pocho* (González Gutiérrez 1999), to an extraterritorial insider entitled to citizenship rights has been used to construct an ongoing but increasingly uncertain collaboration between the state and its migrant diaspora. Our initial questions include the following: What specific projects has the state of Guanajuato initiated to recapture the loyalties and tap the resources of its migrants, to engage their material and social capital? How does the state seek to involve the migrants in projects that it sponsors? What social constructions of "migrant," "community," and "citizenship" (or more precisely, "dual citizenship") inform this discourse? How are these social constructions symbolized, understood, and enacted in the policy-making discourses of the state and with what effects?

We then turn to the issue of the agency of the migrants as extraterritorial citizens. How have these initiatives been received, modified, or transformed by the migrants? What are the effects of their agency? What consequences are emerging on both sides of the U.S.-Mexican border from this new politics of transnational migrant reincorporation? Who are the winners and losers in the politics of extraterritorial citizenship?

Celebratory readings of political changes in Mexico since the dawn of the twenty-first century have suggested that we are witnessing the authentic birth of Mexican democracy because of changes in party competition and the replacement of the national hierarchy by a reformist PAN leadership under Vicente Fox (Diamond 2000). Enthusiastic accounts of the emergence of extraterritorial citizenship by Mexican migrants have likewise depicted these developments as signs of a new democratic opening "from below" (Thelen 2000). Sometimes these two celebratory narratives are even combined, as in Fox's frequent attempts to portray the political reincorporation of Mexico's transnational migrant population as a key dimension of the rebirth of a vital Mexican civil society. But perhaps this enthusiasm is premature. The changes at the top and from below are real enough, but they do not necessarily entail a wholesale transformation of Mexican political culture.

Such political changes are necessarily mediated by actors and institutions of the state and civil society "from in-between" whose practices may be affected by changes from above and below but who also can be expected to embody longstanding understandings of how politics is normally practiced. For seventy years the Mexican state was viewed in the prevailing political culture largely as a mechanism for incorporating new clientele groups into state-controlled projects by exchanging various forms of patronage for partisan political support. At the regional level in many parts of Mexico PRI cadres still control political office and maintain influence in many state and nonstate institutions whose decisions affect everyday state and local political life. Moreover, research on the track record of the PAN in those states where that party has held governmental power for several years suggests that it may be premature to expect the PAN to act as a force for democratization of Mexican civil society (Middlebrook 2001; Spencer 2001). Perhaps, indeed, the clientelist pattern of political incorporation has staying power, even in those parties that have advanced a successful electoral challenge to the PRI. How much then is new in the extraterritorial politics of PAN and how much has a familiar clientelist ring?

Since the mid-1990s the reintegration of el migrante into the Mexican "global nation" (R. Smith 1998) has become inscribed in the discourses and practices of the main political parties and in their public policies. The male migrant in particular has been the target of state-sponsored discursive and policy initiatives, having been recast as a quintessentially heroic figure—a courageous border crosser with deep cultural roots "at home"—where home can be taken to mean the nation, the region of origin (e.g., the guanajuatense homeland) or the local village of origin. In Guanajuato, all three geographical scales have been depicted by the panista political class as concentric sites of cultural embeddedness that localize while simultaneously transnationalizing the meaning of citizen loyalty and political obligation. El migrante is also viewed by these state-centered actors as an important source of capital—both physical and social—a vital source of remittances, business investment, community development initiatives, and political leadership roles.

Each year 32,500 migrants from Guanajuato travel north to the United States, making it the second largest state in México in sending population. By various counts Guanajuato has generated between 670,000 (official) and two million (estimated by the political elites interviewed) transnational migrants that are current residents of the United States. According to documents provided by the state of Guanajuato, in 2000 over 90 percent of the state's migrants were men. This estimate must be treated with skepticism, since there is growing evidence from other sources (e.g., Canales 2003; Consejo Nacional de Población 2006; Woo Morales 2000) that for at least a decade women have constituted a growing percentage of Mexican migrants to the United States. Recent data on the gender composition of Mexican migrants in the United States show that 44 percent of resident migrants are women (Consejo Nacional de Población 2006). The discrepancy in estimates of the gender composition of Mexican migrants may be explained in two ways. First, these estimates are derived from data sources that are noncomparable. The larger figure of 44 percent female migrants is based on what migration researchers term the "immigrant stock" resident in the United States, whereas the data provided by Guanajuato state officials relies on surveys conducted in Mexico that tend to undercount women because they rely on the self-reporting of male "household heads" regarding the migration patterns for their entire families and do not capture the migration northward of entire families (personal communication with Ofelia Woo Morales, October 26, 2006). Secondly, it remains true that male migration tends to predominate in Mexico's rural communities, while a majority of the growing number of female Mexican migrants come from urban areas (Comisión Estatal de Apoyo Integral a los Migrantes y sus Familias 2005, 57). Yet even accounting for this general rural-urban difference, the 90 percent estimate is high. For example, a recent study places the proportion of male migrants from Yuriria, the municipality in which our case study is located, at 82 percent. Although this figure is still quite high, the portrait of "el" migrante as exclusively male is not as definitive as official representations claim (Byrnes 2003).

One in four households in Guanajuato have at least one member with migrant experience in the United States. In localities with a population of less than fifteen thousand, one out of three households experienced migration from 1993 to 1996. The migrants tend to be concentrated in traditional migrant-receiving states in the United States, with California, Texas, and Illinois the guanajuatense migrants' main destinations. However, in recent years the guanajuatense diaspora has been more broadly dispersed, with migrants finding new destinations in several southeastern and central states.

In 2000, officially estimated remittances sent to Guanajuato amounted to $650 million (dollars are U.S. unless otherwise noted), ranking it third among Mexico's thirty-two states. In this chapter we analyze the Mexican regional state's political offensive to capture a lion's share of these remittances and show how this has played out in Guanajuato and in California. We first specify how the PAN-dominated government of Guanajuato has responded to the national state's previously discussed decentralization of authority over migrant programs to the state level. We identify key features of the policies and programs first developed under Guanajuato's then governor Vicente Fox to reincorporate migrants into state-sponsored development initiatives. We then explain the political and economic objectives of these efforts and analyze the political dynamics by which the migrants who are the targets of this political offensive have both accommodated to and resisted the state's efforts to embrace them.

Constructing the Transnational Guanajuatense Political Subject

In the mid-1990s, the state of Guanajuato, under the leadership of Governor Vicente Fox, introduced a series of interrelated programs intended to command the loyalty of its migrant community. These programs were subsequently repackaged and consolidated under the administration of Fox's successor, Juan Carlos Romero Hicks, and his state secretary (*secretario*), Juan Manuel Oliva Ramírez, an influential member of the panista political class who was elected governor of Guanajuato in 2006. This consolidation was detailed in a sweeping policy document prepared by the state agency Consejo Estatal de Población de Guanajuato (COESPO, Guanajuato State Population Council) in 2001. The policy report, supplied to us by Oliva, summarizes the philosophy of migrant reincorporation underlying the state's policy initiatives and spells out and justifies its logic. Following a research procedure that anthropologist Arturo Escobar has elsewhere termed "institutional ethnography" (Escobar 1995), we now subject the COESPO report to close critical scrutiny.

Guanajuato state officials project a deeply gendered vision of migration and its consequences, viewing the migration of young males who leave (*"los que se van"*) as a loss to the Mexican nation and to the female family members they have left behind (*"las que se quedan"*) (Byrnes 2003). The COESPO report reflects this patriarchal social construction. Five programmatic targets of the regional state's political project are identified—the migrant, his wife, children, extended family, and community. This gendered division of labor reflects the state's view of the migrant as exclusively a male subject. The male migrant is conceptualized in the COESPO report primarily as a "remittances provider" who requires a set of conditions that will ensure a steady flow of remittances to the family he has left behind. Consistent with a neoliberal modernization agenda of promoting "productive" as opposed to "unproductive" financial flows, the report declares that public policies must (a) promote inexpensive remittance services to reduce "unproductive losses" due to high transaction costs; (b) establish a framework encouraging the migrant to save and invest to ensure an eventual "dignified return" to his community of origin; and (c) channel the migrant's investment dollars into various microenterprises in his native community.

The migrant's wife is represented as a potential bearer of human capital useful to the future economic development of the state. She is said to need training and work experiences geared to the development of entrepreneurial skills. The report recommends that governmental institutions target appropriate training, labor, and educational policies to the wives of migrants. As potential "entrepreneurial women" migrant's wives are envisaged as needing access to microcredit, technical training, and assistance in marketing and commercialization of products. The migrant's wife is further depicted as a kind of irrational "other" who needs help in "remittance management" through state policies designed to develop her intellectual capacities to manage the family's resources. She is viewed as needing to be modernized by encouraging her to invest, save, and optimize remittances rather than consume them. Finally, health–related institutions are to disseminate both general health information and specific birth control methods to migrants' wives. It is clear from the all-encompassing character of these interventions into everyday life that the realization of the neoliberal goal of creating entrepreneurial women entails a significant set of public policy interventions by the state. Far from withering away, the regional state of Guanajuato is assuming a central role in the reconstitution of the transnational family.

The migrant's children and extended family are likewise brought under the umbrella of targeted state policies. The report details existing policies and new policy proposals whose central objectives are to upgrade children's human capital while at the same time reinforcing, or even expanding, the family's social capital by "re-creating" extended-family obligations. This would implicitly extend the normative claims that less immediate members of extended families who remain behind in local communities in Guanajuato could make on transnational "remittance providers." To accomplish this goal the COESPO report emphasizes educational programs and family-centered policy initiatives that promote specific family, social, and cultural values. The document argues that the migrant's family requires "better integration" and advocates the identification of "new family models" that would raise the migrant's consciousness of the values of "family identity" while addressing the "transculturization" affecting transnational families.

Specific policies aimed at consolidating transnational families include (a) a "voluntary insurance" scheme to be paid for by the migrant in support of his transnational family; (b) the institutionalization of trust funds, enabling the migrant to devote a portion of his resources to his extended family's future social security; (c) educational programs such as access to scholarships financed by a combination of migrant remittances and public funds; and (d) policies designed to reduce the number of school dropouts and thereby increase the state's overall pool of human capital. If the migrant's family were to be reorganized as a site of "small family enterprises" it would also receive assistance from several government organizations that encourage entrepreneurship.

Under the legitimating rhetoric of a public-private partnership for family restructuring the policies summarized in the COESPO report would channel substantial portions of the resources of migrant "remittance providers" either directly, or by influencing the choices of the migrant's wife as "remittance manager," into state-designed and state-run social and educational policies. The role of the state has not been reduced but redefined or even increased in the range of its impacts on everyday family life. Ironically, therefore, while arguments about the "nanny state" may no longer be part of the national political discourse in many advanced-capitalist welfare states, the issue has been reframed in Guanajuato, Mexico, by the panista regional state under the rubric of transnational family restructuring.

This same logic of "partnership" designed by the regional state but financed largely by migrant contributions is carried to the community level. The report recommends infrastructure development policies that require a rechanneling of the migrant's resources into community development schemes in their communities of origin. It identifies several "opportunities" for migrants to support such infrastructure development, particularly in transportation and communication infrastructure such as new or remodeled roads and telephone systems. Also deemed appropriate areas for such 2×1 cost-sharing projects are electrification, pipelines for water service and sewage disposal, and new housing developments. In effect, the long-standing assumption that it is the state's role to provide the infrastructure investment on which the economic development of a region depends is here recast as the transnational citizen's "opportunity" or even duty to share in this role. Likewise, migrants as transnational taxpayers are expected to "volunteer" funds to support their extended families through contributions to health, educational, and social security programs that the state could not or would not otherwise provide to the poorer citizens of rural Mexico by taxing more privileged segments of the Mexican population.

Implementing the Policy Vision

In May 1994 the Dirección General de Atención a Comunidades Guanajuatenses en el Extranjero (DACGE) was created as the lead agency to implement the policy rationale subsequently spelled out in the COESPO report. Between 1994 and 1999 the DACGE, responding to the PRI-dominated federal government's decentralization of migrant policymaking to the state level, created several key programs designed to reincorporate guanajuatense migrants into the lifeworlds of their communities of origin. The most important of these are: (1) the Casas Guanajuato program, which promotes the creation of hometown associations under the auspices of a home-state institutional umbrella; (2) the Mi Comunidad maquiladora investment program; (3) the 2×1 community development program; and (4) the program for mass communication with the migrants.

The Casa Guanajuato Clubs

The Casas Guanajuato program creates nonprofit, hometown-centered "clubs" in the United States to pursue social, cultural, economic, and educational activities designed to build a strong sense of "guanajuatense community" among migrants from Guanajuato. From the regional state's perspective the Casa Guanajuato clubs have four main objectives: to promote "roots-forming" activities among migrants; to establish close working relationships between them and the state government; to serve as a channel of communication between the state and its migrants; and to increase the number of clubs in places where Guanajuato's migrants are concentrated. By March 2001 the state had organized thirty-nine Casa Guanajuato clubs in such large U.S. cities as San Jose, Dallas, Houston, San Antonio, Chicago, Denver, and Atlanta, as well as in smaller municipalities such as Eugene, Oregon; Granger, Washington; Springdale, Arkansas; and Napa, California. Officials we interviewed told us that this program was to be expanded to create one hundred clubs under the PAN administration of Vicente Fox's successor, Romero Hicks, though in the most recently published data there were fifty-two clubs (Faret 2004).

Given the transnational character and broad dispersal of these programs, it is not surprising that the recently departed general director of DACGE, Lupita Zamora, spent 80 percent of her time in the United States, operating from a field office in Dallas while visiting the various clubs. Ramón Flores, the executive director of the DACGE, responsible for administrative and political coordination within Mexico of the state's migrant programs, told us that of the seventy programs organized by DACGE, the Casas Guanajuato program was the most politically important. Flores described the state's interest in creating the Casa Guanajuato clubs:

> Casas Guanajuato is where we have been monitoring and assessing the location and networks of the migrants. What we can't yet do is go to the U.S. looking for guanajuatense migrants because it is just too expensive and overwhelming. But in this case they are already networked into the Casa Guanajuato, and this is one of the main objectives of this program where we can capitalize on existing arrangements and contacts between the guanajuatense migrants. . . . There are twenty-three of these offices in all the States, and we are still the number one, the best. . . . A few years ago we were asking for all the governments to take care of immigrants, and nobody paid attention to what we were saying. But once they realized that migrants are an incredible political force [conceptualized by Flores as twenty million potential voters capable of electing a president] they started to take care of these people. Now everybody wants to help people who live in the states. Everybody acknowledges that we are the best and better consolidated. . . . Two years ago most of the states in Mexico were trying to open offices in the States like Casa Guanajuato. (interview with Ramón Flores, Guanajuato, Guanajuato, March 20, 2001)

Just how does this program, touted by Flores as a model for constituting the transnational Mexican nation, work? What is it political logic? What are its political practices? To gain a sense of the cultural and political dynamics of the Casa Guanajuato connection we conducted participant-observation field research in February 2001 at a two-day *reunión* (gathering) of the Casa Guanajuato clubs of northern California in San Jose. The *reunión* was held in a rented facility for community organizations and activities with a large convention hall. The event was co-organized by DACGE and the leaders of the region's migrant clubs. Various high-level political elites from Guanajuato participated in the formal and informal activities we observed, including an induction ceremony for the presidents of the northern California clubs. The first day of the meetings was restricted to migrant leaders and state officials. It was devoted largely to a lobbying session in which the presidents of the migrant clubs expressed the needs of their communities of origin and of the migrant population in general to the state authorities, including the secretario to the governor of Guanajuato, the general director and the executive director of DACGE, and the secretario to the president of the Municipality (county) of Yuriria, from which many of the northern California migrants had come.

The second day of the *reunión* was a festive and symbolically rich *convivio* attended by two hundred migrants and their families. Music was provided by a *rondalla*, a folk band from Salinas, California. While adults enjoyed food and beer, their children played games for prizes and were entertained by clowns. These informal celebrations preceded a remarkable round of symbolic rituals designed to honor the migrants and raise their awareness of their guanajuatense and Mexican roots. A giant Mexican flag was unfurled. A local performer sang the Mexican national anthem. The audience stood, saluted the flag, and joined in the singing. The U.S. national anthem was then sung. Next, Guanajuato's state secretary, Juan Manuel Oliva, gave a welcoming speech. Key governmental figures from Guanajuato, the Mexican consulate, and the Casa Guanajuato leaders were introduced to the audience. Other notables were introduced from their seats, including, much to our surprise, our field research team. Following the introductions, the five selected presidents of new Casa Guanajuato clubs in northern California were called forward from the line of notables standing in front of the stage. Each was presented with a certificate and a Guanajuato banner symbolizing their new status. Each leader, in turn, was asked to raise his hand and pledge his support to Guanajuato and its state-sponsored projects for community betterment.

At this point a dramatic gesture occurred, reflecting what we have found to be a more general migrant perception of the pervasive corruption typifying Mexican political life. The club president from San Jose, after being named regional president for northern California, called on the government officials to raise their hands (as he and his fellow club presidents had done) and pledge to work with honesty to fulfill their promises to the migrants in California and Guanajuato. Interestingly, when the migrant leader finished his speech, the state officials chose not to respond directly to his symbolic challenge, perhaps because doing so would tacitly acknowledge the validity of the migrants' view.

Instead, the ruling political class turned to the highlight of the afternoon—the unveiling of a scale model of a statue in honor of el migrante that was planned for placement in the town squares of various cities in Guanajuato. The monument depicted a male figure with no eyes, because when the migrant leaves he cannot see where he is going. The figure had no mouth or ears, because the migrant doesn't understand the language of the land he has come to. The figure was naked because, when the migrant left, he had nothing to take with him. Yet the figure was supported from behind by a smaller female figure to remind the migrants of their wives, parents, and children. Both figures are emerging from a tree with large roots sunk deep in the soil. A small Mexican flag was added to the model during its unveiling to remind the migrants of the nation that, in, the words of Secretario Oliva, sadly saw them depart but has never forgotten them. After unveiling the statue, Oliva announced that it would be constructed very soon in five municipalities in Guanajuato and invited the

Fig. 1. The Guanajuato regional state's representation of the heroic migrant unveiled. Photo by Pat Smith.

Casa Guanajuato clubs to propose a place for its construction "here in California, wherever you think would be appropriate—a plaza, a street, a park, etc." (speech of Juan Manuel Oliva, Casa Guanajuato Reunión, San Jose, February 4, 2001).

It is important to be aware of the nested character of the migrant programs developed by the Guanajuato's political elites. The Casas Guanajuato are the key points of communication through which the state seeks to incorporate migrant leaders into the other dimensions of its relatively sweeping policy agenda. When Guanajuato's political elites attend meetings of Casas Guanajuato in various U.S. cities, discursive practices move in two directions. On the one hand, the political elites listen to pressures from below expressed as the "community needs" of the villages of origin *as perceived by the migrant leaders.* For example, in response to my question "Do you get frequent visits from Guanajuato authorities?" Chavela, the only female investor in the El Timbinal maquiladora, replied:

> Lupita Zamora visited us about six months ago, and we expect to see her again around March or April. She is very busy and travels wherever there is a Casa Guanajuato club. Usually when she or others come Ángel [Ángel Calderón, the migrant leader of the Casa Guanajuato in Napa] calls all of us so that we get together for a meeting. And we pass her our requests. I am sure she is tired of listening to our claims, but we do it to help others there. We have insisted that everyone in the town have piped water service [as well as] more classrooms for the children. We have asked her for the road to be paved, so that we can get in and out of Timbinal faster, [and] for a good clinic, with all the medicines and equipment. Those are mainly the things we talk about at the meetings. Also she asks us about our needs here, and we tell her what we need. (interview with Chavela, Napa, California, January 24, 2001)

At the same time that the migrants lobby the state "from below," the panista political elites use these occasions to sell their preferred policy initiatives "from above" to the migrant members of the clubs in order to enlist them in their preferred corporatist projects.

Consider an example drawn from *Programa Mi Comunidad,* a documentary video used by the state to promote its maquiladora program:

> How did you know about the *programa* Mi Comunidad and why did you decide to become an investor?
>
> INVESTOR: When I lived in Chicago, in 1997, I used to belong to an association called Casa Guanajuato. It was here that authorities from the state of Guanajuato came and presented us with a business plan for creating maquiladoras. We analyzed the proposition and decided to invest. So this

Fig. 2. Secretario Juan Manuel Oliva (center) and other state officials from Guanajuato exchanging views with migrant leader Ángel Calderón in the presence of the research team, Michael Peter Smith (second from right) and Gustavo Galindo (right) at Casa Guanajuato Reunión, San Jose, California. Photo by Pat Smith.

is really a joint venture between migrant workers and locals. It is a great example of working together and making this dream come true. (Gobierno del estado de Guanajuato, 1998)

In short, the Casa Guanajuato clubs have been used by the PAN political elites as a vehicle to reconfigure migrants' social locations by reshaping their dreams and relocating their identities. The other policy initiatives promoted by the panista political class have been advanced through the discursive space created by the institutionalization of the Casas Guanajuato as the principal point of connection between guanajuatense migrants and the state.

Mi Comunidad

The Mi Comunidad program was initiated by the Guanajuato state government in 1997 to channel the flow of dollars back to migrants' communities of origin in the form of "productive investment" rather than household reproduction. The program was initially planned and implemented during Vicente Fox's term as governor. DACGE executive director

Ramón Flores administers Mi Comunidad. The program taps into the economic resources of guanajuatense migrants by inviting them to invest in textile maquiladoras in their places of origin. The state policymakers hope this program will economically develop the poorest municipalities in Guanajuato in the short run and that in the long run it will reduce immigration to the United States. In 2001 fifteen *maquilas* were in various stages of operation in Guanajuato. Six others were being constructed. The program had created jobs for 339 people and had attracted $2.2 million in investment by migrants in Guanajuato's municipalities and rural villages (García Zamora 2002).

The migrants provide all of the capital investment for these maquiladoras. The state coordinates a series of legal, managerial, and technical services provided by three principal sources: the state government; state-financed educational organizations such as the Centro Interuniversitario del Conocimiento (CIC, Interuniversity Knowledge Center), which provides training and certifications for technical personnel, machine operators, and managers; and the staff of DACGE, which provides technical consultation on legal, accounting, financial, and marketing activities as well as a loan to supplement the migrants' initial investment. As succinctly described by Flores, "The migrants are the capitalists and we are the enablers" (interview with Ramón Flores, Guanajuato, Guanajuato, March 24, 2001).

In the Napa–El Timbinal partnership, migrant leader Ángel Calderón initially persuaded two dozen guanajuatense migrants living in Napa to invest in the textile factory in their native community of El Timbinal, a small village in the southwestern part of Guanajuato with an official population of 718 (Instituto Nacional de Estadística, Geografía e Informática 2000), although various informants estimated it at less than three hundred. This partnership forms one of several translocal connections linking El Timbinal and the 250 migrants from El Timbinal who were then living and working in the city or county of Napa. The capital for the firm was entirely provided by the migrant investors. In addition to its technical and administrative support and the negotiation of transnational production contracts, the state also provided start-up financial support with a relatively high-interest $50,000 loan. It also gave symbolic political support to the project through a formal inauguration ceremony for the maquiladora in 1999 led by Governor Fox. This was the first time in its history that the semidesert agricultural community was accorded such a high-status visit.

According to Ramón Flores, the state's plan for the maquila scheme was to have each factory start small with local production for regional markets, then to have the factories in Guanajuato collaborate with one another to fulfill large global textile production contracts. Their long-range goal was to have each maquiladora move up the commodity chain of global production by developing its own unique products for global export. In Flores's words:

> The first phase is to work with local companies. Actually, these local companies subcontract [to] companies in the state. In the middle term we want to give the maquila direct links to American companies—80 percent maquila and 20 percent our own product. In the long term we want to create our own products—20 percent maquila and 80 percent our own products, which is what constitutes the real profits. . . . Our own eight maquilas are organized in such a way that they will be integrated into a big company. So when Levi's comes to us and tells us fifty machines is nothing, we need two hundred, so, if we are talking eight maquilas we can join resources. We want to make more efficient maquiladoras in order to secure quality with clients like J. C. Penney and [then] create our own fashion center. (interview with Flores, Guanajuato, Guanajuato, March 20, 2001)

The idea of Guanajuato as a center of fashion design and production, a kind of Mexican version of middle Italy (on the regional development of the "Third Italy," see Cenzatti 1992) was very much part of the initial planning vision of the Fox administration in Guanajuato. In a speech at the inauguration of the maquila in Guanajuato, José Muñoz, the director of the state-financed Centro Interuniversitario del Conocimiento, alluded to the lure of Levi's 501 jeans as a global commodity, and then made this rhetorical prediction:

> In this program we, the planners, have a dream that in the future Guanajuato will present the world with its own design brands, with its own fashions that will make us different from the rest. We dream of having a line of jeans, the "1810s," that have to do with our independence movement, or a more fashionable line of clothing, "Yuriria," the name of a woman. We dream like this, but at the same time we are rushing to accomplish these dreams. . . . In a few months, with the governor's authorization, we will create the University of Textiles, with specialized courses in design, marketing, and commercialization. (speech from documentary video *Inauguración de Maquiladora "El Timbinal,"* gobierno del estado de Guanajuato, 1999)

Two years after this speech, with Vicente Fox in Los Pinos (the Mexican equivalent of the White House) and another PAN governor in power, we asked Flores to comment on the materialization of this dream:

SMITH: Is the fashion center in the works yet?

FLORES: Not yet.

SMITH: There is a university here. Is there a textile and fashion department?

FLORES: No, but there is some thinking about that. El Timbinal is working on its own product. They have achieved [enough] quality to compete in international markets.

SMITH: What product do they make?

FLORES: They make baby sets [boxed sets of baby clothing].

GUSTAVO GALINDO: When the maquila of Timbinal was inaugurated the CIC director talked about a textile university that could be ready in months.

FLORES: Actually, it's not the same guy. There is a new director now [*laughs*]. I don't know if they are going to continue with the same plans. His name is Roberto Contreras Zárate. I haven't met him yet. (interview with Flores, Guanajuato, March 20, 2001)

The development of Guanajuato as a center of fashion design is at best still in the "thinking" stages. According to Flores, the component maquiladoras that have moved from regional subcontracting to global contracting have begun to develop their own products. The maquila in El Timbinal, for example, has developed a prototype for a boxed set of baby clothing, which state planners told us they hoped to promote and market in the near future. Although this may eventually happen, a recent policy evaluation study by a Mexican social scientist from the Autonomous University of Zacatecas (García Zamora 2002) has criticized the Mi Comunidad program, for, among other things, its unfulfilled marketing plans.

Moreover, when we visited the maquila, all of the women on the sewing machines were piecing together bright red and blue adult-sized "Spider-Man" costumes, under a transnational contract from the U.S.-based Target department store chain. When asked how he gets contracts for the maquila in El Timbinal, the factory manager, Salvador, explained: "My contract comes from the U.S., from a broker from Chicago I know from my earlier maquiladora jobs. We call him 'Spider-Man.' . . . Everything comes from abroad: the fabrics, the patterns are already cut from the U.S. We just assemble it here and send it back" (interview with plant manager Salvador, El Timbinal, Guanajuato, March 21, 2001). The assembled costumes were timed for marketing in the United States several months before the release of the film *Spider-Man* in 2002. In March 2002 we found that adult Spider-Man costumes were selling at a store in Los Angeles for $44 each. When the retail price was mentioned to Ángel Calderón, he said, "We got $1.50 each for the costumes" (interview with Calderón, Napa, California, April 20, 2002). Despite the grandiose promises of the panista political class in Guanajuato, the migrant-owned maquila in El Timbinal was still very much a subcontracting firm situated at the low end of the commodity chain of global textile production. This has made it highly vulnerable to fluctuations in global demand.

Fig. 3. Spider-Man costumes assembled in El Timbinal maquiladora on display in a storefront in the Westwood section of Los Angeles. Photo by Pat Smith.

Other Policy Initiatives

Other state policy initiatives have rounded out the political offensive of the panista regional state. The most significant of these is the 2×1 program. Dos por Uno was initiated with the goal of community development and improving infrastructure in the poorest communities in Guanajuato. Its main objective has been to attract the resources of the migrants by a shared funding arrangement in which, for every peso "invested" in their communities of origin by guanajuatense migrants, the state provides two pesos. Secretario Oliva pointed out that some of the municipalities in his state offer a match of as much as "four for one" to create public infrastructure such as sewage disposal, electric power, and new schools. As we shall see, the implementation of this program in El Timbinal involves the migrants extensively in the local politics of the Municipality of Yuriria, where they must compete with scores of other villages to secure matching-funding arrangements.

In addition to its "transnational partnership" programs, the state of Guanajuato finances several media initiatives to create a favorable image of the state, shape the cultural identity of guanajuatense migrants, and provide appealing images of "home." A variety of television programs, radio broadcasts, informational brochures, newspaper sections and features, and a migrant-centered magazine are part of the panista regional state's political offensive to construct a transnational guanajuatense subject and channel migrant resources into state-centered development schemes.

Me voy pa'l Norte is a weekly television program focusing on rural communities in Guanajuato and the migration phenomenon on both sides of the border. It is produced in Guanajuato and televised both in the state and in Dallas, Texas. It is also distributed more broadly in the United States via the Latino TV networks Teleamérica and Univisión. The state-sponsored radio program *Caminos de Guanajuato* features themes of general interest to guanajuatense paisanos in the United States. Its programming stresses the traditions and culture of Guanajuato while featuring human-interest stories of men and women represented as constructing the "new Guanajuato." The program originates in Santa Rosa, California, and is broadcast in U.S. cities with high concentrations of guanajuatense migrants such as Napa, Fresno, Chicago, Houston, Dallas, Atlanta, and Denver.

A third vehicle for building a strong sense of guanajuatense identity among transnational migrants from Guanajuato is the cultural affairs magazine *Pa'l Norte*, twenty thousand copies of which are distributed free to guanajuatense paisanos in the United States. The magazine is produced by state officials and edited and printed in the state's print shops. *Pa'l Norte*'s feature "The Migrant's Page" has been created and coordinated in collaboration with the newspaper *Correo*, which circulates statewide in Guanajuato and on the World Wide Web in the United States. *Correo* provides migrants and their families with information about changes in laws affecting migration, stories of migrants' experiences, and advice from and the addresses of state agencies that may help migrants and their families in case of emergencies. "The Migrant's Page" also invites migrants to write to the editors with their stories and concerns, under the slogan: "Write to us and don't forget this is your space." This symbolic gesture is a departure from the otherwise one-way flow of communication between the regional state and its migrants. Significantly, "your space" has proven to be a slogan that the migrants have taken very seriously. Through the Internet version of the newspaper *Correo*, and its Migrant's Page, we first learned of a growing rift between the state and its migrant diaspora, as the migrants have used "their space" to voice objections to the implementation of the Casa Guanajuato program under the direction of its new leader, Secretario Oliva.

Constructing Dual Citizens: The View from the Regional State

Despite their heroic social construction of the migrants in public discourse, in practice the political class sees el migrante in a different light, as a kind of friendly cash cow who is a limitless source of physical capital investment and social capital for state-initiated projects, yet one that remains a relatively passive citizen, a predictable font of future electoral support for those in power.

In an interview in his office in Guanajuato in March 2001, Secretario Oliva expressed this contradictory view of the migrant. Oliva has significant political influence in both Guanajuato and on a national level. In addition to his key administrative position as the governor's secretario, a post equivalent to that of a state minister, Oliva simultaneously served as a senator from Guanajuato in the upper house of the Mexican Congress. Before occupying these positions he served as president of the PAN in Guanajuato from 1993 to 1999 and helped secure the party's presidential nomination for his friend and fellow guanajuatense, Vicente Fox. Shortly before Fox's successor, Romero Hicks, completed his gubernatorial term, Oliva was named the PAN candidate for governor. He was handily elected to that post in July 2006, winning 58 percent of the vote. In our interview with Oliva in 2001, he summarized his political and administrative role as secretario to the governor as follows: "My role is to increase the link between Guanajuato society and the guanajuatense community abroad in the U.S.; to educate the community about the government plan of the governor; and to build support abroad for this project and hopefully recruit support for this project for the next six years" (interview with Secretario Oliva, Guanajuato, Guanajuato, March 22, 2001).

In light of his influential role in Guanajuato's political system, several passages from our interview with Oliva are noteworthy. They spell out vividly his and, by implication, the PAN's understanding of transnational migrant networks and their interplay with state policy-making structures and practices. They also reveal the panista conception of transmigrants as an emerging political force in Guanajuato and in Mexico's political development. Perhaps most pointedly, they highlight the continuing corporatist logic underlying the panista regional state's social construction of dual citizenship within cross-border neoliberal opportunity structures.

When asked to reflect on his conception of dual citizenship for Mexican migrants, Oliva said:

> El migrante needs to understand and to develop a double gratitude to offer
> the best qualities of his country—his principles, values, traditions—to the

second nation that has opened its doors with welcoming arms, so that he can enrich his second homeland. The Mexican people and culture have a lot to contribute to the U.S. culture, with our skills, our approach to life, our joyful way of doing things. This kind of dual loyalty is possible and would help overcome the "indefinition" of the Mexican, the guanajuatense. My job is to strengthen and contribute to the development of the North American fatherland. (interview with Secretario Oliva, Guanajuato, March 22, 2001)

Oliva's vision of dual citizenship as "dual loyalty" elides the question of the rights of citizens and focuses instead solely on the responsibilities of subjects. In so doing, he provides an ideological legitimation of the neoliberal policy premises of the COESPO report. This representation of el migrante stresses the dual citizen's duties to the Mexican and U.S. nation-states while saying nothing about the voice of the migrant in state or subject formation. The migrant as political subject is constituted as loyal and grateful and thus, by implication, as a contented and quiescent citizen.

Following from this logic, Oliva views the guanajuatense migrant as a kind of transnational taxpayer, a key source of state revenues. The migrant's "double gratitude" is viewed as a necessary motivating force for obtaining the funds needed by the panista state to finance its preferred economic and social policies. Institutional restructuring is being undertaken to rechannel the flow of migrant remittances into state policy initiatives in health, education, housing, and social insurance. Oliva described the restructuring as follows:

There are some government institutions that will have very specific roles. For example, we are trying to get COESPO to be in charge of administering and designing all the matrixes of surveys, studies, and statistics that will be conducted for all municipalities. Second, we are going to develop common strategies to deal with state or national problems specific to immigrants. For example, we are proposing that in terms of social security, migrant families qualify for voluntary insurance. It would then be the task of the municipality, the state, and the national government to determine how those resources that come to Guanajuato directly through the migrant be directed to establish a voluntary insurance [plan] for the families of migrants either in communities or health clinics. We are also looking into ways to address the needs of the wives of migrants through organizations such as the Instituto de la Mujer at a state level and the Desarrollo Integral de la Familia, a municipal agency that deals with the women's role in the development of the family. . . . That way we would look at aspects such as health remittances, education, and housing. . . . There is the issue of transferring some of the remittances, which account for around $650 million that immigrants send to Guanajuato. (interview with Secretario Oliva, Guanajuato, March 22, 2001)

When pressed to focus on the political participation of transnational migrants on both sides of the U.S.-Mexican border, Oliva saw little difficulty in negotiating the tensions of duality. In the following exchange he provides concrete examples of transnational political actors that are contributing to the political development of Guanajuato to bolster his optimistic view of the question of dual citizenship:

> SMITH: On the dual side of citizenship, how do you envision people becoming active political citizens in both places? There is the question of voting and basic citizen rights in two places. Talking not about dual loyalties but dual practices, what mechanisms would enable a person to be an active U.S. citizen and at the same time an active participant in political processes in Mexico, in Guanajuato, in voting and forming public opinion?

> OLIVA: Right now the dual vote is a reality. We have some of our migrant population that goes to the U.S. for six months every year . . . who come here to vote and are participating. However, the proposal to reform the law to allow migrants to vote directly from their host country is not a reality yet. First we would need to change the law . . . and then you would have to work out the logistics . . . whether by mail or ballots to make sure this Instituto Electoral para el Extranjero could succeed. There are lots of guanajuatenses living in the U.S. who have not only contributed resources to campaigns but who have actually traveled back to Mexico [to] . . . vote in Mexican elections. We also have migrant presidents. Carlos Guzman, the municipal president of Uriangato, used to be in Chicago. President Pedroza from Ocampa, Guanajuato, is also a Chicago migrant. The municipal president of Jerequero, Juan Soto, is a California migrant. Here we have a "problem" that has become an opportunity for a lot of our paisanos. . . . We are willing to become a bridge between the Mexican migrant vote and the Mexican senators so that the proper constitutional reforms can be made. (interview with Secretario Oliva, Guanajuato, March 22, 2001)

A follow-up series of questions dealt with the extent to which the experience in Guanajuato could be generalized to Mexico as a whole. Oliva's answers indicated just how widespread the political offensive to reincorporate migrants has become in the sending regions of Mexico. They also underlined a complex construction of the "migrant problem" as a structurally driven feature of the Mexican national political economy that Oliva believes should be addressed by state governments in helping to upgrade potential migrants' skills before they migrate and, paradoxically, by the devolution of other unspecified policy responsibilities from the national to the municipal level of policy and governance.

> SMITH: Now that Fox is president, do you envision that the extensive efforts in Guanajuato to make serious connections with the migrant community will become a national model?

OLIVA: Right now twenty states out of thirty-two have adopted the general plan for "communities abroad" . . . similar to what we are doing in Guanajuato. Second, this week Vicente Fox will open the Casa de Atención al Migrante in Santa Ana, California, that will be in charge of dealing with Mexican migrant issues. This office will be the locus for integrating the Mexican [national] government and migrant issues. We also have several states looking at investment opportunities for migrants. What we are witnessing is an increasing attention to the migrant, at least in twenty states of the republic. We meet every three months, the twenty people responsible for dealing with the U.S. migrant agenda, and we are trying to develop a common agenda.

SMITH: What is your vision of the role of the transmigrant in the future of Guanajuato?

OLIVA: First, we need to acknowledge, not just in the Guanajuato case, but in the larger context of Mexico, the lack of opportunities in the labor and education markets. Second, to look at the phenomenon of immigration as an opportunity for the economic and professional development of people. For example, the Dolores Hidalgo Technological University of the North has been teaching English to their students. Migration to the United States in this region has not diminished. On the contrary, migration has been constant with the difference that these students that migrate with English skills have been able to find better job opportunities. So migration has been an important factor in the economic and professional realization of people in Guanajuato. Also, the capacity to generate a vision of immigration such that the paisanos that are in the U.S. can achieve a cultural integration predicated on their Mexican roots. Third, there is also the political connection that could be achieved through the exercise of the right to vote. . . . Guanajuato is the second largest migrant exporter region after Jalisco, so we want to reclaim this notion of the migrant. We want the migrant problem to be perceived as a direct responsibility of the specific municipalities. In the past, migration was constructed as a national federal matter. Now we are looking, under this new administration, for the migration problem to be shared between the national and local governments. In Guanajuato we have forty-six municipalities. We have been able through our guanajuatense contacts overseas to involve thirty-seven out of the forty-six municipalities in selecting officials in charge of dealing with the immigration problem in their specific municipality. Among the specific goals are to identify by first and last name the migrants leaving for the U.S., to identify the family of the migrant that stays behind, and the precise ways the local and federal governments can serve the needs of both the migrant and his or her family. We have thirty-seven confirmed municipalities that have committed to establish an office that will deal with migrant affairs. Our vision is to convert the migration problem, which as of now has been a federal problem, into a municipal problem in which the national government continues to collaborate with the local government in addressing the migration issue. (interview with Secretario Oliva, Guanajuato, March 22, 2001)

The Agency of the Extraterritorial Migrant Diaspora

How does the regional state's image of the male guanajuatense migrant as an acquiescent citizen and provider of "voluntary" state-managed remittances stack up against our ethnographic findings on the practices of the migrants themselves? Ángel Calderón is the recognized leader of the *timbinalenses* in Napa. He was inducted as president of the Casa Guanajuato club in Napa at the ceremony described earlier. The migrant respondents we interviewed were promised strict anonymity except for Calderón, who encouraged us to use his real name in our study. Calderón has become a highly visible public figure featured in U.S. and Mexican press accounts of the Napa–El Timbinal connection (see, e.g., Quiñones 1999 and Hua 2002). He was even invited by President Fox to stay at the presidential residence, Los Pinos, because of his key role in creating the El Timbinal partnership. Calderón has been a far more active citizen of his native village *and* of political life in Napa than the state's model of "double gratitude" would anticipate or than U.S. assimilationists, who see transnational citizenship as necessarily diminishing active participation as U.S. citizens, would predict.

During the past fifteen years Calderón and his network have not limited their translocal ties to El Timbinal to the economic sphere. Indeed, many of the community development projects that Guanajuato now subsidizes elsewhere through its 2×1 program were initiated on a voluntary basis in El Timbinal by Calderón and his fellow migrants nearly a decade before the state created its 2×1 policy. The Napa–El Timbinal migrant network has contributed nearly $50,000 to renovate El Timbinal's church and town plaza and build a kindergarten there. The cast iron benches inscribed with each migrant's name that grace the renovated town plaza symbolize the migrants' local status as benefactors to their home village. The migrants regard these benches as "something that gives us pride." Thanks to the migrants the village now has a reliable potable water supply for a good part of the village. The water project was financed by a combination of migrant contributions and a $5,000 gift from Sutter Home, a Napa Valley winery where some of the investors and many other migrants from El Timbinal have worked during the past two decades. This arrangement too was achieved by the transnational migrant network as a self-organized project before the group's partnership with the PAN state government.

Despite the migrants' self-initiated community development projects, El Timbinal still has many infrastructure needs, particularly in education, road construction, and improved water supply. Calderón and the other members of the Casa Guanajuato in Napa have been pressing the local state to address these needs. Yet, the local state must consider these demands against the needs and demands of over one hundred other small communities that make up the Municipality of Yuriria, which includes El Timbinal. In contrast, the neighboring Municipality of Santiago Maravatío has only twelve localities and can thus address their needs on a monthly basis. Therefore, as Calderón explained, in Yuriria, "in order to get what you need, the people have to put a lot of pressure on the government authorities, otherwise you would get nothing. It is on a first-come, first-served basis" (interview with Ángel Calderón, Napa, May 9, 2001).

Since the major Napa contributors to earlier community-improvement projects in El Timbinal have become capital investors they have been forced to deal with several contradictions, some stemming from the tension between their earlier role as donors and their new role as investors, others from the character of Mexican political culture. First and foremost, the money they once had available for community improvement has largely been channeled into financing the maquila and paying back high-interest loans from the state. The maquiladora, which opened in 1999, only turned a profit for several months in 2001. To attract supporters for projects eligible for funding under the state's "two for one" program, Calderón was forced to draw on a wider circle of timbinalenses in Napa and elsewhere in California than he needed to before the maquila project was undertaken. Yet the time he could devote to doing so was constrained by his new responsibilities as a microcapitalist. Despite Calderón's impressive ideas, energy, and leadership skills, after he was drawn into the structural leadership role in the state's maquiladora initiative, he had to delay his deeper interest in improving educational opportunities in El Timbinal.

A second contradiction facing the migrants is that, as investors, they have necessarily been concerned with the profitability of the enterprise, at least in the long run. Yet their desire for a return on their investment in the factory has been tempered by their continuing desire to maintain the social status that they earned in the community by their previous activities as transnational benefactors. Thus, for example, when faced with the difficulty of maintaining female workers once they were trained because of a combination of low wages and dissatisfaction with the supervisory practices of the local plant manager, Calderón and his fellow investors doubled the workers' wages and fired the local manager, replacing him with a state-trained manager from outside the local community. This improved labor-management relations in the short run and fit well with the stated long-range desire of several of the migrant investors to return to live in their native community when they retired from their U.S. jobs.

A third contradiction stems from the fact that both roles—the migrants' capital vs. community consciousness—are strongly mediated by family relations. The social relations of the family often intersected in complex ways with both roles in the small community of El Timbinal. For instance, one of the female workers at the maquiladora that we interviewed was the niece of Chavela, the female migrant investor. A consequence of Chavela's willingness to forgo short-term profits as an investor was to raise the wages of her niece, a member of her transnational extended family. More dramatically, if somewhat differently, the fired local plant manager was Calderón's nephew. By making the choices he did in the name of the viability of the maquila and the economic development of his overall native community, Ángel Calderón opened an unwanted rift with his nephew's father, his own brother, who still lives in El Timbinal.

These contradictions among the migrants' multiple role expectations are illustrated in the following series of ethnographic exchanges:

SMITH: When did you start collecting money and thinking about helping your native town?

CALDERÓN: In 1987 someone called me and said they needed money to fix our church at Timbinal; so that time I collected about seven thousand dollars, and I took the money down in December of that year and we painted the church ourselves. Then we needed a school; we needed classrooms, so I collected money again. I think another seven thousand—that was back in 1987. So in November or December of 1990, we constructed two classrooms, for our kindergarten children. Back then we were around sixty; today we are around 250 [migrants from El Timbinal working in Napa]. I really wanted to work in helping with education, because ignorance is the biggest enemy we have. . . . The next project was music, so I hired a teacher, and we gathered around twenty-five youngsters who started learning music in Timbinal. Then the next thing was water for the town. It is very dry there, and about four months of the year we are completely dry. The women have to walk about three miles to get the water, bringing it [back] in clay or ceramic containers. I collected about twenty-three thousand dollars for that project. And we also started to see some politicians and people from the government asking for help, so that by 1995 we inaugurated the water system, and now we have water the whole year. . . . Then we started another project of fixing the plaza, so I collected money again. I sent around thirty thousand dollars and we fixed the plaza.

Later I had in mind to construct a high school, because after *secundaria* [ninth grade] the guys have nothing to do, so they come to the U.S. immediately. I talked to some people here who like to plant and work in the wineries, but I wanted the young people to learn mechanics, welding, things that will help them to come here or anywhere and make money. So I went to the government of Guanajuato. They said they didn't have any program like that but they had the maquiladora plan. So a person from the government came to Timbinal and presented the business plan. We took it, and so far we have invested over two hundred thousand dollars, between twenty-three persons. (interview with Ángel Calderón, Napa, November 14, 2001)

Despite the government's claim to Calderón that it lacked a program to upgrade migrants' skills, the interview with Secretario Oliva revealed that the panista administration does indeed have a program to promote the upgrading of the skills of likely migrants before their migration to the United States. This policy is aimed at boosting the migrants' earning power in the United States and hence the size of their remittances. At the time of our earliest interview with Calderón about the community development projects of his network, he was not aware of the state's skill-upgrading policy and appears to have been steered away from that policy and toward the Mi Comunidad program:

> SMITH: You were already engaged in these projects with other people from Timbinal, mostly what we called "community development" to make Timbinal a better place. You approached the government to partner with you on things you wanted to do, and they said, "We don't have that project but here is what we have." So that was something they already had on the books ready to go. Since then have you gotten involved in any other projects, besides the Mi Comunidad program?
>
> CALDERÓN: I am just working on this one right now. There have been lots of changes in the past two years. If this manager [Ángel's nephew] doesn't work out we will have to change him. We are going to make the last payment for the credit in January [2001] so every six months I collect money again.
>
> SMITH: What are your future plans?
>
> CALDERÓN: The school is my next project. I want to construct six classrooms and inaugurate it in two years. If people don't agree to this project I will construct two classrooms myself. I hope that when the government sees the classrooms they will furnish it and provide the equipment and staff of teachers. (interview with Ángel Calderón, Napa, November 14, 2000)

Calderón pointed out that it would not be a problem to start construction, since he had already raised $2,000 and the PAN municipal government of Yuriria had offered to triple whatever amount the migrants donated for the construction and equipment. But before going ahead, he said, there were several political issues to address. He wanted to clarify to some timbinalenses in El Timbinal and in the United States, before undertaking this project with the PAN administration in Yuriria, that he was not doing this for power, money, partisanship, or any other "dubious reason." He wanted to represent his voluntary efforts as just a desire to help and would like partisan gossip from supporters of all political parties to stop.

This concern suggests a further contradiction of the political and economic development initiatives of the PAN in Guanajuato, stemming from the character of Mexican political culture. In seeking to attract financial support from the migrants to subsidize infrastructure development, panista state policy planners have downplayed the political difficulties entailed in programs that require the collaboration of municipal officials who represent the other main Mexican political parties that have their own agendas, priorities, and networks. It is likely that this barrier of partisan interest and political structuration is the main reason that Secretario Oliva told me that the state had worked "through our guanajuatense contacts overseas" to get municipal officials to set up offices to address migrant concerns rather than simply dealing directly with the local officials, many of whom represented other parties and their clientelist networks. At the street level of politics, where the migrants must act to get things done, this contradiction between a collaborative intergovernmental policy response and a world in which partisanship, patronage, and clientelism continue to matter is vividly apparent. Consider the following excerpts from two separate interviews with Ángel Calderón:

SMITH: When you deal with the local administration, what is it like, good or bad?

CALDERÓN: It depends. I remember this person from the local government to whom I showed the project for the school. He said, "Fine, I'll help you with the material." But we were waiting and waiting and the material never came. Later in another project he helped us a lot with materials and money. The current municipal president is difficult to deal with. He only wants to do it his way, just because he wants to. I think he doesn't even know how to read, but he has a lot of money and was able to finance his political campaign. . . . He goes with whatever the political situation is.

SMITH: What's your sense of how people are reacting to the things you have done?

CALDERÓN: It's funny. I have good friends but also big enemies. Everything was fine until they saw me with Vicente Fox. But I haven't seen him more than six times.

SMITH: Thinking about El Timbinal, there have been some changes that you promoted, but how do the people that are not part of the migration process feel about that? Is there a division in the community?

CALDERÓN: In the beginning, I think everyone was my friend. . . . We put together some money for the renovation of the church. Later for the water I collected a little more than twenty thousand dollars. And there was a mayor in Yuriria that was working together with us. He was from the PRI. In those years there were elections and the PAN won. Then people in the community started saying that I was from the PRI, and when they saw me with Vicente Fox at the inauguration of the maquiladora, they couldn't figure out what kind of party loyalty I had, and some of the community members didn't like that. I told them that I am not a politician and only care to do works for our community. Since then it has been hard to have everyone working together. (interviews with Calderón, Napa, November 14, 2000 and May 9, 2001)

Calderón's skepticism about partisan politics reflects his frustration with the continuing significance of the taken-for-granted clientelist political culture of Mexico, a persistence that penetrates the dynamics of the translocal and transnational politics in which he is engaged. Despite his skepticism, Calderón remains actively concerned about the future of his native community. On the first day of the *reunión* in San Jose, in February 2001, we observed him negotiating with the secretario of the PAN municipal president of Yuriria over the location of the first paved road connecting El Timbinal to a nearby village. Calderón wanted a nine-mile road that connected El Timbinal directly to the county seat, rather than the three-mile road the municipality was prepared to build to connect it indirectly to the municipal center. He said that he was able to persuade the local political authorities that if they must build only the three-mile road they should at least extend it to El Timbinal's central plaza rather than ending it at the edge of town. In a subsequent interview he stated that although the migrants had put up their money for the more limited road project, the state still had not delivered on its promise of 2×1 matching funds. This example of translocal politics played out in the context of preexisting networks of patron-client relations illustrates just how difficult it has been for the migrant leader to even fight for the crumbs of the regional state's vaunted 2×1 program.

Whose Transnational Citizenship?

What has been the play of political agency in the multifaceted Napa–El Timbinal connection? What implications does this case have for the future of Mexican migrant extraterritorial citizenship? The efforts of the panista regional state to constitute a transnational guanajuatense political subject have clearly sought to capitalize on the migrants' existing regional pride and their translocal networks and practices. Before the state identified Napa as a promising site for a Casa Guanajuato club, the Napa migrants from El Timbinal had already pursued several successful self-organized translocal projects for the betterment of their hometown. Because their community and regional pride is quite strong, the timbinalense migrants were initially willing to engage in policy collaboration with the Guanajuato government. Over four years they invested $200,000 in the Mi Comunidad maquiladora. They also formed a Casa Guanajuato club to institutionalize their previously informal social network for community betterment in their village of origin.

Politically, however, the migrant investors never embraced the partisan and clientelist logic underlying the PAN's policy initiatives. The members of the migrant network have made sacrifices to promote community development in El Timbinal. They favor dual citizenship and deem themselves as capable as those who remain in Mexico (if not more so) of full participation in the Mexican political system, from municipal to presidential politics. Yet, as activist extraterritorial citizens, the migrants remain suspicious of Mexican political parties as institutions. Thus, their initial collaboration in panista policy initiatives has not translated into political loyalty to the PAN.

Indeed, the intensity of their skepticism concerning partisan clientelist politics became vividly apparent in a crisis of confidence in the Casas Guanajuato program that erupted in December 2001. The leaders of several Casa Guanajuato clubs, including Calderón, expressed public dissatisfaction with the state's role in the Casas Guanajuato initiative and suggested that they would no longer collaborate with the state. The issues involved in this grassroots rebellion included: (1) the departure of Lupita Zamora, who was viewed by the migrants as a responsive head of the Casa Guanajuato program; (2) allegations that Secretario Oliva had hijacked the resources of the state's migrant programs to promote his political ambitions in a pre-campaign to become Guanajuato's next governor; and (3) claims that the state had not delivered on its commitments to the 2×1 and Mi Comunidad programs.

When interviewed about his break with the state in March and April 2002, Calderón expressed deep distrust of Mexican politicians in general and of Oliva in particular. In his view, Zamora was fired because she tried to gain control of the funding for Casas Guanajuato from the secretario who was diverting money from the organization into his gubernatorial precampaign. The state not only fired her, according to Calderón, it lied about her departure, putting out a cover story that "she went to work in another state," while casting aspersions on her fiscal integrity. He once thought that Governor Romero Hicks was "a good guy" but now sees him as politically weak. He sees a "complete lack of political leadership at the state level in Guanajuato." Furthermore, he pointed out, the mayor of the Municipality of Yuriria had failed to deliver on a promise to provide road improvements for El Timbinal and to meet with migrants and El Timbinal residents to discuss community needs: "I invited him to Timbinal because we were supposed to have a meeting. . . . He says, 'OK, we will be there.' They never show; they never show." Calderón regards Oliva and Romero Hicks as even less responsive. In contrast to his earlier direct access to Vicente Fox, under Romero Hicks and Oliva, "Mr. Governor never answers anything: e-mails, faxes, telephone calls. They never answer anything" (interview with Ángel

Calderón, Calistoga, California, April 20, 2002). Perhaps most significantly, Calderón holds the regional state responsible for his reluctant decision to close down the El Timbinal maquila in December 2001, the same month that he broke with the panista regional state. He explained that under Fox, as the maquila was being built, he was promised and received needed technical and business support:

> The people [in Timbinal] are campesinos, they are not industrialists. They don't know nothing about it, they don't have that mentality. And we are not investors either, we are paisanos. . . . And last year we were making profits, not too much, but we were making profits last year. And everything was fine, until September 11th. . . . We were running the maquila through this company, Confecciones Tula, which has a big contract with businesspeople in the United States. . . . So right after September 11th, I understand that this company closed. . . . Many, many in Irapuato, in Guanajuato, closed down and we are part of them. And I know we were working slow, but we were working. At least we kept that twenty. From twenty to sometimes we were working with fifteen people, but sometimes we have thirty people. We kept them working for three years. But this time we closed in December. (interview with Ángel Calderón, Calistoga, California, April 20, 2002)

In the face of these many disappointments Calderón remains resilient. He hopes to market the maquila's "own product," the baby sets, in the United States through merchandising contacts he has made with the assistance of the Mexican consulate in San Francisco. If this works out he may try to reopen the factory on an as-needed basis to fill the orders he is able to obtain. He will remain active in the Casa Guanajuato organization translocally and promote the betterment of his hometown by working on upgrading the local school. He explained that, in any case, the Casa Guanajuato in Napa was always just his informal migrant network that kept connected and still makes collective decisions informally as they always have done. They only had "formal" organizational meetings when visited by officials of the Guanajuato government.

Meanwhile, on the state's part, Ramón Flores was dispatched to Napa in an unsuccessful effort to mend fences with Calderón and bring him back into the fold. As of this writing, he says he will steer clear of collaboration with the state even if there is a change in leadership at the top. He sees the need for wider changes in political life in Mexico that encourage performance on the part of politicians and the emergence of leaders who teach people how "to be ambitious, or to be a dreamer, or to be the best."

Whatever the long-term outcome of the crisis of confidence in the Casas Guanajuato initiative, several vexing contradictions characterize the PAN's now-disrupted political offensive. Politically, there is a contradiction between the social construction of dual citizenship as "dual gratitude," which implies malleable political subjects, and the practices of the state, which enabled timbinalense migrants to become a local business class and legitimated their bargaining with state and local officials over state infrastructure investment in El Timbinal. Vicente Fox added considerably to Ángel Calderón's political and social status by choosing him as a kind of "model migrante" for migrant reincorporation. He did so by touting Calderón's maquiladora and community development initiatives and inviting him to appear with him on U.S. television and to spend the night in Mexico City at Los Pinos. This is heady stuff indeed, a set of moves more likely to produce a sense of political efficacy and empowerment than to promote mere "dual loyalty." Indeed, this enhanced sense of efficacy now appears to extend to both sides of the transnational border, for Calderón and his network are increasing their political involvement in local ethnic politics in California while continuing to practice transterritorial citizenship.

There is a further contradiction between the economic and status logics underlying the state's migrant initiatives. A stated economic goal of the Mi Comunidad program is to create employment in sending villages that will make future migration less necessary. This elides the fact that all of the workers in the El Timbinal maquiladora are women while most of the state's migrants are men. More important, the patriarchal symbolic politics used by the state to promote Casa Guanajuato clubs inscribes the male migrant as worthy of heroic status, as the dominant figure in heroic statues to be placed in Guanajuato's town squares. Psychologically, by enhancing the social status of el migrante, this political ritual is likely to encourage more male migration from Guanajuato to the United States rather than less.

If the state of Guanajuato were to follow through on its original plan of developing the state as a regional design center, the economic conditions for reversing the long-term dependence of the state on migrant remittances might be established. These might at least partially offset the status incentives toward increased migration found in the Casa Guanajuato program. Yet this does not seem to be in the cards anytime soon. This case study suggests that the state's neglect of sustainable economic development will generate more migrants and render Guanajuato ever more dependent on migrant remittances. These circumstances, in turn, are also likely to help produce less grateful and more demanding extraterritorial citizens.

The programs developed by Guanajuato's political elites depend heavily on migrant remittances. As already noted, the regional state has even developed policies to upgrade the skills of potential migrants before they migrate. Recall that a technological university in Guanajuato has been teaching English to its students with the expectation that those who migrate with English skills will find better jobs and, by implication, have more resources to devote to their transnational role of remittance provider. In light of this policy of upgrading skills before migration, the panista regional state's other stated policy goal of decreasing migration seems to be largely a rhetorical gesture used to legitimate a political offensive that otherwise takes for granted the structural political-economic roots and enduring character of U.S.-Mexican migration and builds this very logic into its remittance-seeking public policies.

Part of the problem of changing the Mexican political culture stems from the fact that for over seventy years there has never been much carry-over of policy commitments or even personnel from administration to administration, as one cadre of political elites replaces another every six years, even if they are in the same political party. This patronage-oriented practice seems to be continuing in Guanajuato, as the panista administration of Hicks and Oliva have replaced experienced administrators from the Fox administration and reoriented programs like Casas Guanajuato to serve different political ends. If the panista regional state accordingly fails to use redirected remittances to live up to its infrastructure development promises because of the continuing significance of clientelism in Mexican state and municipal politics, as has been the case in El Timbinal, the state's overall political offensive is likely to fail. The state's extraterritorial citizens seem increasingly capable of sorting out promise from performance and acting on that basis.

A final contradiction characterizes the PAN's effort to socially construct a pliant form of transnational citizenship. Recall that in response to a question concerning steps being taken to promote voting and political rights across borders, Oliva elides the basic issue of extending political rights to Mexican migrants, claiming that "the dual vote is a reality." To support this claim he notes that some migrants already have contributed to electoral campaigns in Guanajuato, others have returned to Mexico to vote, and still others have returned to Guanajuato to be elected presidents of their municipalities of origin. The examples given by Oliva, although wide in scope, are quite limited in scale. The Mexican migrants who voted in the last two presidential elections, either through absentee ballots or at *casillas especiales* on the border, numbered in the tens of thousands out of the millions of voters who were potentially affected by comprehensive national legislation allowing migrants to vote in presidential elections. Those who have contributed to electoral campaigns in Guanajuato are arguably also a tiny fraction of Guanajuato's transnational migrants. Those who have returned to their communities of origin to be elected *presidentes municipales* are more likely to be "return" rather than "transnational" migrants and "dual" citizens.

Finally, Oliva wishes "the migrant problem" to be viewed as a "direct responsibility of the specific municipalities," rather than "constructed as a national federal matter." This devolutionary policy stance conflicts with the fact that it is precisely at the federal level that political reforms allowing Mexican migrants the right to vote from abroad must be enacted. This radical separation of policymaking from politics raises the question of just how willing the political elites in Guanajuato are to wake up the slumbering giant of the "transnational citizen" by fully extending the right to vote to those who may not match their social imaginary of "double gratitude."

Recrossing the Border: The Politics of Translocality

In the past five years, Ángel Calderón has become networked into the power-knowledge venues of local political life in Napa, California, as well as those of El Timbinal, Guanajuato. He and his migrant network have assumed an activist role on both sides of the translocal space that now constitutes their transnational experience (map 1). The causes and consequences of Calderón's growing involvement in U.S. local and ethnic politics are spelled out in chapter 7, where we focus on the emergence of this second face of transnational citizenship—migrant politics in the U.S. context. For now, suffice it to say that Calderón and his network have been able to transfer the social and political capital they acquired in Guanajuato to the U.S. side of the border. They now regularly interact with prominent leaders in political and civic affairs in Napa. They are active participants in electoral politics and issue-oriented campaigns to advance the interests of migrant farmworkers. They have begun to take full advantage of their newly acquired political access, legitimacy, and electoral influence. Calderón's citizen participation in Napa now parallels his extraterritorial citizenship in El Timbinal and Guanajuato. He and his migrant network are far more active citizens of their native village and of local political life in Napa than the Mexican regional state's model of "double gratitude" would anticipate or than U.S. assimilationists and nationalists like Samuel Huntington would predict.

The question remains whether Ángel Calderón's transnational migrant network is likely to expand its political involvement beyond ethnic and issue-oriented local politics to become engaged in other arenas of U.S. politics at the state and national levels. At first glance there is little direct evidence that the clubs organized by the state of Guanajuato in U.S. communities are moving beyond their focus on Mexican local and regional politics to assume a wider interest-group role in U.S. politics. However, developments among migrants from other Mexican states, particularly the political practices of the Zacatecan transnational activists we have studied in Los Angeles, suggest that this form of dual political engagement is indeed emerging and that cross-border political participation by migrants in Mexican political development is thus not a zero-sum game.

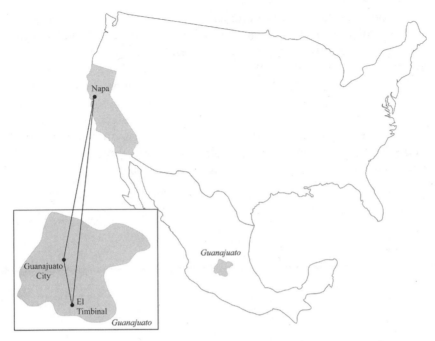

Map 1. The trans-local spaces of guanajuatense extraterritorial citizenship

The Migrant as New Political Subject

This extended case study of the construction of extraterritorial citizenship in Napa–El Timbinal is only one of many such state-migrant political connections shaping the transnationalization of the Mexican political system. Given the scale of migrant remittances and the potential voting power of the migrants, it is hardly surprising that all three major Mexican political parties now seek to forge links with transnational migrants by playing on their residual regional attachments and capitalizing on their translocal connections. Twenty-three Mexican states promote programs similar to the Casas Guanajuato initiative. The changing political dynamics seen in this case study and other research on the politics of migrant hometown and home-state associations suggests a very wide range of agency driving these transnational migrant associations, ranging from highly state-centered to autonomous and even oppositional (cf. Kearney 1995a; Goldring 1996; Levitt 2001b; Fitzgerald 2000; R. Smith 2003b).

Despite the claims of many globalization theorists, this case study has shown that the state has not withered away as a disappearing relic of the end of modernity. Instead, politically constructed state policies, implemented at the regional and local levels, are differentially but ubiquitously mediating the flows of transnational migration, cultural production, and political practice flowing across borders. State policies, legitimating discourses, and institutional practices such as those examined in this book are key elements through which transnational citizenship is being constituted as migrant networks both accommodate to and resist state-centered actors in diasporic projects pursued at various geographical scales. As migrants become involved in the institutional politics of the state they are not merely passive objects of state power or capitalist logics but active agents in the social construction of the practices of transnational citizenship.

4 The Social Construction of "Migrant-Led Productive Investment"

Migrant remittances sent to Mexico have skyrocketed over the last decade, from just under $3.7 billion in 1995 to over $23 billion in 2006 (Banco de México 2007), an increase of over 500 percent. By 2004, Mexico was receiving more remittances than the total sent from the United States to all of the countries of Latin America and the Caribbean—including Mexico itself—as recently as 1999 (Lozano Ascencio 2004a). According to the Banco de México (2005) the increase is a result of both better reporting mechanisms and an increase in remittance flows. Although the official reporting system may be overestimating remittances by including other cross-border monetary transfers (see, e.g., Lozano Ascencio 2004b), a key dimension of the increase in recent years is the rise in the use of formal transfer mechanisms over more traditional informal carriers, a change that allows for more accurate measurement by government officials.

In recent years, international institutions, including the World Bank, the International Monetary Fund, and a variety of organs tied to the United Nations have heavily promoted the use of such formal transfer mechanisms to make remittance flows more transparent and to enhance the "development potential" of those flows. The first of these objectives is intimately tied to international initiatives to fight money laundering and squelch the financing of terrorism. Market mechanisms have been emphasized in this search to enhance the use of the formal sector. Officials in international and state-level institutions attribute the increase in formal transfers in recent years to the growth of and increased competition in the remittance service industry, which has led to greater access and lower costs for consumers (Hernández-Coss 2005).

The promotion of formal money transfer mechanisms is one indicator of the renewed attention government officials, donor organizations, and international institutions are placing on the potential of migrant remittance flows to spur development in migrants' home regions and communities. As a result of this widespread attention, a significant consensus has emerged among migrant-sending states, philanthropic foundations, and international financial institutions about the importance of channeling remittances toward job-creating enterprises in migrant-sending countries, regions, and localities.

Interest in the relationship between migration and development is not new. In the context of Mexico-U.S. migration, for instance, there were intense debates on migration and development throughout the 1980s and 1990s (see Binford 2003 for a review of those debates; see Cohen et al. 2005 for a challenging response to Binford). Adopting the typology first presented by Richard Jones (1995), Binford has argued that the competing positions in these debates can be usefully characterized as "structuralist" and "functionalist" (Binford 2003, 310). The structuralist approach, represented by Tiechart (1981) and Mines (1981) among others, argued that remittances create dependency on migration in sending regions and trap migrant-sending communities in a self-perpetuating cycle of migration. In Binford's account, by the 1990s proponents of the functionalist approach, such as Durand (1994), Jones (1995), and Massey and Parado (1998), presented more positive assessments of the "development potential" of remittances, which they viewed as contributing to development in a variety of ways, including through direct investment in rural businesses and through the multiplier effects generated by remittance income spent on consumption and social reproduction. These debates largely petered out by the mid-1990s as the proponents of the structuralist and functionalist approaches reached an impasse (Goldring 2004).

It is perhaps not surprising, in the context of heightened U.S.-Mexican migration and increasingly vocal opposition to it from nativist movements in the United States, that these issues would resurface. What is surprising, however, is how these issues have brought back into prominence the language of "development," since the very idea of international development has came under such severe attack in the last two decades. With the ascendancy of neoliberal globalization by the mid-1980s, the "development" ideal seemed beset from all sides. For some, this represented an epochal shift from the dominance of a "development project" aimed at replicating the transition to modern industrial capitalism in the nation-states of the "developing world" to a "globalization project" that eschewed such lofty goals in favor of the more limited objective of facilitating the insertion of national economies into a rapidly globalizing economy (McMichael 2000). Proponents of the so-called post-development school went even further, asserting that the ideology and practice of "development" was a Euro-centric and imperialist project that was misrepresented from its very beginnings (Escobar 1995; Esteva and Prakash 1998; Ferguson 1990; Sachs 1992). This loose group of scholars generally argued that the concept and workings of "development" were hopelessly flawed, necessitating not new, alternative forms *of* development but alternatives *to* development.

In the face of the scathing critiques of the development ideal and the significant transformations of the global political economy in the past two decades, what sense can we make of the "remittances-to-development" agenda pursued by various agents of "migrant-led-development" at the contemporary neoliberal moment? What is the role of the migrant in this discourse? How do the transnational practices of Zacatecan migrant leaders and activists conform to or deviate from the discursive ideal of the development community?

In this chapter we address these questions by examining the recent interplay of the leadership of the Los Angeles–based Zacatecan Federation of Hometown Associations of Southern California (FCZSC) with the "development" agenda of the global development apparatus. As the role of migrant remittances in official development discourse gained prominence in recent years, Zacatecan hometown association leaders have increasingly engaged with state-centered actors in Zacatecas and with what has come to be termed the "international donor community" in promoting remittance-driven, job-creating investment in Zacatecas. This newfound objective for the FCZSC represents a significant shift from the social and infrastructure projects that HTAs have successfully pursued in past decades. While those earlier projects brought Zacatecan HTA leaders into negotiations and relationships with officials from local, state, and federal levels of government in Mexico, this new move has brought them into a wider range of relations than those forged in earlier years.

Many scholars of neoliberal globalization might be inclined to see the participation of HTA leaders in these collaborative projects as nothing more than co-optation. This has certainly been a common neo-Marxist theme regarding the politics of cooperation by NGOs and other grassroots actors with neoliberal states and international institutions (see, e.g., Petras 1997; Dolhinow 2005; Yaworsky 2005). Because such interpretations reject all political practice short of revolution, we find such arguments not only politically paralyzing (Block 2005), but intellectually unsatisfying. The reality is much more complex. The migrant leaders we have studied, like most grassroots political actors, are not cultural and political dupes. They are driven by their own hopes, desires, and dreams—one might even say "interests"—and are not simply blindly obeying the dictates of more powerful actors and forces. This means that these collaborative "partnerships" involve complex negotiations between a variety of social actors and interests. In short, they entail a great deal more agency than a co-optation interpretation would allow.

The Politics of "Anti-politics"

James Ferguson's now-classic work *The Anti-Politics Machine* (1990) provides insights from his seminal study of the "development industry" that remain relevant to our understanding of the contemporary "remittance-to-development" discourse and practice. *The Anti-Politics Machine* sought to explain the machinations of the development apparatus in Lesotho in the 1970s and 1980s. Inspired by Foucauldian notions of discursive power and governmentality (Foucault 1991), Ferguson explored the disconnection between the discourse of "development" promulgated by such institutions as the World Bank (and, in Lesotho, the Canadian International Development Agency) and social realities in Lesotho. He argued persuasively that, given the structural requirements of the "development" discourse, development planners tend to construct representations of "less developed countries" that present those places as amenable to the types of interventions that the "development apparatus" is capable of undertaking. What this means is that the problems faced by "less developed countries" are always presented as technical in nature rather than political. The problems are envisaged as emanating from a perceived lack of some important structural feature of a modern economy. In short, "the economy" has needs that can be remedied by the apolitical and technical interventions of the development institutions. In the end, "development" discourse and its conceptual apparatus serve to depoliticize poverty and inequality, turning these maladies into technical problems to be solved through the plans and projects drawn up by "development" experts.

Precisely because this decontextualized, apolitical, and technical account of the "development" problematic is a *mis*representation of the social, cultural, geographical, and historical specificities of particular "less developed countries," the interventions of development institutions nearly always result in failure. The development apparatus, according to Ferguson, is particularly ill equipped to deal with the intractable problems of "underdevelopment" because such problems would require significant political actions that "development" institutions are unwilling to undertake. After all, they "are not in the business of promoting political realignments" (1990, 69).

The one institution, the nation-state, that could arguably undertake the types of actions that might lead to more successful "development" projects as in Lesotho, for example, a forced de-stocking of oxen, is unwilling to take on such politically unpopular tasks because the state's interest in "development" projects is to shore up political support and control, not to potentially undermine them. Far from placing the state in a vulnerable position, one of the main impacts of "development" projects is to increase and solidify the bureaucratic state apparatus. So, given its propensity for failure, what explains the continuing power of the "development" discourse?

Ferguson argues that, while "development" may rarely be deemed successful in terms of its own stated objectives, it must be fulfilling other, albeit unintentional, purposes that explain its continued application. Drawing on Foucault, Ferguson argues that it is most fruitful to think of these unintended consequences not as "side effects," but as "instrument-effects." These effects are twofold: first, "development" discourse has powerful "conceptual effects," depoliticizing the issues and thus undermining political contestation by presenting resolutely political issues as technical "problems" to be addressed by the interventions that the development apparatus is designed to provide; second, there are important "institutional effects" of the failure of development policy, which lead to an expansion of bureaucratic state power. Importantly, Ferguson's Foucauldian understanding of power suggests that these institutional effects are not the intentional results of the "development" project, meeting the interests of the ruling elite or any other powerful subject, but instead emerge "counter-intentionally through the working out of a complex and unacknowledged structure of knowledge in interaction with equally complex and unacknowledged local social and cultural structures" (1990, 270). Thus, for Ferguson, the most important consequences of development practice are not consciously willed by a powerful subject but are the unintentional result of the clash between the ahistorical and decontextualized structure of the (global) "development" discourse and the historically contingent (local) social and cultural structures they confront.

Ferguson's book offers a number of promising tools for contemporary ethnographic interrogations of the "development industry" and its global interventions. First, he helps to turn the study of development away from any abstract, macrolevel account that would present "development" as an inexorable and unilinear historical process of social change leading to a certain end state, namely the modern industrial capitalist economy. Taking Ferguson's lead, by contrast, moves us toward a more grounded enquiry taking into account all of the messy and contingent details of the practices, discursive and otherwise, of, in our case, migrants, the state, and the international development institutions. Second, his work nudges us to look beneath the official discursive representations of "development" and its objectives in search of the unstated goals that might explain its surprising resilience in the face of such glaring failure.

Although Ferguson's book does provide important theoretical insights, the contemporary significance of the analysis has been deeply affected by the large-scale transformations in the global political economy in the years after his field research. As Edelman (2000, 8) perceptively argues, one of the central assertions of Ferguson and other "post-development" theorists— namely that "development" serves to expand and strengthen the state—flies in the face of the ideology and preferred practices of neoliberal globalization that has become hegemonic in policy-making circles in the last two decades.

We should be wary, however, of the tendency in many accounts of neoliberal globalization to overemphasize the diminishing role and capacity of the nation-state in the present period. Long ago in *The Great Transformation* (2001 [1944]), Karl Polanyi showed us that any sustained effort at laissez faire was a recipe for disaster. This lesson has not been completely lost on today's neoliberal ideologues and policymakers, despite repeated assertions to the contrary. Thus, while the early years of neoliberal reform were characterized by an intensive "roll-back" of state functions and services, the initial period was quickly followed by a new round of *re*regulation, a veritable "roll-out" of the state (Peck and Tickell 2002, 384). In light of these trends, we find it more useful and accurate to conceptualize the current period as one characterized by new forms of state regulation, such as those revealed in Guanajuato in chapter 3, rather than the superseding of the state by global capitalism and transnational corporations.

Despite Edelman's tendency to fall into a "hyper-globalist" (Held et al. 1999) view of neoliberalism that sees state powers being evacuated by higher level forces, his fundamental point about the "post-development" school, or what he terms the "postmodernist anthropology of development," does still hold: this literature, particularly in its early incarnations, largely overlooks the neoliberal turn. In Ferguson's case, of course, this is not the result of some theoretical blind spot but is a function of the historical period he studied— 1979–84—just before the wholesale application of the neoliberal model.

One effect the neoliberal model has had on "development" has been to substantially increase the range of actors making up the development apparatus, including the incorporation of parts of the burgeoning NGO sector. A second impact of the neoliberal model concerns its reach into the political sphere. It seems much less plausible in the neoliberal era to argue, as Ferguson does (1990, 192), that development institutions are hesitant and in fact unable to effect large-scale political-economic transformations. Structural adjustment programs, perhaps the most obvious manifestation of neoliberalism in the "developing world," have made patently obvious the capacity and the willingness of international financial and development institutions to impose lending conditionalities as a means to obtain significant political and structural changes in their recipient states.

Finally, in addition to these historical grounds, Ferguson's work can be interrogated and extended along more substantive lines. This requires abandoning the overly structural reading of the power of discourse in favor of a more agency-oriented theoretical perspective (see M. P. Smith 2001) that views the discourse of "remittances-to-development" not as a determinative structure but as a contested field in which the targets of "development" are capable of talking and acting back. Such an approach undermines the view of the development discourse as being necessarily depoliticizing. Instead, our approach recognizes that the various social and political actors engaged in the development problematic are driven by different political perspectives and interests. As these come together and clash in the public realm there is always the potential for transforming dominant discourses, structures, and forces that are not timelessly enduring, but instead always in the making.

A clear recognition of the ascendancy of neoliberal globalization necessarily leads the ethnography of development along new lines. This does not require a return to highly localized studies of the "underdeveloped" peoples on whom "development" is being done, but instead requires an interrogation of the polyvocality of development discourse because its institutional apparatus is made up of a broader range of political actors, from the global-level financial institutions to the representatives of national states and the grassroots. Key questions animating agency-oriented ethnographic accounts of the development apparatus include: What are the roles of the national, regional, and local states in neoliberal "development"? What role do international development institutions play? In what ways have nonstate, grassroots actors become articulated with official "development" schemes? Is this simply co-optation, or is something else at play? Are grassroots actors capable of exercising political agency in these contexts, or are their concerns necessarily depoliticized by technical representations of the development problematic?

The Discursive Contours of "Migrant-Led Development"

What are the main contours of the top-down development discourse constructed by Mexican and U.S. states? How has the Inter-American Development Bank framed its discourse about the "migration and development nexus" and the "productive potential" of migrant remittances? Addressing these two questions serves to place the ethnographic portrait of our research subjects' engagement with migrant-led development initiatives squarely within the larger political-economic context of North American neoliberal globalization.

Neoliberal Development Discourse in the United States and Mexico

Within the context of the neoliberal U.S.-Mexico partnership, market mechanisms have become a kind of magic wand for public officials in both nations for promoting the productive use of remittances among Mexican migrants. Surrounded by all the fanfare of the United Nations-sponsored "International Conference on Financing for Development," held in Monterrey, Mexico, in March 2002, Presidents George W. Bush and Vicente Fox were presented with a report from the Partnership for Prosperity that they had created two years earlier. The aim of the P4P initiative was to "foster growth in [the] less developed parts of Mexico . . . harness[ing] the power of free markets to boost the social and economic well being of citizens, particularly in regions where economic growth has lagged and fueled migration" (Partnership for Prosperity 2002). The idea that free markets and private enterprise are the most desirable and effective vehicles for economic growth and development, which was the backbone of the P4P project, continues to be the dominant approach of the Bush administration in addressing issues of global poverty and inequality. At the meetings of the G8 in 2004, for example, President Bush succeeded in gaining support for his "private sector-led development" proposals that represent "economic freedom and entrepreneurship as key drivers of job creation and poverty reduction" (Group of Eight 2004).

In both major policy formulations, the theme of putting migrant remittances to productive use takes a prominent place. Consistent with the overall framework of these proposals, the "remittances-to-development" agenda is best achieved, according to the Bush doctrine, through the market. The Bush administration's discourse on development thus relies heavily on the hypothesis that remittances can be channeled toward productive investment by encouraging more competition in the transfer services industry, removing constraints on this market and pushing migrants into formal banking institutions ("banking the unbanked" in the official lingo).

President Fox's public address illustrates how remittances became an important development tool on the Mexican side of the U.S.-Mexico transnational space:

> One of the greatest concerns of Mexican workers in the United States was that all of the money they sent home would reach their family members. This worry has diminished now that we have different businesses providing remittances services; however, our paisanos complain about the high costs of these transfers, which is why we are establishing agreements with businesses . . . [reducing] the cost of these transfers . . .

We could have opted to establish some sort of government and state mechanism to fulfill this task, but we believe in . . . private enterprise . . . so that our paisanos can see more benefit from their efforts and their work.

Similarly . . . we should be sure to support nationally the program that exists in various states so that this "Two for One" program would allow for the investments and transfers that our paisanos send to go not only to consumption, as they do currently, but for them to go toward investments in their communities . . . [and] in productive projects . . . that the paisanos themselves and their family members in their communities will be owners and share-holders of. That will allow for the financing and generation of the sources of employment that are needed in order to be able to hold on to the young people of the future. (President Vicente Fox, "Commitments to *El Paisano*: Remittances and Services," Guanajuato, March 3, 2001)

Fox's language provides a clear demonstration of the particular form in which the Mexican government now embraces and seeks to engage Mexican migrants living abroad. During the presidential administrations of Salinas, Zedillo, and Fox the Mexican state crafted a coherent set of migrant reincorporation policies that sought to capitalize on the political, social, and economic resources of Mexican nationals whose lives straddle the border. Fox's language makes clear just how deeply these migrant reincorporation policies have become enmeshed with the neoliberal ideological project that is hegemonic in both Mexico and the United States.

It is in this context of the dominance of the neoliberal ideological and institutional model that we must try to make sense of migrant-state relations in the U.S.-Mexico public sphere. Seen through the optic of the neoliberal Mexican state—as Fox's pronouncement makes clear—migrants' political claims and social concerns are to be addressed through the market and private enterprise. They and their families remaining in their communities of origin are heralded not as citizens, or even as transnational families, but as potential investors and shareholders in "productive projects" capable of generating employment opportunities, putting a halt to migration, and, in the process, transforming the historic role of these communities as sources of migrant labor for the United States. (For an alternative discourse on migrant-led productive investment see Moctezuma Longoria 2002a.)

The Remittances-to-Development Agenda of the Inter-American Development Bank

The market fundamentalism at the core of the Mexico-U.S. partnership has been extended into the realm of state-migrant relations. Migrants and their remittances have been envisioned as essential contributors to neoliberal "development" by state-level elites—if they can be effectively and efficiently incorporated into financial markets. But, other than President Fox's mention of the inclusion of "productive projects" in the Mexican state's 2×1 (now 3×1) matching-grant program, how have these policy visions been translated into practice? How are migrant remittances represented by and incorporated into the policy schemes of the "global development" apparatus?

The discourse on remittances and development constructed by the Inter-American Development Bank has become increasingly institutionalized in the first decade of the twenty-first century. We have strategically chosen to highlight the IADB discourse because, among all the organizations that make up the international "donor community," the IADB has become the leading promoter of reconfiguring remittances as a development tool. Since 2001 the IADB, through its Multilateral Investment Fund (MIF), has worked throughout Latin America and the Caribbean to promote a vision of migrant remittances as a development tool to be utilized by states in the hemisphere. The MIF has commissioned studies and convened conferences across the region to discuss remittances and their potential impact on development, as well as funding a variety of regionwide or nation-centered projects.

As a result of the IADB's intensive work in the area over the last half decade, the MIF program on remittances has now developed an elaborate discursive model of the role and impact of remittances in the development of migrant-sending regions in particular states. This model is centered around a two-pronged remittances-to-development strategy. The first objective is to increase the financial resources available to remittance recipients. The second is to increase the development impact of those remittances. Not surprisingly, financial markets are the key arena through which the MIF hopes to achieve its goals. As stated in one of the program's key strategy documents, "To achieve this [dual-pronged] goal the MIF has been trying to stimulate private sector forces in the remittances market. In order to strengthen the remittances market, MIF seeks to support every aspect of the market that could promote competition" ("MIF Strategy and Program on Remittances").[1]

In line with the goals of the other major international financial institutions mentioned above, the MIF program focuses heavily on constructing a consensus around the importance of lowering remittance transfer costs and moving remittance senders and receivers into the formal financial sector. This is realized through a healthy dose of advocacy and good old-fashioned consciousness raising. In terms of lowering transmission costs, the MIF

---

1. This and other policy documents cited here are drawn from the website of the MIF's program on remittances, http://iadb.org/mif/remittances/index.cfm.

claims to have undertaken "a systematic campaign of *awareness-raising* and the *knowledge dissemination* [that is] greatly raising the awareness of policymakers and key stakeholders as to this important issue" ("Advocacy: Remittances Principles").

As a result of this systematic consensus-building campaign, the MIF and its partners have constructed a set of "core principles" for each of the "key stakeholders" in the "remittances market": remittance-service providers, public authorities, and civil society. Financial institutions are implored to improve transparency, use new and appropriate technologies, promote "fair and competitive" pricing, form partnerships, and expand their financial services. Civil society is expected to "leverage" the "development impact" of remittances and "support the social and financial inclusion of transnational families into their communities." Finally, governments are asked to improve their data collection on remittances, facilitate the "mainstreaming" of remittances into the formal financial sector by "improving" the regulatory environment, promote the benefits of financial services among their citizenry, and, in typical neoliberal fashion, are cautioned to "do no harm" and "avoid attempts to tax, overregulate or otherwise take actions that impede the flow of remittances" ("Advocacy: Remittances Principles").

The market-oriented neoliberal discourse of the MIF program on remittances is probably best illustrated by reference to the policy study "Remittances 2004: Transforming Labor Markets and Promoting Financial Democracy." This policy brief, first presented at the IADB/MIF conference "Sending Money Home: The 2004 Map of Remittance Flows to Latin America" in New York in March 2005, succinctly presents the conceptual apparatus governing the MIF's discursive model of remittance-led development. "Remittances 2004" begins with what might be read as a standard Marxist account of international labor migration—stating, for instance, that "the basic equation in the Americas, and throughout the world, is quite simple: developed countries need migrant labor, and families back home need remittances. . . . So people move 'North' by the millions, and money moves 'South' by the billions":

> Call it the case of the missing billions. For generations, millions of migrant workers have been sending billions of dollars back to their home countries to support their families. But these flows of both money and people have been hidden in plain sight for decades. Why? Because the money is sent regularly in small amounts, usually outside the formal financial system; and the workers typically live on the margins of society. All of this is now changing. (Multilateral Investment Fund/Inter-American Development Bank, "Remittances 2004," New York, March 2005)

The migration process is presented in a neoliberal manner as "profoundly entrepreneurial," as migrants—"like entrepreneurs who seek markets around the world"—crisscross the globe "in search of comparative advantage." Interestingly, the language of transnationalism is employed to argue that, the migrants' entrepreneurial spirit notwithstanding, "the driving force [is] . . . a commitment to family values. . . . These are transnational families, living and contributing to two countries, two economies, and two cultures at the same time." In recognition of the profound effects of these transnational migration flows on global labor markets, the report stresses the need to adopt "new rules and mechanisms to meet the modern realities" of migrant labor in world labor markets (Multilateral Investment Fund 2005).What might this vague reference to "new rules and mechanisms" mean? Is this a gesture toward liberalization of immigration policies in the industrialized North, a plea for open borders? Not in this neoliberal development recipe. Instead, this call for new rules and mechanisms is an allusion to the goal of moving remittance providers and recipients into the formal banking sector, which the report terms "financial democracy." After estimating that only some 10 percent of remittance recipients "have access to" bank accounts and other financial services, the report envisions that, by the end of the decade, "millions of poor people can be brought into the financial system, and remittance can be leveraged by linking flows to local microfinance institutions, home mortgages, and even the securitization of bonds." Returning to the individual/familial-level emphasis, remittances are presented as "individual decisions made in the best interest of individual families." In the neoliberal utopia presented in "Remittances 2004," the challenge for the MIF and its collaborators is simply to give migrants and their families "more options to use their own money" because when migrants and their families have those options "they will do the rest" (Multilateral Investment Fund 2005).

Consistent with neoliberal premises, the remittances-to-development discourse of the Mexican and U.S. states and the international financial institutions situates the potential for migration-led development with the individual migrant entrepreneur and the market. In the IADB's ambitious vision of financial democracy, market-driven, inclusionary changes in the formal banking and money transfer industries offer to make every poor migrant and remittance recipient an entrepreneur. The rhetoric of "financial democracy" and the concomitant expectation that it might miraculously transform millions of poor migrants and their families into entrepreneurs conveniently ignores the actual dimensions and importance of remittances.

Official statistics show that the aggregate amount of worker's remittances to migrant-sending countries has grown substantially over the last decade.

In Mexico this increase in remittances has not made great strides in reducing poverty (Lozano Ascencio and Olivera Lozano 2005), much less given the mass of remittance recipients a large pool of disposable income or savings that could be directed toward "productive investment." Nevertheless, persistent poverty in Mexico, particularly in its rural hinterlands, has forced Mexican state officials to seek partnership with migrant hometown associations in order to channel the collective social and economic capital of these associations toward job-creating productive investment.

Collective Remittances: From "Social Infrastructure" to "Productive Investment"

The organized Zacatecan migrants in southern California have been trail-blazers in developing transnational public-private partnerships with the Mexican state to promote community development. As noted in chapter 2, beginning with the administration of Governor Genaro Borrego (1986–92), the Zacatecan federation in southern California began cooperating on community development projects with the state and municipal authorities in Zacatecas, helping to finance potable water projects, schools, electrical and telephone services, nursing homes, and more (see, e.g., Mestries 1998). That early cooperative program, in which migrants provided the bulk of financing for these projects, eventually became institutionalized as a matching-grant program in which migrant contributions were matched peso for peso by the state government. Over the years, that initial program has gone through a number of incarnations, increasingly incorporating additional partners.

For a brief period in the early 1990s the matching-grant program was extended to the entire country under the auspices of the neocorporatist Solidaridad Internacional program of President Carlos Salinas, only to be axed as a consequence of *el error de diciembre,* the economic meltdown of December 1994 that caused large-scale capital flight and a swift decline of currency reserves over the final year of the Salinas administration. Although the program technically survived in Zacatecas even after the Solidaridad Internacional program was terminated, it was not until the late 1990s, during the governorship of Ricardo Monreal Ávila, that it experienced a real resurgence, expanding from a budget of just under $50 million pesos (US $5 million) in 1999, the first full year of his administration, to well over $150 million pesos by the end of his six-year term (Delgado Wise, Márquez Covarrubias, and Rodríguez Ramírez 2004).

After assuming the presidency in 2000, Vicente Fox expressed keen interest in the program. Given the entrepreneurial nature of the migrant-investment schemes he promoted as governor of Guanajuato in the 1990s it

Fig. 4. An early "productive project" in Jomulquillo, Zacatecas. Photo by Pat Smith.

is not surprising that Fox would try to create a hybrid of the "social infrastructure" and "entrepreneurial" approaches followed by Zacatecas and Guanajuato, respectively (Torres 2001). By 2002, with renewed success in Zacatecas and lobbying from migrant leaders, the 3×1 program for migrants[2] was expanded to the federal level. By October 2005, the program had added an additional private-sector "partner," with the new 4×1 program including a $1.25 million contribution from the First Data Corporation, the parent company of Western Union and Orlanda Valuti, two giants in the remittance transfer business (Inter-American Dialogue 2005).

Although some small-scale productive projects were financed by the early state-level program in Zacatecas, the bulk of projects in both state and federal programs have been "social projects" providing community infrastructure and recreational resources clearly understood to be public goods and not for the personal enrichment of individual investors or HTA leaders. Yet, as early as 2001 the leadership of the FCZSC began promoting the creation of a 2×1 program with the federal and state governments to help finance job-creating productive projects by migrants in their hometowns

2. On its expansion to the federal level, the program was initially baptized Citizens' Initiative 3×1 and was open to migrant HTAs and community-based organizations in Mexico as well. Following the first year of implementation, the program's name and structure became the focal points of intense debate among the Zacatecan migrant leaders due to their perceptions that program funds were being diverted to the politically motivated projects of mayors across the state. Because of the pressure this provoked, the name was changed to its current form in 2004.

(Gómez 2001). Since that time, the idea of transferring the energies of migrant hometown associations toward economic development and productive projects has gained real momentum.

One indication of this added momentum is the increasing attention of international foundations toward the transnational activities of HTAs. For instance, in 2003 the FZCSC received a $214,000 grant from the Rockefeller Foundation's North American Transnational Communities program. That money was intended to help the Federation build "its capacity to promote and sustain sustainable strategic philanthropic investment in Zacatecas" (Rockefeller Foundation 2003, 73). Such "capacity building" funding allowed the FCZSC to install a computer lab in the Federation's building and to provide basic computer training to club and HTA leaders. More important for our purposes, the Federation hired one of its HTA leaders in a full-time position as philanthropic director in Los Angeles to promote productive investment and to employ a project coordinator in Zacatecas. The complex networks linking the FCZSC in Los Angeles to the community development agendas of the three levels of the Mexican state, the international donor community, and the global development industry are represented visually in map 2.

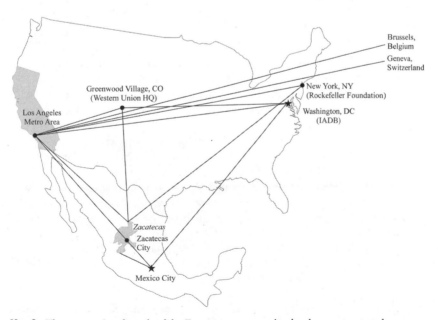

Map 2. The transnational reach of the Zacatecan community development network

The Migrants' Perceptions of "Migrant-Led Development"

What has driven the migrant leaders of southern California to promote a move from their traditional "community development" activities toward "productive projects" in their home communities? Is their view of migrant-led development wholly consistent with the vision expounded by the U.S. and Mexican states and the international financial institutions? Or is there some dissonance between the views from above and from below?

Migration as Option rather than Necessity

In our conversations with migrant HTA leaders, the objective of turning migration into a choice for rural Zacatecans was often the principal reason these grassroots activists were promoting the turn to productive investment. It might seem somewhat contradictory for these migrant leaders, whose own lives, for the most part, have been enriched through the migration process to be so desirous of stemming the tide of migration to El Norte. However, a careful analysis of their complex descriptions of this goal, and the migration experience more generally, help to explain this apparent contradiction. Consider first the voices of three prominent FCZSC leaders: Efraín Jiménez, the philanthropic director of the FCZSC; Guadalupe Gómez, a former president of the Federation; and Martha Jiménez, one of the Federation's most active female leaders. These transnational migrant activists express a good deal of the complexity of sentiments shared by most of our interview subjects:

> We want to create a solution for emigrants. All Zacatecans [now] come to the United States because they have to. And we don't want that. We want that to be an option, not a necessity. For a Zacatecan to stay, who lives in Zacatecas, we want them to have that option to come to the U.S. if they want to . . . but not a necessity. Because right now they don't have [any] choice, they have to come over here. (interview with Efraín Jiménez, Los Angeles, May 13, 2004)
>
> I'm concerned about the future of our communities in Mexico. And we're concerned about the future of Mexico. We have the resources to develop [into] another Canada or another country that can one day say that its citizens will travel not because they have to but because they want to. They want to come here because they want to go to Disneyland, because they want to go to Magic Mountain. You know, that's got to be the objective one day, the long-term objective. (interview with Guadalupe Gómez, Los Angeles, May 14, 2004)
>
> [Migration] will never stop, because, for instance, in Zacatecas it's a way of life: you go north. It's a way of life to look for better opportunities. That's why people like us come, because there is no hope over there. Why did my father come to the U.S.? Because cattle died. Because it never rained. . . . So it's about a necessity. (interview with Martha Jiménez, Los Angeles, March 24, 2005)

On their face, these assessments illustrate two important points. First, migration from Zacatecas is experienced, or at least represented, as an economic necessity and as a communal expectation or rite of passage in migrant-sending communities. Second, these voices suggest that even if economic development and job creation is "successful" in Mexico's migrant-sending regions this is still unlikely to put a stop to migration, as some people will continue to "choose" to migrate in search of the ever-illusive "better opportunities" and greener pastures represented in timeless myths of the journeys to El Norte.

But even more important, these excerpts grant us access to a subtext underlying the turn to productive investment. That these migrants, who are among the proverbial handful of Mexican migrants who have met with real economic success in the United States and thus sustain the migration myth, would not fully endorse migration as a livelihood strategy might come as somewhat of a surprise. And yet they express an ambivalence about the migration process that negates any undifferentiated view of its impacts on individuals and communities. This ambivalence toward the migration experience and toward the differential opportunities available to migrants in the United States was most strikingly expressed in our interview with Manuel de la Cruz, a former FCZSC president and now PRD "migrant deputy" in the Zacatecan Congress. He began with a nationalist reading of the dangers of U.S.-bound migration:

> Mexico does not need to be sending so many migrants, for so many people to be leaving. It is a real shame. They arrive in the United States and they don't have any rights. They work and work, and everything that they should receive in benefits is retained by the U.S. government even though the United States didn't spend a single penny creating that source of labor. Here when they study, the students that are most successful finish their degree and they can't find work. So they go to the United States. That is terrible! It's dreadful! What can we expect of a country like Mexico if it continues like that? It's going to continue diminishing; it will dry up. Or the time will come when we're like Puerto Rico. Damn! [*laughs*] A commonwealth of the United States! (interview with Manuel de la Cruz, Zacatecas, Zacatecas, June 25, 2004)

Within moments, however, de la Cruz recognizes that "my interests are over there, and the only thing that is here is my wish that Mexico progress. My children are there, my houses are there, everything is there, and here is where my heart is at [*laughs*]. What can you do? What can I do?"

These ambivalent feelings, perhaps more amplified in the discourse of the state's first migrant deputy than among most migrants, are a testament to the enduring legacy and continued sting of racism, discrimination, and exclusion that Mexicans face in their everyday lives and engagement in political affairs in the United States. This dark side of the migration experience helps explain why these successful migrants are so strongly in favor of slowing migration, of giving potential migrants other choices.

Productive Projects: The Next Step toward Progress?

How do the migrants envision their desired transition from "migration as necessity" to "migration as option"? What are the obstacles to its enactment? HTA leaders are deeply concerned about the future of their home communities. The activities of their clubs are, by definition, aimed at the betterment of those communities through the construction of public infrastructure and the provision of more modern urban amenities. The success that migrant leaders have experienced in creating the matching-grant program and funding projects in their home communities has helped to propel them into more expansive forms of community involvement. Thus, for the leaders of the FCZSC, their participation in the various incarnations of the 3×1 program led to more far-reaching consequences as these migrants gained social and political capital that could be mobilized for other ends. Luin Goldring, for instance, notes how the Zacatecan HTA leaders' participation in the 2×1 program provided an interactive arena where the discursive and political projects of "migrant-led" and "state-led" transnationalisms confronted each other and gave migrants a space to "renegotiate the[ir] relationship with the national state" in ways that challenged traditional corporatist and clientelistic readings of state-society relations in Mexico (Goldring 2002, 70).

The sense of efficacy generated by these productive engagements with state structures and government officials empowers migrant leaders to act in increasingly political ways in other spheres of their lives. For the FCZSC this empowerment enabled certain of its leaders to take on a fuller and more explicit engagement with politics in both the United States and Zacatecas, as well as a turn to more comprehensive views of the possibilities and requirements for migrant contributions to community development in their "home" state.

The turn to productive investment and job-creating projects by the FCZSC, although still in its infancy, represents just such a comprehensive vision of community development as migrant leaders seek to move beyond simply contributing to basic infrastructure, urban services, and cultural and recreational amenities. The following excerpt from our interview with Manuel de la Cruz illustrates how migrants view this move beyond "social projects":

> BAKKER: So then you view positively the transition that the FCZSC is making from social projects to productive investment?

DE LA CRUZ: Of course. Because we've already taken the first step. You can't do a productive project if you don't have communication links or the basic services, like sewage, potable water, schools, clinics. But, if we already have them . . . we already did that.

BAKKER: So it's a second step?

DE LA CRUZ: It is the next step, the second step; it is obligatory that we begin and establish productive projects to continue progressing. We cannot stay like that. We cannot leave the villages abandoned, beautiful. We can't do that. So that our people no longer have to migrate or stay over there, jobs have to be created. (interview with Manuel de la Cruz, Zacatecas, Zacatecas, June 25, 2004)

Despite de la Cruz's rhetoric, it is not clear that migrant-government collaborative projects have completed the "first step," providing the communication and infrastructural networks that would be necessary to attract investment and generate the employment opportunities that might help change *zacatecanos'* perception of migration as a necessity. Another of our interview subjects, Felipe Delgado—a longtime migrant leader and successor to de la Cruz as official representative of the Zacatecan government in the United States—spoke frankly about the difficulty of attracting investors due to the state's deficient transportation and communications infrastructures. For example, Delgado told us, "Roads are more difficult than in the United States. [Imagine] if you are creating glass or products like [that]. We have to work a lot in order to have an infrastructure [like there would be] in any other part of the world. So, I do promote my state in different ways, but it is very difficult" (interview with Felipe Delgado, Los Angeles, California, November 13, 2003).

This voice from the regional state identifying infrastructural barriers to the successful attraction of investors and job-creating enterprises begins to pierce the utopian representations of migrant remittances as a potential development tool. Although in the official discourse of the international financial institutions and the U.S. and Mexican governments the problems facing migrant-sending regions are largely the consequence of a lack of capital that could be remedied by channeling remittances toward investment, the migrant leaders we spoke with were fully aware of other barriers to a healthy economy. The migrant leaders did not express the same optimism as the policymakers that the economic causes of migration might be resolved simply because "the missing billions" of migrant remittances had suddenly been found by national and international policymakers.

The types of contextual barriers that migrant leaders identify range widely. For some, the main problem is the unclear and uninviting policy and regulatory environment in Mexico; we were told by one pessimistic federation leader, for example, that Zacatecan HTAs still preferred "social projects" to "productive projects" because "the laws aren't clear" and that "they tax you based on your investment, [not] on your profit" (interview with Felipe Cabral, Hawaiian Gardens, California, May 15, 2004).

A recurring theme in our interviews was the difficulty facing the agricultural sector. Small-to-medium–size agricultural producers have been devastated throughout the country as a result of trade liberalization and cuts in government supports in the neoliberal period. Yet, migrant leaders diverge on the cause of the problems faced by the state's campesino sector and the potential solutions to those problems. Felipe Delgado, for instance, who makes his living as the co-owner of a family-based furniture manufacturing business, identified the oversaturation of markets with traditional agricultural crops as causing economic hardship for campesinos. However, Delgado does not suggest that this is simply the result of supply outstripping demand; he told us instead that "in our state we have a problem year after year, that we just grow beans: beans, beans, beans. By the end of the year we have thousands and thousands of tons of beans." While arguing that there is "no market" for so many beans, Delgado, far from attributing this to abstract market forces, points to an identifiable agent that affects campesino livelihoods—the market intermediary or *coyote*—telling us: "The *coyotes* buy a kilogram of beans for nothing," paying the producers perhaps twenty cents per kilo, whereas "in the market you find that it is $1.70 a kilo."

Echoing an opinion shared by other regional state leaders, Delgado's solution is to bypass the *coyotes* and move toward nontraditional, export-oriented production. In this vision, greenhouse production is the preferred solution for two reasons: first, because their controlled environment can save on costly electricity and scarce water resources; and second, because greenhouse production of nontraditional produce, such as bell peppers and tomatoes, can be effectively timed to fill a niche in the U.S. market, providing these products during the two-to-three-month period when competitors from the United States and the Mexican state of Sinaloa have finished their harvest. In recent years Zacatecas has seen a significant increase in greenhouse production, but, according to an official with the Secretariat of Economic Development in Zacatecas, "it is very hard to convert the traditional farming guys to greenhouses" because of the cost—about $1 million per hectare of greenhouses. Consequently, at the time of our interview, there were only twenty or so hectares across the state dedicated to greenhouse production (interview with Robert Barker, Zacatecas, Zacatecas, June 24, 2004).

Other migrants would prefer to see the concerns of these "traditional farming guys" addressed more directly. Francisco Javier González, for example, an HTA leader who heads the FCZSC's political offshoot Frente

Cívico Zacatecano, hoped for a much more immediate and practical solution to the economic woes of the state's campesinos: state-mandated price guarantees. In speaking about what he had expected from the "democratic transition" promised by the insurgent PRD gubernatorial candidacy of Ricardo Monreal in 1998, González recounted a conversation he had with the then governor-elect:

> I told [him], "Ricardo, if you are going to do something, you have got to fix the prices on beans, on corn, on cattle, so that people can work." That is one thing that we wanted from democracy: that prices be set once and for all, for campesinos mostly, so that they wouldn't have to be battling it out at the very end. (interview with Francisco Javier González, Norwalk, California, November 13, 2003)

Taking this or other actions to address the interests of the campesino sector is likely a necessary component of any economic recovery, if for no other reason than the resistance of campesinos to economic modernization plans that would require them to abandon their livelihood strategies and traditional cultural identities that are so tied to the land. The resilience of campesinos and their resistance to being incorporated into state-directed economic transformations has led to a striking irony in the labor market of Zacatecas, this land of massive labor emigration: potential investors report that the state does not have an abundant labor supply! For example, in the *municipio* (municipality) of Jerez, one of the state's largest with an estimated fifty-five thousand inhabitants, Taiwanese investors invited to invest in Jerez by migrant mayor Andres Bermúdez balked at a project in 2005 after a labor market study revealed that the *municipio* did not contain the requisite stable labor force of five hundred employees that could commit to full-time, year-round employment. An insider in the Jerez municipal government under the then newly elected Mayor Bermúdez (see chapter 5) explained the *municipio*'s failure to attract the investors by recounting the population's response to the queries of the labor market researchers: "Half of them said, 'Sure, it's just that at planting time [I'm not available]. And when it's time to irrigate, I'm going to have to go irrigate. And when it's time to harvest, I'm going to have to go harvest'" (interview with Raymundo Carrillo, Jerez, Zacatecas, August 9, 2005).

Iskander (2005) reports a similar finding from the state of Guanajuato, where migrant-funded maquiladoras faced chronic labor shortages as workers, once trained, left for higher-paying positions in other more traditional textile-producing regions or dropped out of the labor market after receiving remittances from relatives abroad. However, as the above quotation suggests, in Zacatecas the labor shortage appears to be much more related to people's attachment to the land and the agricultural cycle, that is, they are resisting proletarianization (see Eckstein 2001 for a similar discussion regarding Cuba's campesino sector).

The Dialectics of the State in Migrant Discourse

The role of the state in migrant discourse is complex and apparently contradictory. As the result of the deep-seated corruption engrained during the PRI's seventy-one-year rule, the state, and the political class that controls it, are vilified and represented as a primary cause of the dismal economic conditions that make migration a necessity. Migrants' ringing criticism of the state does not, however, lead to the adoption of an antistatist, market idolatry. Instead, migrants attribute a strong and important role to the state in the development endeavors that they are engaged in. Bringing these two views together helps to capture the FCZSC leaders' complex view of the state and to set such views apart from the antistatist logic of neoliberal ideology.

One way that the migrant leaders' views of the state emerged during our interviews was through their discussions of the meaning and importance of migrant participation in the generation of public goods and infrastructure. Our interviewees fell into two camps in discussing the importance of their participation in the various matching-grant programs. One set of migrants saw their participation in the matching-grant programs as part of their attempt to gain greater recognition and expanded rights for migrants in a political context in which their opponents often asserted that such recognition and rights should not be extended because migrants' residency abroad resulted in them becoming "disconnected" from the necessities and desires of the state's true inhabitants. Another set of migrants adopted a contrasting position that focused on the fiscal limitations facing government in Mexico that rendered it incapable of meeting all of the country's infrastructural needs.

In reaction to their opponents' charges of being disconnected, the first group highlighted migrants' voluntary cooperation in activities that were really the state's responsibility. This position is well articulated—in strikingly transnational terms—in the following excerpt from our interview with former FCZSC president Guadalupe Gómez, responding to a question about how he and the other leaders remain "connected" to realities on the ground in Zacatecas:

> We go over there to find out what the needs are in different communities, and we support those clubs that are helping these communities obtain those services through this 3×1 program. You know, we are talking about very basic services that are the responsibility of the government. It is the responsibility

of the government to provide potable water, sewer systems, and electricity. A very basic system, right? Well, we are not only doing that, we are building roads, we are paving streets, we are enriching the life of the people that are there. And . . . we don't have to. We're American citizens. I'm an American. I vote here! So tell me that I am disconnected, when I travel the whole state, different communities where we have clubs and I see all of these needs. (interview with Guadalupe Gómez, Santa Ana, California, May 14, 2004)

Manuel de la Cruz expressed the contrary view, responding directly to the arguments of other migrant leaders that they are voluntarily providing what is actually the government's responsibility:

Everybody says "it's the government's obligation." Well, yeah, but the government has got to cover a lot of areas. It would be impossible for the government to come to this place if it has these other priorities over here. But if you, as an organization, offer, "I've got 33 percent to build a project here," when that is money that is outside of Mexico, that is not even in Zacatecas, only if that government bureaucrat were crazy would they not accept what we're offering. (interview with Manuel de la Cruz, Zacatecas, Zacatecas, June 25, 2004)

These competing positions are best understood within the context of the ongoing political struggles for migrant political empowerment unfolding in Zacatecas and throughout Mexico. The differing social and political positionings of the migrants within these struggles is clearly related to the rhetorical devices they use in vilifying and/or heralding the migrant and the government. Thus, it comes as no surprise that migrant agents of the regional state, like de la Cruz, the former "official representative" of the state government, defend the state as doing the best it can with limited resources, whereas migrant leaders, like Lupe Gómez and his allies, who are struggling to gain political power while maintaining autonomy from the state take the opposing position.

Despite the politically motivated disagreements of these opposing camps, migrants' representations of the meaning of migrant participation in the matching-grant programs share a basic understanding of the fundamental role of the state in providing collective goods and promoting improvements in people's livelihoods. This is not altogether surprising, even in the neoliberal era, when confined solely to the provision of public infrastructure, but this shared interpretation takes on greater importance for our understanding of the politics of neoliberalism when the state's role is seen as extending deep into the sphere of production, that semisacred realm of neoliberal ideology that is supposed to be evacuated by the state and left to the "private" forces of "the market."

This extended view of the role of the state in both the provision of public goods and infrastructure and in production is precisely what we find in migrant discourse on remittances and development. In the following excerpt from our interview with Martha Jiménez, she expresses a fairly radical vision of the role of the state in facilitating the transition to productive projects:

> If we are able to transition to create the productive projects, we are going to be able to make people stay there a little bit longer. If we are helped by the Mexican government to create real sustainable projects that can create jobs, we can make it. We're going to make the Mexican government, through the Economy Department, create the means necessary where, if I want to have a maquiladora that treats people with justice and pays good salaries, I can have it. (interview with Martha Jiménez, Los Angeles, March 24, 2005)

This is far removed from the pie-in-the-sky neoliberal discourse in which promoting competition among remittances service providers and providing migrants' access to formal financial institutions would single-handedly unleash migrants' pent-up entrepreneurial energies and thus bring "development" to their home communities. In the migrants' view the state should continue to play a fundamental role, indeed an expanded one, in the economy.

Although there are surely differing opinions on what it would mean for the Mexican government to "help" migrants to create sustainable projects and to "create the means necessary" for those projects to provide justice and fair salaries to their employees, an FCZSC project being carried out with the financial assistance of the Rockefeller Foundation and the technical assistance of the Development Studies Program at the Universidad Autónoma de Zacatecas (UAZ, Autonomous University of Zacatecas) gives some indication of what the zacatecanos have in mind (see Delgado Wise, Márquez Covarrubias, and Rodríguez Ramírez 2004 for the policy prescriptions coming from the UAZ team). As described to us by the Rockefeller-funded philanthropy director, Efraín Jiménez, the migrants' vision includes the direct participation of the state and federal governments in the financing of productive projects: "It is my work to look for a way to persuade our government to match our investment in certain projects." In fact, Jiménez's goals go even farther. Here is how he explained the reasoning behind his campaign proposal, during his losing bid for the presidency of the FCZSC in 2004, to create a 4×1 program that would include the participation of the U.S. government:

> What I would tell them is, "If you want to stop immigration, instead of spending millions of dollars on building that big fence . . . you are trying to

stop people who have brains, they are going to find a way somehow to go through the fence. You are not trying to detain cows. Instead of spending those millions of dollars on those fences that set us apart more than we are already, why don't you spend those millions of dollars on creating jobs in Mexico?" (interview with Efraín Jiménez, Los Angeles, May 13, 2004)

Migrant Agency in Reworking Neoliberalism

How are we to understand the engagement of the Zacatecan migrant leaders with the remittances-to-development agenda of the international institutions and the U.S. and Mexican states? Is the FCZSC's cooperation in the revamped 3×1 program and its turn to the promotion of "productive projects" indicative of co-optation, of a full-scale adoption of the neoliberal premises of the remittances-to-development discourse?

Although the political imagination and practice of the Zacatecan migrant leaders studied here do not constitute a frontal assault on the neoliberal project, their proposals and activities do help to illustrate that politics do indeed exist in neoliberal restructuring and reregulation and that they do matter. To be sure, in rejecting an interpretation of the politics of migrant-led development as nothing more than submission to the dictates of the hegemonic model and discourse of neoliberal globalization, we should not overly valorize the resistance and contestations of the Zacatecan migrant leaders. As Sarah Radcliffe has recently noted, direct protest and "coordinated rejection" of neoliberalism in Latin America (and across the globe, one might add) are "severely compromised and perhaps unlikely in the immediate future." And yet, in the face of these daunting circumstances, we do still find individuals, collective organizations, and even some regional governments engaging in myriad "contestations, reworkings, and compromises with neoliberalism" (Radcliffe 2005, 328). It is precisely within this dialectic of accommodation and resistance to the hegemonic neoliberal project that we can appropriately situate the practices of the Zacatecan migrant leaders: they may not articulate a fully formed alternative to the dominant model, but the development-oriented projects they pursue, and the significant role that they reserved for an active and interventionist state in those projects, represent a significant deviation from the legitimating discourse of neoliberalism.

It would, however, be a mistake to portray the Zacatecan migrant leaders, or even their leading organization, the FCZSC, as a single, unitary, and coherent political subject. As Luis Eduardo Guarnizo has pointed out, and as our own research subjects readily acknowledge, in the Zacatecan case the leaders of migrant clubs tend, on the whole, to be affluent entrepreneurs whose experiences and life chances at their present stage of life are quite different from those faced by the mass of migrants. Given the heterogeneity of the Mexican migrant community, divided as it is along class, ethnic, gender, political, and regional lines, Guarnizo suggests that the assemblage resulting from contemporary transnational migration should be conceived of as a "transnational social formation" instead of relying on the idyllic imagery of a more egalitarian and homogeneous "transnational migrant community" (Guarnizo 1998, 73; cf. Portes 1998). This is clearly an important conceptual shift, and it deserves sustained attention in analyses of the potential of migration and remittances to contribute to development and positive social change. In doing so, we should recognize the crosscutting nature of these lines of cleavage and avoid any kind of class reductionism that would view these migrant leaders as necessarily constituting an emergent class of migrant elites that was not itself riven with multiple divisions.

In the case of the Zacatecan migrant leaders under study here, for example, it is quite clear that, while they largely share a common class position, they are divided along numerous other vectors of inequality, including gender and different social class origins. They differ as well in terms of other social divisions such as political ideology and degree of partisanship, nonpartisanship, or antipartisan orientation with respect to the changing Mexican political landscape. With respect to gender, for instance, "migrant leadership" is almost exclusively a male domain, and we have found that gender divisions are a cause of constant tension for the few female club leaders that manage to take on leadership roles in the FCZSC (see Goldring 2001a and b for a more extensive analysis of gender division within the FCZSC). Divisions based on social-class background tend to play out in terms of the patterns of accommodation or resistance to the emerging power structure and party alignments in Zacatecas. Those from more working-class or peasant backgrounds tend to be more resistant to efforts by the PRD-dominated state government to shape their activities and uncritically gain their support. The divisions among migrant leaders with respect to partisanship result in the formation of three identifiable political groupings within the FCZSC: that of Zacatecanos PRImero, a U.S. affiliate of the once-dominant PRI party; a group of PRD members (many of whom are former members of the PRI) who have parlayed their support and closeness to previous PRD governor Ricardo Monreal into influence and positions within the regional state government; and the Frente Cívico Zacatecano, whose members have attempted to adopt a more independent position vis-à-vis all of the Mexican political parties following their break with Monreal in the early years of his administration. Inasmuch as these political divisions and distinctions, detailed in chapter 6, represent real political and programmatic differences, they are not simply rhetorical markers within an otherwise indistinguishable political class. They force us to view the FCZSC not as a unitary subject but as an arena of contention, the site of contested meanings and diverse political projects. These very distinctions within the heart of the Zacatecan hometown associations reveal just how politicized the issues of "migrant-led" development are.

Equally important, the political thrust of the projects that the FCZSC is pursuing, in collaboration with the neoliberal Mexican state and other institutional actors, diverge widely from the orthodoxy of neoliberal ideology. This pronounced divergence helps us to see that present-day remittances-to-development discourse and the official talk of "the market" as a panacea that could miraculously transform poor migrants and their families into entrepreneurs are not so fully "de-politicizing" as the work of Ferguson would lead us to expect.

Finally, the political engagement of the Zacatecan migrants with the Mexican state highlights the importance of the continuing legacy of earlier political regimes and structures that are not so easily pushed aside with the imposition of a new economic model. In the context of the reigning political-economic model, states may attempt to promote a new neoliberal form of "market citizenship" (Schild 1998; Harvey 2001; Goldring 2002). However, our emerging transnational citizens' understandings of the role and responsibilities of the Mexican state in guaranteeing the general welfare are not so easily jarred from the mooring of earlier modes of political representation and legitimacy. This suggests the need to depart from the sweeping assertions of those who would see the formal economic changes wrought by neoliberalism as also effecting broad and diffuse sociocultural changes, such as "a renewed faith in the market" or a dismantling of traditional nationalist sentiments and resistance to imperial domination (Portes 1997).

Migrants may hold no romantic yearnings for a return to the corrupt and semiauthoritarian past of one-party rule in Mexico, yet they are not easily swayed by the political elites' abrupt about-face in eschewing the revolutionary nationalism of the past in favor of a more accommodationist neoliberal project of North American integration. Enduring popular mistrust for the ruling elite tends to dispose migrants and other citizens toward a healthy skepticism and disbelief in the face of the lofty promises of politicians and planners. In the end, the migrant leaders are neither the victims of a depoliticizing remittances-to-development discourse nor lifeless recipients of broad and diffuse sociocultural changes brought about by neoliberal reforms from above, but historically situated, living and breathing human beings capable of seeing and acting politically.

PART 3

||||||||||||||||||||||||||||||||||||||||||||||||||||||||||||||||||||||||||||||||||||||||||||||||||||||||||||||||||||||||||||||||||||||||

El Migrante as
Transnational Citizen

5 Transnational Electoral Politics

The Multiple Coronations of the "Tomato King"

On July 1, 2001, Andrés Bermúdez Viramontes was elected *presidente* of Jerez, one of the largest municipal governments in the state of Zacatecas. Bermúdez, a successful tomato grower, labor contractor, and inventor of a tomato transplanting machine who lived in Winters, California, gained international media attention during his campaign as El Rey del Tomate (the Tomato King). Running under this rubric, Bermúdez, the candidate of the PRD, positioned himself as the prototypical transnational Mexican migrant, and thus as a symbol of the rising power of el migrante in Mexican political life. Bermúdez's campaign and his victory were publicized widely in the Mexican and international press, where his victory was represented as a sign of the transnationalization of Mexican political life.

The Tomato King's victory and its implicit transnationalizing of political power caused considerable consternation among his opponents in the once dominant and now threatened PRI party, who seized on a legal obstacle that potentially prevented transmigrants from participating in Mexican electoral politics. Before the Tomato King could take office, the PRI succeeded in having his election invalidated by a federal electoral court (for failing to fulfill "local" residency requirements) in an ongoing national and transnational political struggle over the meaning of cross-border electoral power. In the face of these exclusionary practices, the Tomato King, who had been deprived of what he saw as a democratic electoral victory in the new transnational political space of Mexican politics, cemented an alliance with another transnational political actor, the Frente Cívico Zacatecano (FCZ), a political arm of the Zacatecan migrant organizations in southern California (Goldring 2002) and joined with supportive public intellectuals in Zacatecas to gain constitutional reforms in the state that now recognize "binational residency" as a legitimate dimension of popular elections. These state-level constitutional reforms paved the way for the Tomato King to stage a dramatic transnational political comeback in 2004.

Once the exclusionary state law had been changed, the Tomato King expanded the transnational electoral coalition of which he had become both a leader and a symbol. He made political allies at multiple sites on both sides of the border, while simultaneously fostering a dynamic *bermudista* social movement at the grassroots level in Jerez. On July 4, 2004, the Tomato King was once again elected *presidente municipal* of Jerez, winning office by a wide margin. He received 41 percent of the vote in a three-way race, defeating his closest opponent by over two thousand votes.

How did this dramatic turnaround come about? What factors help us to understand and explain the bermudista phenomenon? How can we account for the centrality of el migrante in the discourses and practices contributing to the transnationalization of Mexican electoral politics? In this chapter we use transnational ethnography to tell the story of the rise, fall, and dramatic rebound of the most prominent transnational political candidate to emerge in the struggle over dual citizenship in contemporary Mexico. We explore the cross-border electoral politics by which Andrés Bermúdez, the Tomato King, was twice elected mayor of Jerez, Zacatecas. We seek to explain the meaning of his transnational electoral victories and their cumulative impact on the role of "the migrant" as a new social actor in Mexican political development. We advance an agency-oriented perspective that underlines the need to carefully historicize the relationship between transnationalism and citizenship—that is, to map the contingency and agency underlying the changing practices of states, migrants, and transnational institutional networks vis-à-vis questions of transnational citizenship. This is best done by paying close attention to the social and political practices whereby human agents pursue historically specific political projects that extend the practices of citizenship across borders.

Who Is the Tomato King?

Andrés Bermúdez is a successful immigrant entrepreneur with no political experience who decided to put aside his business operations to run for office in his Mexican hometown. Bermúdez was not the first migrant to become an elected official in Mexico. In many migrant-sending regions, the economic clout and improved social status acquired by successful migrants have led them to prominent positions in local politics after their return to their home communities (Alarcón 1988; Fitzgerald 2000). In at least one case during the Bracero program (1942–65), a *presidente municipal* even governed his community from the United States (e-mail communication with Frank Bardacke, June 6, 2002). However, the campaign and election of Andrés Bermúdez were markedly different from earlier examples of migrant political and electoral participation. First, Bermúdez was not a successful "return migrant." Instead, he operated from the United States, maintaining a home, family, and business in Winters, California, and otherwise carrying on a transnational life. Second, Bermúdez garnered an extraordinary amount of national and international press coverage because of his fiery personality and his self-portrayal as a "binational candidate" seeking to transform Jerez into a "little United States" (Quiñones 2001).

How did the Tomato King choose to launch his first transnational candidacy? Who were his initial allies, and what were the key moments in his dramatic rise to international prominence? In December 2000, in the main plaza of the city of Jerez, while donating Christmas gifts to low-income children, native son Andrés Bermúdez publicly announced his intention to seek the nomination of the PRD for the office of municipal president. In so doing, he chose to align himself with the ruling party in the state, which at that time was the main opposition party to the long-ruling PRI regime in Jerez. Although a political unknown, Bermúdez gained popularity among the electorate and slowly began to generate support from PRD activists, largely because of the populist character of his initial campaign rhetoric (interview with Raymundo Carrillo, Bermúdez adviser, Jerez, Zacatecas, September 10, 2002).

Bermúdez's emergent campaign focused on the needs of the inhabitants of the rural villages surrounding the city of Jerez, communities that account for the lion's share of migration to the United States. His stories of the migrant's plight as well as the political opportunities presented by the migrant as a new political actor ultimately won him an overwhelming plurality in these traditional migrant-sending agricultural communities. This campaign strategy proved effective, and Bermúdez prevailed in the PRD municipal primary election in 2001, despite losing the vote in the city of Jerez.

The success of Bermúdez in these rural migrant-sending communities highlighted the extent to which transnational migration had become a central focal point in electoral politics in Zacatecas. For Bermúdez, the migrant experience was deployed as a double-edged discourse. On the one hand, the suffering of el migrante and the loss to *his* family were highlighted. Rather than representing these ills as direct and inevitable outcomes of neoliberal globalization, Bermúdez attributed the negative human consequences of migration to a corrupt political system that made migration necessary as a household survival strategy because the ruling political class had misappropriated the nation's vast wealth. On the other hand, the migration experience also was portrayed as a useful learning experience for migrants such as himself who had experienced class mobility and acquired a binational perspective that gave them a "modern" understanding of how to bring prosperity to underdeveloped localities and regions in Mexico. In this way, Bermúdez openly portrayed himself as a transnational candidate, a living embodiment of the contradictions and bifocality of the U.S.-Mexican transnational experience.

In an interesting twist, which provides further evidence of the transnational nature of the campaign and of Zacatecan politics in general, the only debate among the major mayoral candidates was held in Montebello, California, in metropolitan Los Angeles. This transnationalization of local politics in Jerez and the insertion of el migrante into a central role in political discourse carried significant risks in the electoral arena. The incursion into electoral politics raises questions not only about the meaning of citizenship but also about the legal boundaries of membership and therefore of the rights to formal political participation, such as the right to vote and to run for elected office. El migrante could be portrayed as an outsider who had left the nation and been acculturated into the values and interests of another nation just as easily as he could be held up as a legitimate member of the global Mexican nation. This is precisely the move made by Bermúdez's political opponents in the PRI that eventually led to his disqualification from the mayoral office he had handily won in 2001.

The Legal Challenge to Dual Citizenship

The Tomato King won this five-party election with 47 percent of the vote. However, the president of the PRI in Zacatecas publicly declared during the electoral campaign that the PRI would legally challenge a Bermúdez victory, alleging that he had failed to meet formal residency requirements (Mena 2001). Following Bermúdez's victory, the PRI challenged the outcome in the state courts. The PRI lawsuit was based on three allegations: (1) that Bermúdez was not a Zacatecan citizen; (2) that he did not possess full political rights; and (3) that he did not maintain "effective and uninterrupted residency" in Jerez during the year before the elections. Bermúdez won the initial lawsuit and a subsequent round in the state appeals court. However, PRI officials then took the case to the federal court (Tribunal Federal Electoral, TRIFE) where they expected an audience that was less susceptible to the inclusionary representations of el migrante advanced by Bermúdez and his PRD allies. Just days before he was to take office, the TRIFE stripped Bermúdez of his victory and granted the post to Bermúdez's alternate in the election, Ismael Solís.[1]

---

1. In the Mexican political system, candidates for public office choose "alternates," who are to serve in their place if for any reason they are unable to assume, or continue in, office.

The TRIFE did not address the first two of the PRI's allegations but found Bermúdez ineligible based on the third—that he was not a legal resident of Jerez for the year before the election. This determination was strongly supported by evidence, including media reports placing Bermúdez in the United States at various times during the year in question and, most convincingly, a sworn declaration Bermúdez had made on November 21, 2000, in which he stated that his home was Winters, California (Tribunal Electoral 2001, 68–69).

Bermúdez blamed President Fox for the decision, claiming that nothing had changed in Mexico with the arrival of Fox, whose oppositional electoral victory had been heralded by many as representing a true transition to democracy. Bermúdez also threatened to convince migrants to stop investing in Mexico. His initial disappointment led him to consider giving up the fight and returning to his business in California (Sullivan 2001). Within a few days, however, Bermúdez was energized by the outpouring of support he received from migrants, which included being an *invitado de honor* (honored guest) at Mexican Independence Day celebrations in Los Angeles (interview with Andrés Bermúdez, Davis, California, March 15, 2002). Rejuvenated, Bermúdez committed himself to fighting for the post he had won.

Contesting the Federal Electoral Court: A Transnational Response

By September 10, 2001, Bermúdez was back in Jerez threatening to "jump scale" by internationalizing the conflict (for a theoretical discussion of the politics of jumping scale, see Brysk 1996). Demanding that President Fox intervene to overturn the TRIFE decision, Bermúdez threatened to take his case to the United Nations on the grounds that Mexico had violated the International Convention on the Protection of the Rights of All Migrant Workers and Members of Their Families. He continued his attack on President Fox, arguing that "on one hand, he says he is going to push for legal reforms granting the right to vote to Mexicans abroad, and on the other, he denies us full political rights" (Becerra 2001). In addition, some of those who supported Bermúdez even threatened that an armed resistance was forming to defend his cause. Bermúdez soon backed away from those references, claiming that he was supported by fifteen thousand *jerezanos* ready to "rise up in arms, but [arms] of arguments and reason" (Vacio 2001).

With the events of September 11th hanging over him, Bermúdez chose to abandon his more aggressive efforts to defend his electoral victory and instead sought a negotiated settlement. He was able to broker a deal with PRD officials that called for a public opinion poll to determine who should hold the office. Although a majority of the poll's respondents again chose Bermúdez over his alternate, Solís, the latter refused to step down, claiming that he had the law on his side. Leaders of the opposition PAN and eventually even his own PRD leadership turned against Bermúdez and scrapped the negotiated settlement, leaving Solís free to hold the office. In response, on January 13, 2002, Bermúdez published a letter in Zacatecas newspapers announcing his break with PRD governor Monreal and the state PRD, saying that he would not leave the party but would instead form an internal bermudista faction.

For the rest of 2002, Bermúdez, who had returned to his home in California, avoided direct participation in Zacatecan politics. While reconsidering his political options, he wavered between extensive participation in transnational Mexican politics or a complete turn to ethnic politics in the United States. In our interviews with him at the time, Bermúdez spelled out the three specific options he was considering: (1) the formation of a new migrant-based political party; (2) preparing the terrain for his eventual run for the Zacatecan governorship; or (3) dedicating his energies to the educational, economic, and political advancement of Mexicans in the United States (interviews with Andrés Bermúdez, Davis, California, March 15, 2002, and November 1, 2002). He made clear that the key determinant of his political future was the potential passage of legal reforms in Zacatecas that would permit migrant political participation independent of their place of residence and length of residency.

In December 2002 Bermúdez made a formal and highly public return to Zacatecan transnational political life. From his home in northern California he traveled to Los Angeles where he and his allies in the binational Frente Cívico Zacatecano presented a proposal to amend the Zacatecan constitution. In recognition of the symbolic significance of Bermúdez's experience in bringing transmigrant exclusion to the front burner of the political agenda, these transnational political actors named their proposal La Ley Bermúdez. The proposal sought to gain recognition for "binational residency" and to allow migrants to hold elected office in Zacatecas. Within days of presenting the proposed constitutional amendment in Los Angeles, Bermúdez returned to Jerez where he successfully attempted to reconcile with Governor Monreal and pave the way for his return to Zacatecan political life (Hernández 2002).

These actions indicate that at the beginning of 2003 Bermúdez was leaning toward the second of the three options spelled out above. He explained to us that his reconciliation with Monreal was the price he had to pay to prepare the ground for a possible 2004 gubernatorial campaign. The logic behind this reconciliation was understandable from Bermúdez's perspective as a potential transnational candidate, but it ran directly counter to the non-partisan political logic being promoted by his allies in the FCZ and the Federación de Clubes Zacatecanos del Sur de California (Federation). These two transnational organizations had taken the lead in attempting to construct a cross-party consensus in support of the Ley Bermúdez. The clash generated by these conflicting logics resulted in the FCZ and Federation leaders publicly breaking with Bermúdez regarding his alliance with the governor (González 2003). To underline their nonpartisan stance, when they presented their reform initiative to the Zacatecan state congress, FCZ and Federation leaders renamed their initiative the Ley Migrante, stating: "In the political whirlwind unleashed in 2003, some actions and events could attempt to identify the 'Initiative to Reform the Political Constitution of Zacatecas,' known as the 'Ley Migrante,' with a certain candidate or with some political party. From this point on, we distance ourselves from such a possibility. . . . Among ourselves, we call it the 'Ley Migrante,' not any other name, because it brings together the demands and experience of a plural and diverse social movement . . . of which we are a part" (Frente Cívico Zacatecano 2003). From the perspective of these transnational social-movement actors, this rhetorical move reflects a desire to gain a political consensus on constitutional reform that crosses party lines.

Bermúdez's reconciliation with the governor turned out to be short lived, however. Consequently, so too was the temporary breach between him and his transnational allies in the Frente Cívico Zacatecano and the Federation. Governor Monreal did not back the Tomato King's desire to run for governor, but the PRD did allow him to contest the mayoralty of Jerez in the 2004 party primary. Yet, despite the putative openness of this party primary election, Bermúdez was forced to run against a candidate handpicked by Monreal. The Tomato King did surprisingly well in the primary election despite the governor's opposition, losing by only a handful of votes amid charges of electoral irregularities. Bermúdez regarded his loss as a betrayal by the governor.

This second experience of betrayal by the PRD prompted Bermúdez and his local allies in Jerez to leave the PRD altogether, jumping from being the bermudista faction of that party to constituting themselves as an autonomous bermudista social and political movement. This distancing from the PRD allowed Bermúdez and his local allies to reunite with their southern California migrant allies as well as to consider other alliances in Zacatecas. This exit from the PRD also necessitated that the bermudista movement form an alliance with one of the other registered political parties in Zacatecas if the Tomato King was to gain a position on the ballot. Although Bermúdez apparently considered joining with the once-dominant

PRI, he quickly rejected that option. His success in the 2001 campaign was largely due to a popular rejection of the PRI at the national as well as the local level. In field interviews with local elites and citizens in Jerez, the desire to oust the PRI was repeatedly mentioned as a main factor explaining Bermúdez's victory. Even the losing PRI candidate, Alma Ávila, suggested the following:

> Well, if we analyze our proposals, I think that the proposal that I presented was the stronger one, [and] also closer to the needs of the people. But let me tell you, I belong to a party that is discredited. The citizenry no longer believes in the party. And with Andrés Bermúdez, an expectation arose that he could accomplish what he proposed to do. (interview with Alma Ávila, PRI candidate for mayor, Jerez, Zacatecas, September 10, 2002)

Recognizing that much of the public had lost faith in the PRI, Bermúdez and his supporters eventually entered into a marriage of convenience with the historically weak, right-of-center PAN in Zacatecas. This was an unusual alliance between a neoliberal political party and a populist social movement candidate in the 2004 elections.

Fig. 5. A social welfare office in Jerez created by the bermudista movement to gain electoral support. Photo by Pat Smith.

Narrating a New Political Subject: Constructing El Migrante

What accounts for Andrés Bermúdez's extraordinary success in capturing popular support on both sides of the border? In part, he was able to cash in on a colorful and compelling personal narrative that spoke to the experiences of ordinary people while also drawing extensive media attention both in Mexico and around the world. Bermúdez's impressive rags-to-riches story of rising from poverty to become a wealthy tomato grower, his direct, no-nonsense style, and his trademark look—dressing daily in a black outfit, cowboy hat, and boots—offered plenty of material for the national and international press to publicize this "first" binational candidate.

The novelty of his narrative is that it was compelling to disparate audiences in the United States and in Mexico. Bermúdez's personal narrative closely parallels popular myths of mobility in U.S. society, and thus might explain its popularity in the U.S. mainstream press. But more important for his electoral fortunes in Zacatecas, Bermúdez came to be seen by his supporters in Mexico as a migrant who had fulfilled the "Mexican-American dream," a transnational story exemplifying the possibilities available to Mexican migrants in the United States who had orchestrated their lives binationally yet had "come home" to help those left behind. It

Fig. 6. The Tomato King, on the campaign trail, making an emphatic point to Bakker (far left) and Smith (second from left). Photo by Pat Smith.

was this complex sense of belonging that became central to Bermúdez's winning campaign representations of el migrante, a narrative that remained remarkably consistent throughout his two campaigns.

The political discourse of Andrés Bermúdez sought to mobilize a winning coalition based on a complex weaving together of a multidimensional heroic migration narrative applicable to the Mexican nation as a whole. His narrative appealed to a multifaceted yet contradictory sense of belonging based on articulations of *class*, *status*, and *power* that cut across local affiliations while promising to improve local community life. Alluding to the experiences of the pain and loss that ordinary families feel as a result of migration, Bermúdez emphasized his campesino class origin and emotional experiences on a gut level as key qualifications for holding public office. In highlighting his own negative experiences with migration, he in effect told voters (particularly the women relatives of migrants who remain behind in the rural villages and make up a majority of voters in the municipality of Jerez): I have been there. I understand your problems and feel your pain.

The Tomato King then deftly linked this class identity to a discourse that valorized the migration experience. Bermúdez's *status* as a transnational migrant was represented as offering three advantages. First, it is what accounts for his successful upward class mobility. Second, his experiences in the United States enabled him to acquire the business and technological skills needed to bring economic development to underdeveloped parts of Zacatecas. Third, this status gave him an understanding of an alternative political culture and institutional framework that did not depend on the graft and political corruption that has kept Mexico backward, both politically and economically.

Consider the following excerpts from an interview Matt Bakker conducted with the Tomato King on July 3, 2004, the day before his second electoral victory.

> BERMÚDEZ: Look, I have as much experience as the experience that you acquire in the United States building up a million-dollar business from nothing; where Andrés Bermúdez has the experience of six hundred or seven hundred people working for Andrés Bermúdez; where the payroll of Andrés Bermúdez is around 140,000 to 160,000 dollars. Now, in order to govern, to know how to govern, to understand what it is to govern you have to understand the people. To be a good governor, you have to have been born into poverty to understand poverty. It's not the same to say "that child is cold," than to have felt that, nor "that child is hungry," than to have felt it. That is the experience that Andrés Bermúdez has. But it's so simple, it's so simple to govern: it is speaking the truth and doing what you say. That is the politics of Andrés Bermúdez.
>
> BAKKER: What would you like to bring to Jerez from the political system in the United States?

BERMÚDEZ: I'd like to bring the political system, the free vote, democracy. The free vote, without any pressure. Look, the subdirector of the police department, from here, supported me and now they told him that he's been fired. Principally, that is what I would like to bring. That the people be free, that they forget about the electoral gifts, that they forget about the hundred pesos [for votes]. And that instead they believe they build Mexico. They think, "Well, they give me the gifts and I continue to sleep." No. Wake them up. (interview with Andrés Bermúdez, Jerez, Zacatecas, July 3, 2004).

The Tomato King's populist valorization of the campesino turned successful migrant capable of bringing needed political change is framed against an antipodal representation of an elite "other," namely the corrupt political class at all levels of the Mexican state and society that has enriched itself at great social cost. During elections this power elite has relied on vote buying, which creates passive citizens. After elections the large kickbacks that winning members of the political class skim off construction projects create incentives to spend more and more public resources on public works, which leaves too little available for education, to alleviate poverty, and for productive investment. On a personal level, the ruling political class has never learned the value of hard work, making a handsome living, as they do, not by producing anything of value, but by appropriating other peoples' hard-earned money. In contrast, the defining political slogan of Bermúdez's first campaign, "I have come to give . . . ," embodies just the opposite political ethic. In essence, this narrative expresses the theme that transnational migrant politicians and their traditional counterparts are cut from an entirely different cloth: migrants come back to help the people, whereas the political class only steals from them, as the following excerpts from our interview illustrate:

[There's] nothing harder in changing Mexico. But the government don't want to deal with that. [It] wants to deal, "bring me the money." [Say] I am the contractor, the governor says, "You do this street, how much?" "One million dollars." "Okay, I'll pay you two million dollars. When I pay you two million dollars, you take your million dollars, and give me back my million dollars." That means the money is already washed [i.e., laundered].

And the woman is a widow. Everybody feels sorry for this lady. I started my ideas working and I say, "Well, what's the reason the woman here is alone?" Migration. One time I got two hundred to three hundred women in one place. When I start speaking, when I finished, everybody [was] crying. I tell them, "You see one of these, the sons of these politicians, cross the border? No. Why not? Why do our sons got to risk their lives? Why? . . . Because you appoint these rich, because you give them the power, when you give 'em your money." (interview with Andrés Bermúdez, Davis, California, March 15, 2002)

Once framed in this way, the Tomato King's electoral narrative then expands from class and status considerations to *collective power* as a source of political mobilization and social change. Voters are asked to empower a new political class by voting for Andrés Bermúdez. In so doing, they are told they will be opening the door for the inclusion of more and more successful migrants in the political life of contemporary Mexico.

> SMITH: Do you think that more and more people like yourself are getting involved?
>
> BERMÚDEZ: That's the reason [Governor] Monreal [is] scared. Because if I do, becoming a president and later on maybe becoming a governor, but just say becoming a president and I do the job, in three years there's a lot of guys jumping across the border and try to do it. Because some of the guys called me, you know, some guy from Houston, he's got a big market, he's from Mexico City. He goes, "How did you do it? I want to go back." A guy from Guadalajara, a lot of people called me: "How can I go back and help?" I mean if you go back that government is scared. Scared of losing control . . . of losing power. (interview with Andrés Bermúdez, Davis, California, March 15, 2002).

Like Bermúdez, these migrants are depicted as caring deeply about the transnational Mexican nation from which they have previously been excluded. Like him, they are represented as caring, competent, and free of corruption. Like him, they don't need the emoluments of office that the political class has taken from the national treasury. They simply "want to help" and know how to do so.

Bermúdez's emphasis on fighting corruption needs to be analyzed in the context of contemporary political transformations in Mexico that culminated in Vicente Fox of the opposition PAN defeating the ruling PRI in the 2000 presidential election by campaigning successfully as the "candidate of change." In our interviews, Bermúdez did not seem to have much faith that Fox or any other opposition party politician would successfully transform Mexico's corrupt and authoritarian political cultures. Instead, echoing remarks he heard from the U.S. consul in Monterrey, Bermúdez argued that Mexico would only change if its emigrants were to return from the United States and make the change by bringing a different way of doing things—without corruption (interview with Andrés Bermúdez, Davis, California, March 15, 2002).

The bottom line of this narrative is that by voting for the Tomato King voters will not only empower Andrés Bermúdez, they will empower themselves. Voters will usher in a new political era. They will legitimate the political participation of a new set of migrant political leaders who understand the needs of ordinary Mexicans, have gained much know-how from their migration experience, and are free from the confines of the old political culture of corruption, authoritarianism, and inefficiency. In his own words:

> This campaign represents the future of the migrant. . . . This is the true struggle of the migrant. Because if Andrés Bermúdez fails in this project, the migrant also fails. In other words, I've come to open the doors for the migrant. I can't fail. Because I say to the politicians here that they are not afraid of Andrés Bermúdez, because Andrés Bermúdez is just one person, but if Andrés Bermúdez wins and if Andrés Bermúdez does the things that the people expect him to do, then a lot of Andréses are going to return. Because just like we left to go conquer a country, in order to survive, with that same energy we're returning and from over there we're helping out our communities, our towns, everyone. But we're also human beings that have the right to vote and the right to be elected. And we don't stop being Mexican just by the simple fact that we have left Mexico, like they're ignoring us.
>
> They are afraid of the migrant because we see politics differently. We are a true politics. They are [not] going to be able to buy us off for a hundred pesos or with gifts. That is the difference! Us migrants are not politicians. Us migrants aren't living from politics, nor do we eat from politics. So, we go to another country and we learn to do things, because if we don't, we don't eat, we don't live. (Election-eve interview with Andrés Bermúdez, Jerez, Zacatecas, July 3, 2004)

In short, "los Migrantes" are the future leaders of the transnational Mexican nation; we are the best of you; and together we are "us."

Contradictions of the Bermudista Electoral Coalition

Like Andrés Bermúdez's heroic discursive narrative, the winning political coalition the Tomato King "temporarily sutured" (Mouffe 1988) during his two electoral campaigns was multidimensional. The political practices of the Bermúdez coalition brought together actors occupying different class experiences, ideological orientations, subject positions, and geographical locations. The multiple local, regional, and transnational geographic scales brought together in the bermudista coalition are represented visually in map 3.

In winning the first election Bermúdez allied himself with a number of local and regional actors who had been working, often within the left-of-center PRD in Zacatecas, to incorporate migrants into a social movement to democratize the Mexican state by bringing migrants "back in." These included the local party militants who eventually emerged as a local populist bermudista faction in Jerez as well as a group of public intellectuals,

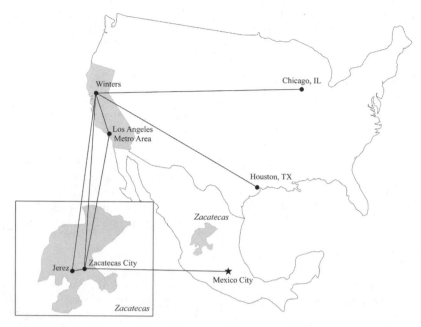

Map 3. Places of power and meaning in the transnational coalition of the Tomato King

including Miguel Moctezuma Longoria and his colleagues from the Universidad Autónoma de Zacatecas, who have both studied and participated in the transnationalization of Zacatecan political life.

Bermúdez also sought allies among members of the fifty highly organized Zacatecan transmigrant hometown associations in southern California. Recall that the only debate of the major candidates for mayor of Jerez during the first campaign was sponsored by the FCZSC and held in Montebello, California. At the Montebello debate, Bermúdez solidified his candidacy and demonstrated the seriousness of his campaign by presenting the only formal campaign proposals (interview with Miguel Moctezuma Longoria, Zacatecas, September 3, 2002).

Following the reversal of his electoral victory by the courts, Bermúdez forged an alliance with the Frente Cívico Zacatecano to obtain state-level constitutional reforms recognizing "binational residency" and facilitating transmigrant candidacies for popular elections. Among its other promigrant provisions, this electoral reform allowed transnational candidates such as Bermúdez to run for and hold office in Zacatecan municipalities by maintaining residence in the state for six months rather than the full year previously required.

Thus, electoral reform produced by transnational social forces set the stage for Bermúdez's second successful run for mayor of Jerez. Underlining

Fig. 7. El Rey del Tomate adorning the back of a glossy campaign brochure

the personalistic and populist dimensions of his coalition, during the second election Bermúdez and his local supporters in the bermudista movement left the PRD altogether, forming an alliance with the ideologically more conservative PAN. This alliance was clearly a marriage of convenience. It allowed Bermúdez to obtain a position on the ballot after he had lost a primary election to a PRD candidate backed by Governor Monreal (amid charges of vote rigging). At the same time, this unholy alliance of neoliberals and populists allowed the PAN, which had never had much electoral success in Zacatecan state or municipal elections, to hitch its fortunes to a populist candidate with proven electoral support from a bermudista mass following. The potentially contradictory character of this coalition is further underlined by the support that Bermúdez and his movement have continued to enjoy from the leftist public intellectuals at the University of Zacatecas, particularly from Miguel Moctezuma Longoria, who was active in drafting and promoting the Ley Migrante and who produced an impressive campaign brochure for the second election touting the Bermúdez legend and its promise of future economic development of Jerez and Zacatecas.

It remains problematic whether the electorally successful but potentially contradictory coalition of transnational migrant entrepreneurs, a neoliberal political party, reformist public intellectuals, and populist-oriented local and regional bermudista movement activists can hold together as Bermúdez attempts to address the economic and social needs of the rural poor who voted for the Tomato King. In our view, the long-term cohesiveness of this coalition is rendered especially unstable by the largely neoliberal agenda of "public-private partnership" that he has advanced during his electoral campaigns. We now turn to a consideration of the "productive investment" theme Bermúdez advanced alongside his heroic migrant narrative. In so doing we consider what is likely to happen when populist democratic–oriented political reforms aimed at empowering ordinary people are combined with neoliberal policy prescriptions intended to empower migrant entrepreneurs and promote local and regional economic prosperity.

The Campaign Discourse on Productive Investment

The multidimensional heroic migrant narrative of Andrés Bermúdez adds an additional layer beyond the representation of the migrant as a new social actor uniquely positioned to transform and expand the political sphere. The migrant is also projected as a pivotal actor in the economic realm, a potential catalyst for economic development and regional prosperity.

In his first campaign, Bermúdez directly addressed the concerns of the municipality's struggling agricultural producers. Capitalizing on his image as an agricultural inventor and entrepreneur, Bermúdez made several concrete proposals for improving the welfare of agricultural producers in Jerez. These included state-financed infrastructure improvements to facilitate small growers' access to existing markets as well as efforts to expand those markets by producing more profitable cash crops, such as bell peppers and tomatoes, for which he claimed to have already lined up buyers from among his contacts and associates in California (Grover 2001).

In this 2001 campaign, Bermúdez combined these agricultural proposals with other economic and community development plans that aimed at providing educational and employment opportunities for community residents and slowing emigration. He claimed to have attracted Taiwanese and

Japanese investors to create jobs in Jerez (Grover 2001). His educational proposals included the eventual creation of a Jerez campus of the state university and the reduction of transportation costs for university students that traveled daily to the capital city, a proposal he had made even before the election.

Discussions with Bermúdez about this suggest that he initially envisioned using municipal power to intervene in the market and obtain results for the public good. Following the first election, as mayor-elect he negotiated with bus-service providers to reduce fares for university students. This was to be accomplished by subsidizing the operations of compliant bus companies. To ensure compliance, Bermúdez threatened to establish a municipally funded bus service, which would reduce noncompliant operators' market share and profitability (interview with Andrés Bermúdez, Davis, California, February 8, 2003). Because the Tomato King was not able to take office in 2001, this use of the power of the local state to improve public services never materialized.

The issues of economic and community development and the creation of employment opportunities in particular were central campaign issues in Zacatecan regional elections in 2004. Jerez was no exception. Andrés Bermúdez continued to speak about the dire material conditions facing the bulk of the municipality's residents and proposed specific solutions to address their economic woes. However, the creative use of municipal power by the local state to address the needs of ordinary residents played a less prominent role in his second campaign. Bermúdez presented a set of economic development proposals that outlined a markedly entrepreneurial vision for local government. These policy proposals contained a curious blending of recipes for attracting businesses, for public entrepreneurship to improve the economy, and for public-private partnerships with migrants to form job-creating enterprises.

His proposals to attract industrial and commercial investment tend to envision a limited role for the local state in encouraging corporations to relocate from other regions of Mexico and the United States through such selective incentives as tax breaks and government subsidies. Yet these proposals, as the following excerpt from our election eve interview with Bermúdez illustrates, do require government to play a creative role in building and administering development sites:

> Listen, to create jobs in Zacatecas there has to be a big commitment and the government needs to invest. It has to build, let's say, shopping centers and go to invite companies from the United States, from Monterrey, from Mexico to come to Zacatecas. But bring them and tell them, "I'll loan you the building for two years. Come and put down your business. Create jobs. I won't

charge you for the water. Just come here and create jobs. If within the next two years it's not working out for you, you can pull out. If within two years you're doing well, then you begin to pay." (interview with Andrés Bermúdez, Jerez, Zacatecas, July 3, 2004)

Bermúdez's agricultural proposals represent the state as playing an activist, entrepreneurial role in economic development, moving beyond simply providing incentives and subsidies. His proposals call on the state to modernize agricultural production and distribution by introducing machinery from the United States and educating local agricultural producers about modern agricultural practices. Modernized agricultural techniques would significantly reduce the costs of production and allow the area to undercut its regional competitors, according to Bermúdez:

> To create employment in agriculture, first we have to look at which lands have water and then bring modern equipment from the United States and teach the campesinos. Bring the equipment that I invented, to plant *chile*, to plant watermelon, to plant everything, all types of vegetable. Where the cost is cut in half. . . . If in Aguascalientes a kilo of *chile* costs twenty [pesos], then we are going to sell it at fifteen and we're going to make more money than they do at twenty. So, you've got to modernize agriculture. We're fifty years behind. We need to modernize ourselves. But the point isn't [only] to modernize ourselves in production. If we're going to modernize ourselves in production we need to find someone to buy it from us. Because if I bring them the machinery and they plant and plant, then when the crop is ready, where are we going to take it? We've got the same problem. So, we've got to figure out where. (interview with Andrés Bermúdez, Jerez, Zacatecas, July 3, 2004)

Although the rhetoric of these proposals highlights their "public" character, the reality is more complex. Given Bermúdez's own economic participation in these proposals, the line between his role as public official and private investor begins to blur. At times this distinction is obliterated altogether. In an interview with a U.S. reporter, for example, he claimed that "I will personally invest $1 million in two canneries that will create 600 jobs–if I win. You have my word on that" (Kraul 2004).

As the above excerpts make clear, similar to their position in the transformation of the political sphere, here too the heroic migrant—and particularly Andrés Bermúdez—is seen as playing the leading role in creating a brighter economic future. Voters were told that by voting for Bermúdez they could assure the support of migrant entrepreneurs in job-creation projects. At the massive rally marking the end of his campaign, Bermúdez suggested that his connections with migrants would lead to two specific projects: an air conditioner fabrication plant and a cannery capable of adding value to the *municipio*'s agricultural products. These contacts would permit Andrés Bermúdez to utilize a "new 3×1 program":

> These realities will be possible because we have reached consensus with our emigrants, agreeing that if Andrés Bermúdez becomes *presidente* the developers of the 3×1, 2×1, and 1×1 programs will no longer allocate their funds toward paving streets or urban infrastructure projects, many of which have been carried out at elevated costs. Instead, they will now put those funds in the hands of migrants in the government, like Andrés Bermúdez, to create jobs, businesses, and employment. (Andrés Bermúdez, campaign rally, June 30, 2004)

It remains an open question whether these types of economic development proposals can generate job opportunities in sufficient quantity and quality to stem the tide of migration to the United States. Andrés Bermúdez himself appeared skeptical that migration levels could be reduced significantly. In recognition of the probability that economic livelihoods in Jerez would continue to depend on dollars sent home by the *jerezanos ausentes* working in the United States, Bermúdez proposed to orient the local educational system toward creating the skills necessary to find meaningful work in the United States:

> One of my projects is to teach basic English from kindergarten through high school. At least when they arrive over there they'll know a little bit of the language. Now, my project is to [set up] workshops to teach them to cook, to become waitpersons, to be tractor operators, to work with computers. All of that. So that the people that leave from here make it there knowing something, an occupation, if we're not going to be able to stop them. (interview with Andrés Bermúdez, Jerez, Zacatecas, July 3, 2004)

This proposal closely resembles similar policies already enacted by the PAN regime in Guanajuato to upgrade the skills and hence the earning power and future remittances of transnational migrants.

The Promise of Change and the Practice of Governance

What are the broader lessons from this analysis of the multiple elections of the Tomato King? What does this political drama tell us about the meaning, impact, and contradictions of migrant political transnationalism?

First, although the political fortunes of the Tomato King emerged from a particular historical context and political opportunity structure, these contextual circumstances are not specific to the translocal spaces forged through jerezano transnational migration, but instead have a wider transnational reach. The electoral campaigns of Andrés Bermúdez brought together two important trends in contemporary Mexican politics: the emergence of new political subjectivities and the diminishing appeal of the nation's political parties. A whole series of new political subjects, with el migrante and *los pueblos indígenas* only the most prominent, have emerged in recent decades and furthered the nation's still incipient process of democratization.

Beginning with the 2001 elections, Jerez, Zacatecas, provided fertile ground for el migrante to emerge as a political subject in regional politics. By the time of the July 2004 Zacatecan municipal elections, Jerez had ceased to be the only site of such mobilizations, as other migrant candidates contended for municipal presidencies. Another migrant, Texas businessman Martín Carvajal, was victorious in the small *municipio* of Apulco while two migrants were elected to the state legislature as required by the new Ley Migrante. These multiple sites of surging migrant political mobilization suggest that the case of the Tomato King is not an isolated phenomenon resulting from the particular conditions of the translocal networks and relations connecting the *municipio* of Jerez and its migrants in the United States.

Declining popular support for the major political parties and the political class they nourish also helps to explain the appeal of the Tomato King's multidimensional heroic migrant narrative. Bermúdez successfully positioned himself as an antipolitician who shared in the traumatic experiences of most Zacatecan families forced to send their loved ones to El Norte because of the state's deplorable economic conditions. He was successful at presenting those conditions as the result of the corruption and misdeeds of the political class and not as being due solely to Mexico's position in the global economy, the region's ecological conditions, or a lack of natural resources. To the extent that the distrust of politics as usual so widely shared in Jerez is present in other regions of Mexico, this provides favorable conditions for the construction of "outsider" political discourses—migrant or otherwise—that champion the displacement of the long-entrenched political class as the route to social change, political transformation, and economic improvement.

Second, the Tomato King's experiences once he took office illustrate the harsh reality that the social and economic transformations promised by migrant would-be politicians are not so easily accomplished, even when they do gain political representation and public office. Once in office, the Tomato King faced significant obstacles that limited his room for maneuver and, consequently, his ability to carry out the bountiful promises of his electoral campaigns. During his short time at the helm of the *municipio*, an embattled Bermúdez faced constant threats from the local political opposition, whose offensive included the occupation of city hall, accusations that

Bermúdez had fraudulently misappropriated municipal funds, and even charges that he had raped a young woman.

As a result, the bermudista administration spent much of its energies fighting back political challenges. Few, if any, of the promises of economic development and renewal came to fruition. In fact, Bermúdez came to express skepticism about the ability of migrant investment to generate local employment opportunities. He confided that he had begun counseling migrants to create marketing outlets in the United States before thinking about building factories or processing plants in Jerez. One of the few campaign promises that was implemented brought two used buses from the United States to provide municipal transportation to the regional university in the capital city.

Despite the lively opposition his administration faced and his inability to carry through on any of his major campaign promises, Bermúdez was able to maintain his popularity among his base. This was accomplished in part by placing blame for the administration's limited accomplishments on an entrenched local elite that he claimed would not let him work. With dramatic flair, Bermúdez struck this chord most forcefully on the occasion of his first Informe Municipal (State of the Municipality) speech in which he lamented the obstacles the local opposition had placed in front of his project and insinuated that he might abandon Mexican politics for good and return to the fields of northern California.

In the end Bermúdez abandoned this "exit" path, opting instead to jump scales within the Mexican political arena. Less than two years into his term, Bermúdez resigned the mayoral post in Jerez to run for federal deputy in the July 2006 elections. That campaign would prove successful and claim the PAN's only victory within Zacatecas's five federal electoral districts. By credibly representing the threat that he—and perhaps other migrants—might enact a full-scale exit from the Mexican political scene in response to the continuing control exerted by the traditional political class, Bermúdez's gestures toward a return to the United States both mobilized support from his grassroots base and weakened the veracity of the political attacks coming from his opponents.

In just over five years, the Tomato King has demonstrated a remarkable ability to triumph in the electoral arena. His three successive and successful campaigns in that short period exemplify the potential for migrant success in the politics of their sending communities and even at the wider regional and national levels. These campaigns have demonstrated that the commitment and tenacity migrant activists bring to their involvement in home-country politics can capture the popular imagination and construct the political alliances necessary to both gain formal recognition of migrant political rights and win popular election.

Just as important, Bermúdez's experience has demonstrated the difficulty of putting into practice the promise of migrant-led social and political transformation. This is not a real surprise, given that the content of his campaign offerings was based on a set of neoliberal policy prescriptions—the promised egalitarian outcomes of which are more utopian than real. The Tomato King's experience also confirms a political truism that has been painfully assimilated by the Mexican people following the nation's "first democratic elections" in 2000: the promise of change and the practice of government are political animals that belong to completely different orders.

6 Institutionalizing New Spaces for Migrant Political Agency

Votar y Ser Votado in Mexico

Much of the existing literature on migrant political transnationalism has focused, as we have done in earlier chapters, on the construction and exercise of transnational citizenship at the level of the local state. In the case of Mexican migration in particular, such studies have tended to focus on the informal negotiations between individual migrants, hometown association leaders, nonmigrants, and local and regional political authorities in Mexico over the boundaries and content of community membership and "substantive" or "extraterritorial" citizenship (e.g., Fitzgerald 2000, 2005; Goldring 1998, 2002; Rivera-Salgado 1999, 2000; R. Smith 1998, 2005). In recent years, however, the activities of hometown associations, migrant political organizations, and some individual migrants have been aimed at contesting the boundaries and formalizing the legal rights of citizenship in the new social space of the "global Mexican nation."

These efforts have increasingly borne fruit. As a result of years of sustained migrant activism, legal reforms were approved in 2005 that grant Mexican nationals residing abroad the right to vote in presidential elections. This was the culmination of years of debate and negotiation involving migrant activists and political elites in discussions about the meaning and content of transnational citizenship for Mexican migrants. Such developments underline the need to push the analysis of migrant political transnationalism beyond the bounds of the translocal level and the informal politics taking place there to consider the wider social and political networks and processes contributing to the formal-legal institutionalization of transnational citizenship.

In this chapter we consider the wider debates within Mexico over the formal-legal recognition of migrants as legitimate actors in the Mexican political sphere. We focus on two recent cases in which formal rights to transnational citizenship have been extended to Mexican migrants in political spaces beyond the locality. To identify and frame the key issues in the political debates about transnational citizenship, we begin by examining the political dynamics underlying the 2005 right-to-vote legislation at the national level in Mexico that granted absentee voting rights to migrants in presidential elections. All of the issues raised in this debate were foreshadowed in the earlier Ley Migrante legislation in Zacatecas, which we discussed briefly in chapter 5. The Ley Migrante spells out the conditions under which migrants may hold office and be represented in the Zacatecas state legislature. Because passage of this law coincided with our fieldwork we were able to interrogate our research subjects about the political processes leading to its passage and their perceptions of the strengths and limitations of its major provisions.

In examining both the federal and Zacatecas cases, we identify the wide-ranging political coalitions stitched together among migrants and their political allies, detail the complex negotiations and debates that these coalitions engaged in with opponents of the political empowerment of migrants and the recognition of transnational citizenship, and address the scope and limitations of the particular forms of transnational citizenship emerging from the resulting legislation. Then we turn to the special cases of two of our principal ethnographic subjects, both former presidents of the Los Angeles-based Zacatecan Federation of Hometown Associations of Southern California (FCZSC), who are playing an ongoing role in Zacatecan political life as a result of the Ley Migrante legislation they both worked to promote. Manuel de la Cruz is currently a "migrant deputy" elected to the Zacatecan state legislature in 2004 on the party list of the ruling PRD. Guadalupe Gómez has been mentioned prominently in the media on both sides of the border as a likely future candidate for governor of Zacatecas under the banner of a hoped for, but not yet incipient, migrant party.

The (Trans)National Politics of Migrant Voting Rights

Federal legislation granting Mexican migrants the right to vote from abroad in presidential elections passed in June 2005, culminating a decades-long struggle by migrant activists. The demand for the right to vote from abroad has been a recurring theme among Mexican migrants throughout postrevolutionary Mexican political history. The demand was articulated as early as 1929 when a California-based delegation to the convention of the Anti-Reelection Party of José Vasconcelos sought the extension of all the rights of citizenship to those Mexicans residing in the United States (Santamaría Gómez 2003). However, this demand did not regain a prominent place on the political agenda of migrants until the mid-1980s, when the Mexican political system began to experiment with electoral competition, laying the groundwork for the slow and still unfolding democratization of its postrevolutionary form of semiauthoritarian one-party rule. During the presidential election cycle of 1988, migrants once again took up the banner of extraterritorial political rights. Thousands of migrants rallied in Los Angeles and in agricultural regions of California at campaign events organized by insurgent candidate Cuauhtémoc Cárdenas. In subsequent years, migrants began to openly solicit the right to vote from abroad as well, fighting for further democratization and an end to the harassment migrants were subjected to by corrupt government officials on their return to Mexico (Martínez Saldaña 1999).

It was not until the later half of the 1990s, however, following the permitting of voting from abroad in that year's historic electoral reforms, that something that could legitimately be termed a right-to-vote *movement* emerged. This movement came together in the wake of the series of legal reforms promulgated by the Mexican government to further cultivate and maintain migrants' ties and loyalties to their homeland. The 1996 electoral reforms eliminated the constitutional requirement that citizens must vote in their local residential districts and opened the possibility for voting from abroad. This reform, combined with the so-called non-loss of Mexican nationality legislation enacted the following year, created both hope and confusion among migrants, politicians, and the Mexican citizenry in general about the overall effect of the two reforms. For example, there were uncertainties with respect to the scope and impact of the dual-nationality reforms. Some migrants were excited about the prospect that this new law offered them a form of dual *citizenship* with full political rights, including the right to vote from abroad. Others were more restrained in their assessment of the law, noting that the reform only applied to the relatively small proportion of Mexicans in the United States who had become naturalized citizens and did not address the needs of the vast numbers of undocumented migrants who were then coming under increasing xenophobic pressure with the passage of such anti-immigrant laws as Proposition 187 in California.

These critical voices among migrants also denounced the law because they believed that the government's extension of dual *nationality* was unduly limited, offering certain cultural and economic rights (like the ability to own property along coastal and border regions) but expressly denying political rights. These lingering questions about the content of "dual nationality" served to divert attention from the extensive enabling legislation that would be required to convert the promise of the right to vote contained in the 1996 electoral reforms into a reality before the 2000 presidential elections.

In late 1997, as migrants were becoming aware of the significant work still necessary to bring the vote from abroad to fruition, some activists began organizing to pressure Mexican electoral authorities to implement the vote. This network of transnational activists began organizing delegations to Mexico in what Martínez Saldaña has called the "emigrant lobby" (Martínez Saldaña 1998). The network, then known as the Coalición de Mexicanos en el Exterior, Nuestro Voto en el 2000, was able to gain some political concessions from parts of the Mexican state and thus to reinsert the migrant vote issue into the wider national political arena in 1998 and 1999. However, the coalition was unable to force the federal legislative and executive branches, then still dominated by the PRI, to implement the right to vote from abroad (Martínez Saldaña 2003a).

The move to extend the vote to migrants did not gain traction at that time because the PRI party-state, preoccupied with holding on to the presidency in the 2000 elections, feared that migrants would support the opposition parties. These fears were not altogether unfounded, given the large-scale mobilizations for the Cárdenas candidacy in 1988 and the symbolic elections held in Chicago and other U.S. cities in both 1988 and 1994, in which the left-center PRD beat the ruling PRI (Santamaría Gómez 2003; Ross Pineda 1999). And yet, despite the strong rhetorical support for the migrants' right to vote advanced by the PRI's partisan opponents, migrant voting was not approved until five years after Vicente Fox broke the PRI's seventy-one-year grip on the presidency. What explains this delay? Were the nationalistic arguments used to question the extension of political rights to migrants little more than "cover" for PRI maneuvers aimed at sustaining its hold on power? If so, why did the arguments persist once the PRI lost the presidency? What explains the migrant activists' eventual success in gaining legislative approval of their demands despite these objections?

Whether or not opposition to extending political rights to migrants was simply a cover for strategies to maintain PRI rule, the arguments themselves were always couched in decidedly broad nationalistic terms. Jorge Carpizo and Diego Valadés, two noted constitutional scholars and occasional public servants under the PRI regime, became the most high-profile faces of this nationalist voice. Their 1998 book, *El voto de los mexicanos en el extranjero* (Carpizo and Valadés 1998), highlighted the potential dangers inherent in extending the vote to migrants abroad and sought to undermine migrant voting rights' chances for approval. Carpizo's essay in that book draws on comparative legal analysis of extraterritorial voting rights to argue that the Mexican case is unique because the number of eligible voters could affect the outcome of national elections and because of the country's "special relationship" with the United States, where some 99 percent of its migrants live. In Carpizo's view, these unique features of the Mexican case present particularly challenging risks of unacceptable infiltration and influence from outside the nation. Carpizo is most emphatic in emphasizing two of these risks. First, echoing Benedict Anderson's (1994) critique of "long distance nationalism," he argues that the election could be decided by voters who, because they had long been absent from Mexico, were disconnected and ill-informed about its present needs and did not plan to return, and therefore would neither benefit from nor suffer the consequences of their decisions (Carpizo and Valadés 1998, 108). Carpizo's second argument is that the vote from abroad could become "politicized" with powerful U.S. interests attempting to influence the outcome of the election (Carpizo and Valadés 1998, 84). Carpizo is particularly concerned about the influence of the mass media in political campaigns and how those media generally express the views of the most powerful political and economic interests (Carpizo and Valadés 1998, 109).

In this curiously dated nationalist argument Carpizo seems wholly unaware of the impact that the globalization of the media and neoliberal policies have had on the boundaries of nation-states. First, it relies on a view of communications media as cleanly organized within national lines. This image of the media suggests that those outlets accessible to the general public in the United States would necessarily be emitting messages consonant solely with "U.S. interests." Such a view conveniently overlooks the fact that much of the Spanish-speaking media in the United States—precisely those media outlets most likely to influence potential voters in Mexican elections—are deeply intertwined with the Mexican media consortia Televisa and TV Azteca. These transnational capitalist alliances would likely impede the type of strictly nationalist media messages that Carpizo envisions.

Second, Carpizo ignores the extent to which the "sovereignty" of Mexico has already been compromised by wider economic and political actors, networks, and institutions "from above" that are advancing a neoliberal agenda. For example, Mexico's policy choices are already constrained by the expectations of U.S. and global monetary institutions. This constraining hand was made visible in a press conference held by U.S. Treasury Secretary John Snow in December 2005 during an appearance in Mexico City. Responding to a question about the impact that a victory by left-center PRD presidential candidate Andrés Manuel López Obrador might have, Snow declared that Mexican economic stability "depends on the continuation of sound policies and if they continue, as I would expect they will, then Mexico will continue to enjoy the benefits of financial stability" (Gonzalez Amador 2005). In Snow's imagery, the mere suggestion that future governments might seek to change course and move away from the strict application of neoliberal economic policies raises the haunting specter of financial instability and economic crisis. This form of neoliberal globalization from above already poses far greater threats to Mexico's national sovereignty than might any putative pressures of transnationalism from below by migrant voters.

The nationalist critique outlined by public intellectuals associated with the PRI such as Carpizo served to structure the context faced by the vote's proponents in the late 1990s. This context was fundamentally altered by Vicente Fox's defeat of the PRI party-state in the 2000 elections and his construction of migrants as "heroes" to the nation. Once migrants were incorporated into the nationalist discourse, arguments based on nationalism no longer led to an automatic rejection of the migrant activists' demands. In the post-2000 political context, the right-to-vote issue maintained a legitimate presence on the national political agenda, reappearing with a vengeance as new election cycles began. In this new context, each of the major political parties began to proclaim their support for the right to vote from abroad. Ironically, this was a mixed blessing for the promoters of the vote, because it generated a multiplicity of proposals and mechanisms for the vote's implementation, with each party seeking to take credit for their particular set of plans. As a result, by 2003 at least fourteen proposals had been submitted to the Mexican Congress, including five from the PAN, four from the PRD, and three from the PRI (Coalición por los Derechos Políticos de los Mexicanos en el Exterior 2004, 353). This legislative jockeying suggests that the theoretical debates over the issue had been sidestepped—all parties now publicly proclaimed that the vote should be extended to migrants living abroad. This focused attention on questions of the legal, technical, and financial means to implement the extension of voting (Peschard 2005).

This change in the terms of the debate was clearly related to a new perception of the potential power migrants might exercise from abroad. Although migrant activists continued to argue that there was widespread clamor for the vote among migrants—drawing on survey evidence that suggested that over 80 percent of migrants would vote from abroad if they could (Pew Hispanic Center 2005; Instituto Federal Electoral 1998)—it became clear to close observers of Mexican politics that nationalist fears that massive migrant participation might decide election results were seriously overblown. For example, one study by U.S. academics estimated that the universe of migrants likely to vote in the 2006 elections was actually quite small, between 125,000 and 360,000 (Marcelli and Cornelius 2005).

In addition to the changing perception of the scope of migrant interest in voting in Mexican national elections, and thus their potential impact, partisan fears that migrants might vote en masse for any particular party were gradually quieted as well. Migrant activists contributed to the increased recognition that the "migrant community" was not a unitary political subject but instead was a heterogeneous political formation that included militants from all of the major Mexican parties. The strategic political logic of one of the principal organizations leading the right-to-vote movement, the Coalición por los Derechos Políticos de los Mexicanos en el Exterior (CDPME), was aimed at building political strength from this very heterogeneity. The CDPME—made up of prominent migrant activists, HTA leaders, journalists, businesspeople, and academics from across the United States, Canada, and parts of Europe—consciously followed a nonpartisan lobbying strategy aimed at generating unanimity among political leaders across the partisan spectrum in favor of the extraterritorial vote. The CDPME leadership credits the group's "plural, independent and non-partisan" identity with its ability to win the struggle for the vote in 2006 (Rodríguez Oceguera 2005). But this emphasis on cross-party coalition building was not always successful, suggesting that the unity constructed by migrants, *as migrants*, across their significant ideological differences and party loyalties faces obvious obstacles and is always fragile and contingent.

Late in the final push for legislation in 2005, for example, a prominent group of PRD-friendly activists in the CDPME broke from the coalition for reasons that were both strategic and ideological. In a June 2005 e-mail announcing the rupture, activists from the Unión Cívica Primero de Mayo, based in Sacramento, California, explained that they had decided to join forces with other political actors who refused to endorse the partisan compromise that would make the mail-in ballot the only mode of voting. In addition to this strategic intent, the Unión Cívica activists expressed a more pointed critique of the overall cross-partisan political logic of the CDPME. They explained that their "second and equally important" reason for leaving the CDPME was

> the discomfort that we feel in belonging to an organization that includes among its member people that are active in extreme right-wing parties in both countries, the United States and Mexico. Because, what use is it that they help us to gain the vote with one hand, if with the other they are placing rocks in the slingshots of Arnold Schwagernegger [*sic*] and Vicente Fox so they can stone us?" (E-mail communication, June 7, 2005)

Despite these unsettling rumblings, the CDPME's political coalition was able to stay the course and broker a compromise that resulted in the historic 2005 legislation that made the vote from abroad a reality in the 2006 elections. How did the political compromise necessary for its approval affect the institutionalized form that the vote will take? What does this tell us about the particular mode of transnational citizenship now taking shape across the U.S.-Mexican divide?

Clearly, the vote-from-abroad legislation approved by the Mexican political class did not constitute a full-scale embrace of the transnationalization of Mexican political life. The compromise legislation brokered by the CDPME activists and their allies contained a number of *candados* (limiting clauses) that have significantly restricted the exercise of transnational citizenship across the North American divide. Principal among these limitations, the legislation restricts the migrant population eligible to cast their votes from abroad to those migrants holding a voter ID card issued in Mexico. It also prohibits electoral campaigns outside of Mexican territory and monetary contributions from abroad and imposes a cumbersome and restrictive mechanism for exercising the vote by mail.

These are more than small technical details. Promoters of the vote from abroad had always sought some form of registration process that would allow for potential voters to obtain a voter ID card without returning to Mexico, yet the compromise bill did not deliver any such program. This restriction severely limited the pool of potential voters. One recent survey suggests that only about three million of the ten million Mexican adults living in the United States hold a valid voter ID card (Pew Hispanic Center 2006). In other words, from the outset this provision of the extraterritorial voting law serves to exclude more than two-thirds of the potential migrant voter base. Moreover, the seven million migrants who do not have a voter ID card would have had to return to Mexico to apply for the *credencial de elector* at one the registration kiosks of the Instituto Federal Electoral (IFE, Federal Electoral Institute) and return personally a second time, up to a month later, to collect the card. Because this time-consuming process entailed substantial individual costs in time and resources, few migrants were in a favorable position to register to vote in the 2006 presidential elections. The fact that some significant proportion of these migrants are undocumented residents of the United States who would face significant obstacles to reentry if they were to temporarily leave the country to obtain a voter ID card in Mexico only complicates the matter more.

The mail-in ballot mechanism added yet another complex step to the process, requiring voters to apply for a ballot via registered mail six months before the election. This placed a further strain on the potential voter base. Some migrant voting-rights activists expressed skepticism about the mail-in mechanism itself, due to the notoriously inefficient Mexican postal service and the relatively steep $9 postage fee. The apprehensions caused by the restrictive elements of the law substantially reduced the number of eligible voters who chose to apply for a mail-in ballot.

Part of the impetus for the strict and exclusionary requirements undoubtedly came from nationalist desires to limit the potential effect of extending the vote to migrants abroad. However, federal election officials hasten to add that the elaborate provisions were necessary to ensure confidence in the nation's nascent democratic institutions. These concerns with the legitimacy of the democratic procedures help to explain the other major restrictions of the law, which prohibited candidates and their parties from campaigning abroad and outlawed the receipt of campaign financing from foreign sources, including from migrants. Enacted to ally nationalist fears of electoral manipulation by "powerful American interests" and the inability to apply national electoral laws outside the nation-state's territorial boundaries, these restrictions limited the information available and the public debate in the "global Mexican nation" regarding the presidential candidates and their competing projects and visions.

Some analysts and government officials suggest that the particular shape given the extraterritorial vote was driven by foreign-policy concerns more than by domestic concerns with electoral legitimacy or desires to limit the impact of the migrant voices. From this perspective, the foreign campaign ban can be understood as addressing the concerns of the Mexican diplomatic corps that candidates expressing anti-American campaign rhetoric during U.S. speaking engagements might jeopardize diplomatic relations (see Hendricks 2006). Others have linked the mail-in ballot mechanism to the more paternalistic arguments of the nationalist opposition to the vote from abroad, which claimed that approving extraterritorial voting rights would only hurt migrants by fueling the fires of anti-immigrant forces in the United States and subject undocumented migrants to potential deportation because Immigration and Naturalization Service (INS) agents might conduct raids at polling centers. In this vein, Carlos González Gutiérrez, a key intellectual designer of Mexican state policy toward migrants in recent decades, has suggested that the most important reason why the mail-in ballot was chosen was because Mexican government officials were concerned about the potential backlash that could be unleashed in U.S. political circles if expatriate voting were public and visible (quoted in Geyer 2005).

Whether driven by an outright attempt to restrict migrant participation, Mexico's foreign policy concerns, or desires to safeguard the legitimacy of electoral results, the legislation's exclusionary requirements and complex registration procedures resulted in a strikingly low number of migrants requesting mail-in ballots. Fewer than forty-one thousand migrants properly requested ballots with IFE by the January 2006 deadline—less than 1.5 percent of the already limited pool of eligible voters (Instituto Federal Electoral 2006a). Of these registered voters, a little over 32,500 migrants cast votes in the July election (Instituto Federal Electoral 2006b).

These figures highlight the limited reach and impact, at least in its initial institutionalized incarnation, of the presidential-level "transnational citizenship" taking form across the Mexico-U.S. border. But what of political developments at the subnational level in Mexico? How has el migrante been formally incorporated into the transnational political life of Zacatecas? What role did the agency of migrant hometown association leaders play in this subnational process of extending the boundaries of citizenship across borders?

The Implosion of Zacatecan Politics in the Los Angeles Federation

Mexican migrant civic organizations, hometown associations, and their federations are often represented as unitary political subjects, authentic voices of "the migrant point of view" in the new political spaces being opened up in Mexico for migrants' participation in the political life of their local communities, their state, and their nation. (See, for instance, Orozco 2000, on the role of HTAs in migrant-led development; R. Smith 2003b on the Frente Cívico as a binational political force; and Moctezuma Longoria 2003b on "the collective migrant" as a new social actor in Mexican politics.) In the case of the Zacatecan Federation of Southern California this image of unitary political subjectivity could not be farther from the truth. As the predictable political rituals, routines, and modes of incorporation that once characterized one-party rule by the PRI began to disintegrate in the late 1990s, new political spaces of partisanship, access, and influence opened up in Mexican political life. These spaces were both oppositional and corporatist. More important for our purposes, the (re)positioning of political actors along the emergent fault lines of Mexican politics was played out not only on the ground within Mexico but also within the Zacatecan Federation in Los Angeles.

Before the political opening, the Federation had become the largest and most institutionalized organization of Mexicans abroad. In the 1980s and early 1990s its leaders had collaborated closely with the PRI leadership in Zacatecas in the comanagement of the state's 2×1 program for channeling migrant remittances and matching state funds into community development projects in the then nearly forty municipalities represented by HTAs (Goldring 1998, 2). The Federation's relationship to the state government in Zacatecas was a model of PRI corporatism. The municipalities represented by the Federation's clubs received roads, school improvements, health clinics, recreational facilities, and basic infrastructure services financed by collective remittances with a double match of state subsidies. In exchange, Federation members provided electoral support for PRI candidates, as members of its HTAs called home at election time to influence the voting decisions of their family members who remained behind in Mexico. Such transnational political practices helped solidify PRI electoral strength in the state, contributing, for instance, to the 74 percent vote in Zacatecas for PRI candidate Ernesto Zedillo in the 1994 presidential election (R. Smith 2003b, 316).

Migrant efforts to influence the votes of their transnational family members did not end with the critical realignment election of Ricardo Monreal, who was elected governor of Zacatecas in 1998 following his break with the PRI and affiliation with the PRD. They continue to be part of the political landscape in Zacatecas, with one key difference—because of increased party and candidate competition accompanying the fragmentation of the PRI and the rise in strength of the PRD in Zacatecas, the direction and disposition of Federation members' voting recommendations to their transnational extended families can no longer be taken for granted. This has increased the relative influence the fifty-five FCZSC individual clubs have with incumbent public officials and their challengers in Zacatecan state and local politics. FCZSC leader Efraín Jiménez described this shifting balance of power:

> The "hero" perception of our people in Mexico is a very powerful asset for migrants since this can be capitalized with politicians and government officials for the good of our community; this power is because of the power the migrant has over the family nucleus. . . . For example, when there is a county, state, or federal election in Zacatecas or Mexico, and if the migrant calls home and tells his relatives who to vote for, his decision will have great influence on his relatives decision. That is part of the "hero image." One migrant's vote in the United States can transform into fifty, one hundred, or a thousand votes in favor of one political party or candidate. (Jiménez 2004)

This power shift, however, has done little to dampen the jockeying for influence among competing leadership groups within the Federation over the group's overall orientation toward politics in Zacatecas. In fact, the political opening has provoked a series of ongoing partisan cleavages, dividing the federation leadership among those loyal to the ruling PRD, those maintaining ties to the PRI, and those who, while politically active transnational citizens, prefer to remain independent of party affiliations in Mexican politics while devoting increased energy to engaging the Federation in ethnic and immigrant empowerment on the U.S. side of the border.

To cope with these internal cleavages and maintain the Federation's nonprofit status, each of the major factions has agreed to keep their partisan and other political differences separate from formal decision-making processes in the Federation. Instead, they have constituted new political action groups that are formally independent of the Federation structure while being entirely composed of different networks of Federation leaders. The two

Fig. 8. The embodiment of the heroic migrant narrative in Jerez, Zacatecas. Photo by Pat Smith.

principal political action groups are the Frente Cívico Zacatecano (hereafter Frente Cívico or FCZ) and Zacatecanos PRImero. The latter is one of two U.S.-based migrant political-action organizations formally affiliated with the PRI in Mexico. It was formed in 1998 largely in response to the emergence of the FCZ as a new force in Zacatecan political life. The FCZ was initially formed in 1998 by a group of Federation activists who decided to support the insurgent PRD gubernatorial candidacy of Ricardo Monreal Ávila. Soon after Monreal took office, because of the way he chose to incorporate one of the FCZ leaders directly into his administrative apparatus, the FCZ split into two factions: those migrant elites who continued to collaborate with Governor Monreal throughout his six-year term, which we will call the *loyalista* faction, and the remaining leaders of the FCZ, who broke with Monreal and seek to maintain an autonomous "migrant" stance toward Zacatecan politics and political parties. Some of the leaders of the second faction, which we will term the *autonomista* faction, have told us they are considering forming the nucleus of a new migrant political party if existing political channels do not offer a sufficiently broad opening for the "democratization" of Mexican politics.

How did this shift from politically quiescent corporatism to uncertainly managed factional strife within the Federation come about? The initial controversy contributing to the eventual formation of the FCZ was a dispute over the relative influence of migrants in the state's 2×1 community development program. In 1996, a small leadership group within the Federation began to question a political restructuring that replaced 2×1 with a federally mandated program known as Fund 26. This shift was part of the neoliberal "new federalism" agenda enacted by the Zedillo government. The PRI-dominated state government in Zacatecas insisted that the Federation go along with Fund 26's new power-sharing arrangement, which devolved power to municipal governments (local mayors and their councils) for decisions on how to spend municipal funds, including the collective remittances of migrants targeted to their localities. (R. Smith 2003b, 314). Following this restructuring, when the Zacatecas governor made his annual visit to Los Angeles in 1996, critics in the Federation confronted the PRI governor and his entourage, demanding a restoration of the previous "partnership" arrangement under 2×1. They expressed their concern that losing control over the disposition of funds they had raised through voluntary contributions would undermine Federation members' trust in the new financial control arrangements under Fund 26. The PRI government in Zacatecas refused to change the "new federalist" devolution, and the Federation's dissenting leadership group was forced out of power in favor of a more accommodating leadership group. The new leadership faction came to be regarded by the dissenters as excessively partisan colluders with a corrupt PRI political machine (R. Smith 2003b, 315).

When Ricardo Monreal openly broke with the PRI in the 1998 gubernatorial election and campaigned for Zacatecan votes in California, the dissenting group decided to support his candidacy. They formally reconstituted themselves as the FCZ, seeking to promote democratization on the Mexican side of the border by breaking the PRI's monopoly on power, electing Monreal and, once he was elected, renegotiating with him the terms of the political relationship between the state and its migrant diaspora. Monreal courted the migrants in California in the hope of benefiting from the influence they exercised over their extended families in Zacatecas. He made three campaign visits and ran radio ads in California and also made numerous campaign promises designed to consolidate support among migrants and their organizations in the United States.

Following his election, Monreal moved quickly (perhaps too quickly) to fulfill one of the easiest of these promises, naming a prominent former Zacatecan Federation president, Manuel de la Cruz, a founding member of the FCZ, to the position of "official representative" of Zacatecas in the United States. Not surprisingly, in light of the fact that that the FCZ was born out of skepticism concerning state manipulation of migrant interests, this choice, and in particular the fact that the new governor did not consult with the FCZ leadership before making it, led to the split in the FCZ.

We interviewed Francisco Javier González, a key member of the autonomista faction in Los Angeles in November 2003, at the time he was serving as president of the FCZ. He characterized the split as a struggle between democratization and "politics as usual." The autonomistas saw the choice of de la Cruz as a continuation of the corporatist political culture in which the people at the top pick collaborators for political positions by pointing a finger at them (*"el dedazo"*) without consulting voices from below, or for that matter from the middle of the power hierarchy:

> That's why we broke with them . . . with Manuel de la Cruz . . . because we believe in democracy. Because we've got two cultures and . . . when he [Monreal] appointed . . . de la Cruz it was "why?" We are struggling so that there could be democracy in the Frente Cívico and over there. Our idea was that in the Frente Cívico we could have chosen the person . . . that would have been appointed. And that didn't happen, and for that reason there were a lot of people that left the Frente Cívico, because they said, "You see. See right there. That same system." (interview with Francisco Javier González, Norwalk, California, November 13, 2003)

In addition to appointing an official representative, once he was elected governor, Monreal proclaimed his intention to implement his campaign promises to support the creation of seats in the legislature to represent migrants, to expand the vote to absent migrants in the United States, and to run the 2×1 program under the old rules rather than the new Fund 26 rules (see R. Smith 2003b, 317–18). These moves were only partially successful in consolidating his support among migrant activists. They ensured the continued backing of the loyalist faction for the duration of his six-year term. This faction was rewarded for its loyalty with gubernatorial patronage. For instance, when Manuel de la Cruz's term as official representative ended, the governor named another migrant Federation and Frente Cívico member and PRD supporter, Felipe Delgado (with whom the governor had gone to school many years earlier in Zacatecas and who had recently lost the presidency of the Frente Cívico to autonomista leader Francisco Javier González), to replace de la Cruz as the state's "official representative." Delgado in turn converted a suite of rooms on the grounds of his family's furniture manufacturing business in Los Angeles into offices suitable for meeting with migrants in his new official capacity.

None of Monreal's efforts to establish enduring ties to Los Angeles migrants succeeded in bringing the autonomista faction back into the fold. The autonomistas mistrusted the governor's commitment to migrants, perceiving it as more opportunistic than genuine. Their skepticism was cemented in 2001 when Monreal turned against the candidacy of the Tomato King, the migrant PRD candidate for mayor of the city of Jerez, Andrés Bermúdez, whom he had initially encouraged to run. This betrayal led to an initial alliance between Bermúdez and the new leadership of the FCZ to enact a law amending the state constitution to enable migrant candidacies for state and local office. As part of their effort to open up the political system in Zacatecas to migrant participation, the autonomistas organized a campaign to secure control of the Federation and maintain its distance from the Zacatecan state. Their efforts culminated in the election of the autonomista FCZ leader Guadalupe Gómez to a three-year term as president of the Zacatecan Federation in 2001.

Gómez's administration of the Zacatecan Federation can best be characterized as a major binational political offensive. On the Mexican side of the border he formed an alliance with the Tomato King to change the Zacatecan constitution to allow migrants to hold office. They promoted a law initially termed the Ley Bermúdez. However, when it appeared that Bermúdez and Governor Monreal might bury the hatchet, the FCZ broke with Bermúdez and renamed the initiative the Ley Migrante. As Federation president, Gómez accompanied the leaders of the FCZ in several lobbying trips to Zacatecas in 2002 and 2003 to encourage passage of the Ley Migrante. Despite the stricture of keeping the Federation out of politics to protect its nonprofit status, Gómez was frequently interviewed by the Zacatecan press on these trips in his capacity as FCZSC president, and each time he advocated passage of the Ley Migrante. Gómez was equally energetic in moving the Federation toward open advocacy of political issues on the U.S. side of the border that advanced the political rights and economic interests of Mexican migrants and promoted immigrant empowerment more broadly (see chapter 7).

In the face of these power moves, neither the governor nor the leaders of his loyalist faction sat on their hands. Led by the governor's first "official representative," Manuel de la Cruz, supporters of Governor Monreal encouraged thirteen individual clubs in the Los Angeles federation to break away and form a new grouping of clubs known as the Orange County Federation. This splinter group immediately gained the recognition of the governor and was thus placed on a fast track to obtain preferential treatment in the local competition for 2×1 matching funds.

These countermeasures in turn triggered a high-profile public conflict between FCZSC president Gómez and Monreal's U.S. representative, de la Cruz. Their mutual public accusations of manipulation and duplicity were widely reported in both the Los Angeles and Zacatecan press. For example, an article in the *L.A. Weekly* in early 2002 featured Gómez's allegations that de la Cruz was engaging in old-style Priísta tactics whose objective was to divide and control the premier immigrant organization in the United States (Quiñones 2002), in the same way that the Mexican state had for over seventy years co-opted the labor, peasant, and civic organizations that constituted the three pillars of its power base. De la Cruz responded by accusing Gómez of using the clubs of the L.A. Federation to launch a political career in Zacatecas by presenting himself as a progressive "agent of change" and exacerbating the differences between the state and the migrants. In light of our conversations with Gómez and other Frente Cívico leaders about creating a new "migrant party" in Zacatecas and offering Gómez as a gubernatorial candidate under its banner, this accusation was not entirely rhetorical.

In early 2003, as the debate on the Ley Migrante heated up in the capital city of Zacatecas and state and local elections of 2004 in Zacatecas moved closer, the two main factions in the Federation, the strategically nonpartisan FCZ and the unabashedly partisan Zacatecanos PRImero, entered into an alliance in support of the Ley Migrante. This alliance proved successful and eventually changed the eligibility requirements for running for most state and local offices in the state and created two seats in the Zacatecan state legislature for "migrant representatives." How did this curious political alliance come about? Who were its main beneficiaries? As eventually passed, how did the Ley Migrante construct "the migrant" as an extraterritorial citizen? Who benefited and who did not from this social construction? What does this tell us about the transnational political power of el migrante?

The Ley Migrante in Zacatecas: Constructing El Migrante as Political Subject

Zacatecas has played a pathbreaking role in the development and implementation of state-migrant policies at the regional-state level. Zacatecan migrants and state officials, for example, were pioneers and leading advocates of the types of matching-grant "community development" projects that we detail throughout the book and that have made Mexico, and Zacatecas in particular, an obligatory point of reference in global policy debates on the "migration-development nexus" (see Iskander 2005). The pioneering position of Zacatecas has also extended to the political realm. In 2003 Zacatecas became the first Mexican state to pass legislation to officially open the regional political system to migrant participation. The constitutional amendments contained in the Ley Migrante made two important modifications. The Zacatecan constitution now (1) recognizes migrants' right to hold office if they can demonstrate that they maintain what the law terms "binational and simultaneous residency," and (2) reserves two seats in the thirty-deputy state legislature for migrants.

The impetus for the Ley Migrante can be located in the experience of Andrés Bermúdez, whose story of transnational political triumph, defeat, and revival was narrated in chapter 5 (see also Bakker and Smith 2003). Bermúdez's emergence on the political scene brought the questions of migrant political participation in Zacatecas to center stage, and his defeat in the electoral courts in 2001 helped to highlight the exclusionary nature of the state's electoral rules, particularly the requirement that candidates for public office maintain a full year of "effective and uninterrupted" residency within the state. In the wake of this legal defeat, the Frente Cívico and their political adviser, Miguel Moctezuma Longoria, a prominent Zacatecan public intellectual, took the lead in promoting legal reforms that would open the state's political system to migrant participation. Within months of Bermúdez's political exclusion, the Frente Cívico and its advisers and allies in Zacatecas had drawn up a "citizen's initiative" elaborating constitutional reforms that allowed for migrant political participation. They then worked to build a political coalition among state-level political elites, the leaders of various HTAs and other migrant associations, and their academic supporters in Mexican and U.S. universities. Their initial proposal had privileged the corporatist migrant identity of HTA leaders, investing them with a special entitlement to hold office by virtue of their contributions to their communities in Zacatecas. By agreeing to broaden the definition and implementation of transnational citizenship, the Frente Cívico leaders and their allies were able to garner enough support from Zacatecan political elites to gain passage of the Ley Migrante by the legislature, its approval by two-thirds of the state's municipal authorities, and the signature of Governor Monreal.

A key element of the initiative's success was the deliberately nonpartisan lobbying strategy employed by the law's promoters. This strategy was described by the FZC's president, Francisco Javier González, when he, along with FCZ and Federation leaders Guadalupe Gómez and Guadalupe Rodríguez, formally presented the citizen's initiative to the state legislature in January 2003:

The worst thing is that this issue [of granting political rights to migrants] has been seen as the flag of particular political parties. As long as this does not change, the situation will continue as it is: we will not have political rights in this country. The Frente Cívico Zacatecano does not have an antipartisan position, [but] we do not want the Initiative Reforming the Political Constitution of the State of Zacatecas [the Ley Migrante] to be partisanized, as has happened when dealing with national-level reforms on this issue. (FCZ press conference, Zacatecas, January 10, 2003)

The members of the Frente Cívico strategically chose to present their initiative as emanating from "organized civil society," presenting common citizens' demands (Moctezuma Longoria 2003b), as a way of evading partisan conflicts that often stifle legislative advances because none of the parties wants to support legislation that is identified with and will be credited to their opponents.

This nonpartisan lobbying strategy butted up against the reality of partisan politics within the state legislature and "organized civil society." Felipe Cabral, a former president of the FCZSC and leader of the migrant political organization Zacatecanos PRImero, described to us how his organization came to join forces with the Frente Cívico in support of the Ley Migrante. Cabral began by recounting how migrants of all stripes are disparaged by political elites and the mass media in Zacatecas:

Right now when [los políticos] think about the migrantes, they think of the dollar sign. . . . But they don't want to give you your rights. . . . When you go to Mexico, they don't treat you like one of them. . . . I see they picture people with pickups from [the United States], big tires, they picture, they take pictures and they publish them in the newspapers. "Look at the migrantes! Look at the migrantes!" you know. . . . And "troca colorada." You know, red truck. "Troca colorada. Look at the migrants and the flags." They make fun of the migrante. (Felipe Cabral, president, Zacatecan Federation of Hometown Associations, Hawaiian Gardens, California, 2004)

While driven by a similar desire to empower migrants within the exclusionary political culture of Zacatecas, Cabral's story differs from the public stance taken by the Frente Cívico. In contrast to the Frente Cívico activists' representation of the initiative as nonpartisan, Cabral noted that a PRD deputy had initially presented the initiative, a fact that led it to face significant opposition from the PRI. In explaining the initiative's eventual approval, Cabral emphasized how *migrants* had constructed a cross-party alliance *as migrants*. Telling us that after a number of meetings with the FCZ leadership he became convinced that "we cannot fight in the United States *migrante contra migrante*," Cabral recounted how this recognition led him to contact the president of the state-level PRI in Zacatecas, José "Pepe" Bonilla, and invite him to meet with members of the FCZ and Zacatecanos PRImero to discuss the Ley Migrante proposal. The partisan identity of Cabral and the other Zacatecanos PRImero leaders was evidently key in garnering the support of the PRI legislative bloc: after the FCZ presented the initiative to Bonilla and asked him to push it with his party, he turned to Cabral and asked, "Felipe, what do you think?" According to Cabral, with his assent the PRI supported the proposal and enabled it to pass (interview with Felipe Cabral, Hawaiian Gardens, California, May 15, 2004). This episode suggests that the meaning of "nonpartisanship," as espoused by the promoters of the Ley Migrante, was not that they were able to form a coalition of grassroots forces existing outside of the partisan divisions of the institutionalized political sphere, but that they constructed a cross-party alliance among migrants and legislators in support of the initiative. It was because of that alliance that the initiative eventually gained enough momentum to win the necessary support at the executive, legislative, and municipal levels to pass the historic constitutional amendments.

Despite this elite cross-party agreement, which cemented legislative support for the Ley Migrante, the public pronouncements of FCZ leaders continually framed their efforts to pass the law as a struggle to realize grassroots democratization. At a press conference in Zacatecas in January 2003, FCZ activist and Los Angeles Federation president Guadalupe Gómez said: "In contrast to those who think that us migrants are passive actors only dedicated to working and sending dollars home, today we are here demonstrating that we are also political subjects, interested in the future of Zacatecas and willing to participate in its democratizing process" (Frente Cívico Zacatecano 2003). Despite this expansive rhetorical flourish, as we shall see, the impact of the "democratic" reforms they promoted, while opening up a space for el migrante, excluded some classes of migrants.

Among its most important provisions, the Ley Migrante now requires that two members of the Zacatecan state legislature be "migrant deputies." In practice, this provision requires each party fielding candidates for plurinominal deputy seats in the Zacatecan Congress, granted on the basis of proportional representation, to place a migrant candidate in the very last position of their party list. After the votes are counted, the two parties receiving the most votes are required to move their "migrant candidate" into the last of their winning positions on the party list. So, for example, when the PRD gained three plurinominal seats in the 2004 elections, those seats were granted to the candidates in the first two spots of the party list and the third to Manuel de la Cruz, the "migrant deputy" whose story we narrate below.

Although the provision of migrant representation in the state legislature would seem to imply that such deputies could become the voice of "absent zacatecanos" in decision-making circles, the migrant leaders we spoke to often expressed a much more limited vision of the role of the "migrant deputy." Efraín Jiménez, the projects secretary and director of philanthropy for the Federation, envisioned the "migrant deputy" as representing the interests of HTAs and their leaders:

> JIMÉNEZ: It is good for us because now we have people who really experience what the migrant is experiencing here. Now they can work down there to promote the well-being of us over here. There is a lot of ways to help us over here and one of the best ways, in my opinion, is to help us organize. How? They don't have to come over here and create clubs and they don't have to do a lot of stuff. They just have to let us work. That's all we ask. If we submit a [project] application and the application from my club gets stuck down there, I am losing the morale. I am going like sssssss. . . . deflating. . . . And all of my members over here, if the project doesn't get approved they don't see any reason why we have to reunite. They don't help us over there. I mean, what for?
>
> SMITH: So these people can be a help in moving these projects forward when they're stalled.
>
> JIMÉNEZ: They would help by [facilitating] the application to go forward and to make the project with quality, to do it good, to do it fast, to give good results. . . . That would be a big incentive for us over here to reunite. And when you reunite here, when you are a club with a hundred members, you start to feel more empowered. (interview with Efraín Jiménez, Los Angeles, California, May 13, 2004)

The expansive democratic rhetoric heralding the importance of the migrant deputy as representing the interests and promoting the well-being of the broader migrant community is subtly turned in such statements toward more limited and particularistic ends. Far from opening the political sphere to the participation and representation of a broad and expansive category of migrants, in this vision the Ley Migrante opens up that space for a much more delimited group: the "collective migrant," that is, the HTA leaders themselves.

Driven by the legal defeat of Andrés Bermúdez, the Ley Migrante also incorporated a new legal construct that recognized migrants' binational residency and their ability to be *"presentes en la ausencia"* (present in absence). The initiative thus addressed the principal legal problem faced by mayoral candidate Bermúdez—his lack of continuous residency within the state for a full year prior to the 2001 election—by the new legal category of "simultaneous and binational residency." This concept went through a number of incarnations as the Ley Migrante bill was modified in the state legislature.

The final version recognized migrants' "simultaneous and binational residency" and granted them the right to hold all offices except for governor if they could demonstrate, at least six months prior to an election, that they possessed: (1) a home in the state; (2) a registered taxpayer ID card; (3) a federal census ID number; and (4) a voter credential card.

This specification of the new legal construct of simultaneous and binational residency clearly excluded a large proportion of the Zacatecan population resident in the United States, particularly those that do not own homes in the state. Nevertheless, in comparison to earlier versions of the bill, the requirements appear strikingly inclusive. In its initial incarnations, the FCZ's "citizen's initiative" sought to restrict the application of simultaneous and binational residency to those migrants engaged in social projects that "benefit" Zacatecas—a class of migrants that they clearly equated with the leaders of migrant hometown associations or similar organizations. Even after the modified bill had been approved, some of our interview subjects continued to suggest that participation in HTAs was the basis for determining simultaneous and binational residency. Francisco Javier González, for instance, told us: "I don't have to be living there [because] I am working for the good of Zacatecas, in the Federación de Clubes Zacatecanos, or in the Frente Cívico. I am working for Zacatecas, I can participate over there. That was included in there, in the law" (interview with Francisco Javier González, Norwalk, California, November 13, 2003).

This representation of the law's requirements is not only a consequence of the migrant leaders being out of the loop when final legislative amendments were made. Their leading intellectual ally, Moctezuma Longoria, writing in an essay prefacing the approved version of the bill, still claims that "the condition [for migrant eligibility] is that they hold 'binational and simultaneous residency,' which is granted if they are involved in social and community activities in Zacatecas from abroad" (Moctezuma Longoria 2003b, 4). Ironically, under this logic even so prominent a migrant activist as Andrés Bermúdez—the very migrant whose experience of exclusion had been the impetus for the reforms—would be excluded from the right to hold office. This eventuality was readily acknowledged by some of our interview subjects, as evidenced by the following excerpt from our interview with Francisco Javier González:

> BAKKER: So only people that work in the federations would qualify? Somebody like Bermúdez that didn't work with a club, the law wouldn't cover him, right?
>
> GONZÁLEZ: It wouldn't cover him. Right now, he has that problem. He's going to have that problem. Or, I don't know how he's working, if he has a club over there where he's at.

BAKKER: I don't think he does. In Napa. Or in Winters.

GONZÁLEZ: Okay, so then he could have a problem. If he spends a year over there then he qualifies under the law, but if over here he finds a club or something, he could probably qualify because he's providing benefits for Zacatecas. (interview with Francisco Javier González, Norwalk, California, November 13, 2003)

Miguel Moctezuma Longoria, the key political adviser in Zacatecas to the Los Angeles-based FCZ, has continued to make the case for this restrictiveness in his numerous publications addressing the strengths and limits of the Ley Migrante. In these writings Moctezuma has enunciated a difference-generating conceptual distinction between the "symbolic identity" maintained by all members of the "binational community" and the "active commitment" of a certain subsector of the migrant community engaged in social and community projects in Zacatecas. According to Moctezuma, in contradistinction to the mass or "common denominator" of Mexican migrants, the Zacatecan HTA leaders have made the transition from a (passive) symbolic identity to an active engagement with Zacatecas and it is this transition that justifies their recognition as a "new extraterritorial social and political subject" (Moctezuma Longoria 2003b, 3). This separation of the HTA leadership from the rest of the migrant community leads Moctezuma to suggest that policymakers might consider granting "differentiated political rights," distinguishing between those extraterritorial citizens who could simply vote and those who could both vote and hold office, based on differing levels of commitment to Mexico (Moctezuma Longoria 2004, 296).

Although Moctezuma argues that his distinction is not based on a discriminatory classification, it is hard to ignore the exclusionary impact that such a classification would have. On the one hand, there is by now overwhelming evidence that the leadership of the HTAs is made up almost exclusively of well-to-do, often business-owning men (see, for example, Guarnizo 1998; Goldring 2001a, 2001b, 2003; Caglar 2006). Accordingly, codifying a legal distinction between ordinary migrants and migrant HTA leaders, and granting full political rights to the latter but not the former, would have the substantive impact of further disenfranchising female migrants and poor and working-class male migrants. Second, this extension of political rights to the leadership of particular organizations smacks of neocorporatism. It would recognize a particular form of continuing engagement with the "home" community (i.e., participation in "social projects"), which is linked to membership and participation in a well-delineated set of organizations (the migrant HTAs). Such a scheme, of course, renders invisible the "engagement" of the hundreds of thousands of Zacatecan migrants who, while not leaders or even active participants in HTAs, are continually engaged in translocal affairs through the maintenance of social and familial networks and the transfer of monetary remittances that help sustain over 13 percent of the households in the state (Rodríguez Ramírez 2004, 21). Far from representing a set of radical democratic reforms, the proposals generated and put forward by the FCZ appear aimed at empowering an elite sector of the migrant community—the "collective migrant," namely themselves.

The Dual Political Subjectivity of the Migrant Deputy

In September 2004, as a result of the "migrant deputy" provisions in the Ley Migrante, Manuel de la Cruz took possession of a seat in the Zacatecan Chamber of Deputies under the banner of the PRD. The consummate politician, de la Cruz brandished a polished campaign rhetoric, presenting himself as a true champion of el migrante who was dedicated to pursuing the interests of migrants in the institutionalized realm of Mexican politics. This self-representation as an authentic defender of migrants did not go unchallenged by de la Cruz's opponents. Many autonomista migrant leaders in the Los Angeles area were wont to point to de la Cruz's ties to the Zacatecan state—as the state government's "official representative in the United States" and as a key political operative for outgoing Governor Ricardo Monreal—in attempts to taint his qualifications as a true representative of el migrante. These accusations were, of course, not unfounded. After all, de la Cruz had been a Monreal loyalista since 1998 and had been rewarded with many a political favor in the intervening years—from the official representative's position, to PRD candidate for federal deputy in 2003, to regional coordinator of the 3×1 program in Zacatecas, and ultimately to the migrant deputy post on the PRD list in the 2004 state elections.

Nevertheless, de la Cruz also had many years of prior experience as a migrant activist and leader since his arrival in the United States in 1973. Over the years, he had helped form migrant sports leagues and hometown associations and was an early leader in the FCZSC, acting as its founding treasurer and as president in the early 1990s. Thus, the battle over whether to identify de la Cruz as an authentic migrant or a government insider is muddied by the multiple and changing roles he has occupied in the last quarter century.

As the migrant community's political infighting over de la Cruz's political adventures played out in the newspapers and political weeklies of Los Angeles and Mexico, the self-representation of de la Cruz as the migrants' champion also began to raise eyebrows in wider political circles across the United States and Mexico. As a result, de la Cruz became a necessary referent for nationalist forces on both sides of *la línea fronteriza*, who saw themselves—in rejecting de la Cruz's political endeavors—as defending sacred national ideals from the corrupting influences embodied in transnational migrants.

What is it about the political identity and practices of de la Cruz that could so successfully unite nationalist forces on both sides of the border in opposition to his political activity? A key part of the answer lies in the theme of "Americanization" woven into the political discourse of Manuel de la Cruz. The peculiar alignment of purportedly "American" elements in that discourse, such as "democracy" and "human rights," appear to be linked to the divergent readings of his practices and their meaning across the U.S.-Mexican divide—divergences that nonetheless led to common perceptions of de la Cruz on both sides of the border as a dangerously transnational threat to "the nation," its interests, and values.

Americanization: Those Who Have "Learned a Little Something about Democracy in the United States"

In an extended interview we had with Manuel de la Cruz in the capital of Zacatecas just days before he was elected migrant deputy in July 2004, he expounded on the factors driving his personal insertion into Mexican electoral politics. He told us that his initiative was propelled by twin motives: (1) to design and promote public policies protecting the interests of migrants living in the United States, and (2) to bring the unique experience of el migrante to bear on the unfolding process of democratization in Mexico. As the "official representative" of the state government, de la Cruz told us, he was often encouraged to run for office by club leaders who told him:

> "We need you to represent us in the government, so that us Mexicans in the United States"—the 25 million Mexicans that we are—"have our own voice in order to have the right to vote. Because all of the deputies and senators and the president of the republic, the governors that go to the United States, only when they're over there with us do they tell us that they're going to help [*laughs*]. When they come back here, 'No, hey, forget about everything.' " (interview with Manuel de la Cruz, Zacatecas, Zacatecas, June 25, 2004)

This encouragement from a set of migrant leaders was combined with de la Cruz's own concerns with corruption in the existing political class, which he contrasted with his experiences in the United States. After denouncing the existing state of affairs in the Mexican political system as "a vile corruption," de la Cruz suggested that "those of us who have learned a little something about democracy in the United States have to do something. . . . There are so many things: the very laws, security, human rights, so many things that we need and that we have learned from the United States" (interview with Manuel de la Cruz, Zacatecas, Zacatecas, June 25, 2004).

According to de la Cruz, it is this concern with corruption and the desire to bring to Mexico some of the democratic elements "learned from the United States" that stokes the fears of nationalist political forces in Mexico. These nationalist fears materialized in a pointed way in 2003 when de la Cruz was stripped of his elected post as a federal deputy from the PRD party just hours before taking office. Although officially the overturning of the electoral results was based on a recount of votes in several districts, de la Cruz situates the cause in the fear of the political elite of the political encroachment of "Americanized" migrants:

> There is a big fear in Mexico and in all of the governments that the American influence is going to come to Mexico [*laughs*]. I lived that, I felt it, and four hours before I was to be sworn in, Fox says, "Over here in this *municipio* and in that one, in this state and in this other one there have been bad votes and we are suspending them and you no longer are the winner" [*laughs*]. So they didn't let me make it. How come? It is the influence that they don't want us to arrive, because of that fear and so they invented that. But, I wouldn't be able to fight it all by myself. The doubt that remains is that there is a president of the IFE, that is, the highest authority on elections, and he signed the document for me. He says, "You are a federal deputy." That is not given to just anyone. So, what can you make of that? [*laughs*]. Once they give you the signed letter, it means that you're it. It can't just be given out like that; if so, they would give it to everyone. But later I understood it and somebody told me, "We can't accept it quite yet, we're afraid of those who are returning, that they might come back influenced by the Americans." (interview with Manuel de la Cruz, Zacatecas, Zacatecas, June 25, 2004)

Based on the substance of de la Cruz's narrative, we might be tempted to view the opposition to his candidacy and the "Americanized" influence he brought to Mexican politics as nothing more than an instrumental tactic of the ruling political elites intent on conserving their hold on positions of power. This seems to be the suggestion of de la Cruz when he told us, for instance, that the opponents of migrant political empowerment and representation in Mexican politics "are really a very small group":

> DE LA CRUZ: It is just the legislators, not the Mexican people. And why the legislators? Because it has been converted into a vicious circle in which by traditions and dynasties they've been there for forty-three years and they fear that someone will come and break that circle, to come in and remove them. That is the fear. It is not a fear of the influence from America; that is simply a myth. It is a myth that they are propagating. They spread it because they fear losing that position. Because many of them that are there already know that their great-grandchild, although not even born yet, will end up there.

BAKKER: They are going to be a deputy.

DE LA CRUZ: [*laughs*] That's it, that is what they fear, but there's nothing else. The real Mexican people are happy that it's like this, the people of Mexico, everyone except that group of legislators. They are not, and they aren't going to be, because for their entire lives they have been living from the Congress. That is the big problem. (interview with Manuel de la Cruz, Zacatecas, Zacatecas, June 25, 2004)

Despite this assertion that it is only the political class—from which de la Cruz excludes himself—that opposes his political ambitions, and that of migrants more generally, it is worth noting that de la Cruz and his "Americanized" politics also have been the object of criticism "from the Left and from below," to use the language in vogue among the adherents to the antipartisan Zapatista social movement. For instance, the leftist writer Adriana López Monjardín—writing in the Zapatista-inspired journal *Rebeldía*—characterized de la Cruz as part of the "militarist ultra-right that exists in every party" (López Monjardín 2003, 24–25) because of his support for the U.S. invasion of Iraq and his pronouncement that the war's detractors in Mexico were exhibiting an "emotional reaction" because of their fears that their family members might be engaged in the war (see also *La Jornada* 2003).

If these are the reactions to de la Cruz's transnational politics from both the Mexican political elite and the grassroots Left, how have his politics been received by nationalist forces in the United States? One might assume that de la Cruz would be treated sympathetically in U.S. political circles, given the fact that his politics in Mexico have been so widely interpreted—at least in the political realm—as being "influenced," if not manipulated, by "the Americans" and, potentially, pursuing policies consistent with "American interests." However, de la Cruz also has raised hackles among right-wing nationalists in the United States. For example, he has become a prominent symbol of the erosion of "patriotic assimilation" bemoaned by the Hudson Institute's John Fonte in his campaign against "dual allegiances" (see Fonte 2005). In the mind of Fonte, de la Cruz is no friend of the United States:

Mr. de la Cruz is not promoting pro-American values in Zacatecas. He was elected as a member of the traditionally anti-American Democratic Revolutionary Party, the PRD. Look at the web site of the California PRD, which is the political home of many naturalized American citizens. It contains lies about the United States, including the charge, quote, "the Mexican migrant who lives in the United States is without human rights." Not true. In 2003 the California PRD web site contained pictures not only of Che Guevara but of Lenin as well. So much for the promotion of American values. (Fonte 2005, 4)

Although this reactionary hyperbole misses much of the nuance of de la Cruz's transnational politics, it captures the other side of the nationalist response and suggests how the hybrid identities of contemporary transnational migrants manage to raise suspicion and opposition from nationalist forces in both sending and receiving countries. De la Cruz's "error" is to take seriously the ideals of democracy and human rights and to seek their realization throughout the entire space in which migrants orchestrate their lives across the Mexican-U.S. border. Adopting the principle of global human rights over the particular "national interests" of either Mexico or the United States subjects de la Cruz to nationalist criticisms from both sides of the border.

Consider the following comments made by de la Cruz as migrant deputy in denouncing the actions of Mexican federal and state migration authorities rounding up Central American migrants in Zacatecas: "We Mexicans are becoming what bothers us so much about the migration authorities in the United States, we should be more humane, but above all more brotherly, with our Latino communities. If we don't, we're falling into the same vicious circle as the Americans" (Chacón 2005). Such statements are likely to further raise the ire of American nationalist critics such as Fonte, who would see such allusions to human rights abuses by U.S. migration authorities as "lies about the United States," while at the same time they are viewed by Mexican nationalists as "too Americanized" because it brings the U.S.-based representation of "Latino" identity into Mexican political discourse.

The same logic driving his criticism of migration officials in both countries leads de la Cruz to promote supranational solutions to the migration "problem," which pushes the envelope of the neoliberal imaginary of "free movement" but which is also likely to sit uneasily with Mexican nationalists. For example, in our interview de la Cruz described his vision of a free trade agreement consistent with its abstract principles:

> I hope that the moment will arrive when . . . the free trade agreement is truly a free trade agreement—an agreement of the free movement of peoples as well. Not only the movement of raw materials, not just the best tomatoes, not just the best meats, . . . but also of people . . . like they do it in Europe. If over there in Europe they have a euro, why can't there be a dollar here? (interview with Manuel de la Cruz, Zacatecas, Zacatecas, June 25, 2004)

This suggestion that the dollar might become common currency throughout North America is expressed almost as an afterthought in de la Cruz's dream of open borders. Ironically, this image of Americanized pesos ("dollarization") is only likely to increase Mexican nationalists' fears that de la Cruz and other would-be migrant politicians have been unduly influenced during their stay in the United States. This hybridized currency idea is equally unlikely to appeal to U.S. nationalists such as Huntington who would likely see the move as diluting the patriotism of ordinary Americans by adding another gray area to the symbolic universe they must deal with in an incipient postnational world without borders.

Americanization Revisited: The Migrant as Governor?

During our ethnographic conversations with the autonomista FCZSC and Frente Cívico leader Guadalupe Gómez, we extensively discussed his future hopes and personal political ambitions in Zacatecas, where his name has been mentioned in various political circles as a potential future migrant candidate for governor. What Gómez called his "American" experience played a key role in this discourse. Despite their political differences on questions of accommodation or resistance by migrants to Mexican party political leadership, Lupe Gómez and Manuel de la Cruz share with each other (and with the Tomato King) a remarkably consistent view of the endemic corruption of Mexican "politics as usual" and a willingness to appropriate selective elements of their "American" experience to rectify this situation. For Gómez, Mexican state and local politicians tend to be out of touch, overpaid, and corrupt. It is migrants like him who are really doing the job of providing the basic services the political class has failed to deliver. In his view, migrants are better informed about everyday problems in Zacatecas than the political class because their transnational connections keep them in regular touch with ordinary Zacatecan citizens. In contrast, the ruling political elites of Zacatecas are indifferent, uncaring, and disconnected:

> Politicians [are] so out of touch because they don't care. They live off of public money. They get paid pretty good, better than politicians here in the United States. . . . The state assemblymen in Zacatecas, they make as much money as an assemblyman here in the state of California—that's the fifth economic power in the world. . . . Why are they making so much money? (interview with Guadalupe Gómez, Santa Ana, California, May 14, 2004)

Unlike traditional politicians, who are out of touch with the needs of ordinary people and do nothing for them, Gómez depicts HTA leaders like himself as fully in touch with the needs of ordinary Mexicans and willing and able to do something about them. He highlights the numerous ways that HTA leaders keep informed about and stay connected to their communities and state of origin:

I listen to the radio a little bit from Mexico and I read the newspapers too, and I travel about eight to ten times a year. We go over there to find out what the needs are in different communities, and we support those clubs that are . . . helping these communities obtain those services. We are not only doing that, we are building roads, we are paving streets, we are enriching the life of the people that are there. . . . So tell me that I am disconnected, when I travel the whole state, different communities where we have clubs and I see all of these needs. How come we are seeing those needs and . . . those politicians, they don't see them? (interview with Guadalupe Gómez, Santa Ana, California, May 14, 2004)

In the course of our interview Gómez expressed the same sort of fear and loathing of Mexican politics as usual that characterized the political discourse of the Tomato King. Gómez's political logic, like Bermudez's, turned their financially successful business careers in the United States and their experiences with U.S. political culture into virtues necessary to transform and democratize Mexican politics. After he detailed numerous examples of the corruption that he characterized as deeply rooted in the Mexican political culture, we asked Gómez whether he thought that migrants were in a better position than people who live in Mexico to get rid of the corruption he described. His answer highlights the virtues of migrant leaders' successful economic fortunes as a necessary buffer against class domination by wealthy Mexican elites, who routinely, in his view, bribe local politicians in their municipalities to do their bidding:

We're in a better position. Well, first of all, because people in Mexico are poor, they don't have the resources. So it's very easy to come to somebody that has never had anything in their lives and to just, you know: "Here, keep your mouth shut, take this. If not, we get rid of you. So you choose." . . . With us, I'd say that we already made some money. We have some resources and we live well here. So we don't have to be on our knees . . . over there. So we can push an agenda that's good for the entire country, instead of for one's self. Look, this is not working in the fields; I've got air conditioning here, I'm fine! . . . The Tomato King, for example, he doesn't need the money. . . . He's got the money. So, who in the town, who of the wealthy people there are going to come to him, "Hey, if you're building a road"—and it's happened in the past—"here, if you go around my property, here's twenty thousand dollars." . . . That's how the roads are built in Mexico. Wealthy people say, you know, "I don't want this road to take apart my land." And instead of building a straight road they go around it because of this guy. That wouldn't happen under the administration of the Tomato King as a governor, for example. . . . It wouldn't happen under my administration. . . . The safety of people would come first. (interview with Guadalupe Gómez, Santa Ana, California, May 14, 2004)

At this point our conversation turned to questions of Gómez's possible political future as a migrant gubernatorial candidate in Zacatecas. He said that he had been "induced" to think about the possibility of running for governor by various potential allies and that, while he was intrigued by the prospect, he nonetheless saw it as risky because he would have to run on a campaign of stamping out corruption, which is a means of livelihood for many members of the political class. If forced to deal with the risks involved in fighting corruption, Gómez again invoked his "American" experience as offering lessons that might be applied in Mexico:

> Gómez: If I were to go over there, I would have to have twenty security people around me, twenty-four hours, 365 days out of the year . . . because there [are] so many political groups, or power groups, very special groups, if you can understand me, that I would probably have to deal with. I would put half of the mayors in jail if I had the proof. If someone came forward and gave the proof I would have to use some system like the ones that we have in the United States. Over here we have a system, we have a system where even, for example . . .
>
> Smith: I notice that the mayor of Compton just went to jail for three years.
>
> Gómez: Yeah. For example, I would have to install a system like the one that the IRS has. If you point a finger at somebody, they will get something out of it: 10 percent. And give them immunity. In other words, some big fish will go to jail and some smaller fish around 'em will have to be off the hook, even though they did wrong. That's what the United States does anyways. (interview with Guadalupe Gómez, Santa Ana, California, May 14, 2004)

Despite his misgivings about the risks of running against endemic corruption, Lupe Gómez recounted the many ways by which his political engagement in various venues of Zacatecan state and community politics had implanted within him the idea that he might someday become a successful migrant candidate for governor of the state. Favorable grassroots popular reactions to the projects sponsored by his Federation first ignited his ambition:

> We did a lot of projects, and I feel that my best reward is that when I go back and I see people, when they grab you and tears come out of their eyes and they thank you and they say, "If it wasn't for you, we wouldn't have this." So, you know, you just continue going . . . you're on your mission. And it's up to the point that they even mention me to run for something. (interview with Guadalupe Gómez, Santa Ana, California, May 14, 2004)

This revelation prompted the following exchange in which Gómez specified the role that favorable newspaper and television coverage of his political trips to Zacatecas have played in his thinking:

SMITH: What have you been mentioned for and what would you consider?

GÓMEZ: Somebody started a rumor that I might run for governor. And of course that reached the press and that became a national story. I have all of the newspaper clips. . . . *La Jornada* in Mexico is a national paper. What did they say? "The campaign for governor of Zacatecas already crossed the borders." It says heading this list is my name, and so I'm pretty sure that people in Mexico were concerned. When we submitted the migrant law we had all of the national media there: Televisa, Azteca, and all of the major newspapers. *Reforma.* We were at the state assembly and they told me, "We know you are the main promoter of this," and of course I wasn't, it was the Frente Cívico, I was just accompanying the president. But, of course, you know, being the president of the Federation, it carries a lot of weight [*laughs*] . . . and then and so okay: "You are the main promoter of this law. If it passes are you going to run for governor?" [*laughs*] And I said, "Well, thank you for asking." And I told them: "First things first. Before you run, you walk. . . . Before you walk, you crawl. Let's pass the law and we'll see."

BAKKER: You left the door open, didn't you?

GÓMEZ: I was not surprised that they asked, maybe because over here [in Los Angeles] newspapers called me. And after that I spent time over there giving interviews to different radio stations and newspapers. The next day I went to my home in Jalpa, Zacatecas, in a little community called Santa Juana. I was invited to the radio and, same thing, them asking me, "Are you running for governor?" . . . I said, you know, first of all . . . I take it as a compliment. I haven't said anything to that effect and I know that people have asked me that and I know that these rumors reach the press, but . . . I guess that's probably due to the importance that the Federation of Zacatecas Clubs of Southern California has, has accomplished or has reached. I have to believe that's the case and just like any band the singer gets all the attention. (interview with Guadalupe Gómez, Santa Ana, California, May 14, 2004)

Later in our interview Gómez told us that even before all of this favorable media coverage he had received e-mails from political activists in academia from several Mexican states offering him their political support. He went on to describe phone calls from oppositional activists in municipal politics throughout Zacatecas urging him to consider running for governor and telling him he could count on their support. Invoking the anticorruption theme at the heart of the political subject position Gómez has assumed, he offered the following illustrative anecdote:

One guy even told me, he said, "Look, my mayor is doing something wrong here. He's forcing me to give him a receipt for thirty thousand pesos a month." This was a department head of . . . the water department in one of the municipalities. . . . People were already letting me know that there was

something wrong. But if I became governor, my first priority is [to] attack
this cancer that we have, this corruption. (interview with Guadalupe Gómez,
Santa Ana, California, May 14, 2004)

In that same interview Gómez outlined a broad long-term strategy for political incorporation of migrants into the Mexican electoral system.

> We can start with the vote for president and then we can go to Congress and
> do other things. Once we do that, I am sure that the president will help us.
> Anybody who wants to be president is going to come in and say, "Let's do
> this and let's push this too." The parties have to cater to us because they know
> that we eventually we will end up voting. It's going to take time. It'll proba-
> bly take a decade, or fifteen, twenty years. But . . . I think we will be able to
> vote not only for president of Mexico [but] for Congress and Senate and for
> governors of Zacatecas. I think we can do that. Why not? We are becoming a
> force. The twenty million Mexicans that are here in the United States are
> pitching in more to the economy than one hundred million people that are
> over there. They have asked me if that's why we want to be able to vote. I've
> said, "No. That is not the reason. The reason is because we are Mexicans."
> (interview with Guadalupe Gómez, past president, Zacatecan Federation,
> Santa Ana, California, May 24, 2004)

From Electoral Reforms to Political Power

In this chapter we have seen the important role played by nationalist considerations in the compromise legislation limiting the effect of voting from
abroad in the Mexican presidential elections of 2006. Despite years of arduous political mobilization and grassroots lobbying by an extensive network
of migrant activists, the vote-from-abroad legislation finally approved by
the Mexican federal Congress in 2005 contained significant political *candados* and exacting requirements. These restrictions on the absentee-voting
process resulted in a dismally low number of migrant voters taking part in
the election: of the estimated 8.5–10 million Mexican migrants living in the
United States and potentially eligible to vote (Marcelli and Cornelius 2005;
Pew Hispanic Center 2006), only 32,621 actually did so (Instituto Federal
Electoral 2006b).

Migrant activists from Los Angeles working politically in Zacatecas
have had greater success in opening up the subnational political system in
their state and its municipalities to migrant candidacies for public office.
In the 2004 election cycle, because of the political dynamics of constitutional reform, Zacatecas elected two migrant mayors as well as two migrant deputies to the state legislature. FCZSC members active in the
Frente Cívico and Zacatecanos PRImero participated in an important

way in the passage of the Ley Migrante reform that made this political opening possible.

These state-level reforms may well have more far-reaching effects in the future if the role of migrants in Zacatecan political life becomes normalized and more fully legitimated. There is some indication that this is already happening. Lupe Gómez, one of the leading FCZSC activists, is being seriously considered as a future candidate for governor of Zacatecas. There are ongoing discussions about creating a migrant political party that could advance such candidacies. In addition, Andrés Bermúdez, the first migrant mayor of a major Mexican city, has parlayed his populist credentials as a reformist mayor to catapult himself into the federal legislature, winning a federal deputy seat under the PAN banner in the 2006 elections.

Although the advance of migrant incorporation into the Zacatecan, and now federal, political arenas is obviously important, our analysis of the emerging spaces of formal transnational citizenship would be incomplete if we did not simultaneously address the continuing exclusions accompanying recent developments. Our story of the implosion of Zacatecan politics in the HTAs of Los Angeles helps to bring these exclusions to light, highlighting this key tension in the dialectic of transnational citizenship as it is now emerging across the U.S.-Mexico divide. The politicization of the Los Angeles HTA leadership and their engagement with partisan politics "back home" has undoubtedly contributed to a democratization of Zacatecan politics, furthering the gradual dismantling of a political system fundamentally characterized by corporatism, corruption, and patron-client relations. However, this democratic opening has done little to open up spaces for the meaningful participation of more marginalized migrant groups, such as women or the poor.

The political strategy adopted by those migrant activists who have managed to gain a foothold in the Zacatecan political arena heavily depends on combining populist anticorruption rhetoric with the promise of honest and efficient administration. The capacity of these migrant leaders to deliver on their promises of democratic reform if and when they actually take office is tied to their hybrid "Americanized" identity—their self-presentation as economically successful, politically democratic, and capable of generating productive investment in Zacatecas and its municipalities. On the one hand, this representational strategy may prove effective in generating electoral success from a populace longing for democratic reforms and economic development that might make migration more of a choice than a necessity. However, once political candidates win elections and must govern they enter a preexisting political space with prevailing cultural norms and an extant political class. Political culture, whether one of corruption or of anything else, is not quickly or easily changed, even with the election of insurgent politicians promising to transform it. To govern, migrant insurgent candidates who win elections must deal directly with nonmigrant political elites who are unlikely to welcome either continuing charges of systemic corruption or the importation of "American" practices to end it.

Equally important, the political-economic location of Zacatecas as a poor, rural state in the neoliberal context of NAFTA poses significant structural constraints on the transformative promise of bringing productive investment to the state. Although the energy and determination of the migrant HTA leaders cannot be underestimated, the rising expectations generated by their increased involvement in Zacatecan political life could easily lead to disillusionment if their political agendas do not result in a quick reversal of the state's long-standing economic marginality and stagnation. If this prognosis is correct, can there be any doubt that the exporting of migrants is likely to continue as the state's leading growth industry?

We will return to this larger question in the concluding chapter of *Citizenship across Borders*. Before doing so, however, we must still address a crucial dimension of transnational citizenship—a dimension we have chosen to call its "second face." In chapter 7 we will explore this second face of transnational citizenship by considering the engagement of migrant activists from the Mexican states of Guanajuato and Zacatecas in a wide range of political spaces on the U.S. side of the North American divide.

PART 4

The Two Faces of
Transnational Citizenship

7 The Second Face of Transnational Citizenship

Migrant Activists Recross the Border

In previous chapters we have examined the Mexican face of transnational citizenship by detailing the ethnographic findings of a series of separate, yet interrelated, extended case studies that have slowly begun to reveal the complex emergence of Mexican migrants as cross-border political subjects and transnational citizens. In this chapter we turn to the second face of transnational citizenship—migrant politics in the "receiving" context. It is useful to begin this shift to political spaces on the U.S. side of the border by recalling Arjun Appadurai's conception of "post-nationalism" as a trope intended to capture the waning power of "receiving" states such as the United States to incorporate transnational migrants into loyalty to their host society. Appadurai sees migrant communities in the United States as "*doubly loyal* to their nations of origin and thus *ambivalent about their loyalties to America*" (1996, 172, emphasis added). How accurate is this representation of reality in the case of Mexican migrants? In our research on Mexican migrant political transnationalism, we have found a far more complex dialectic of identity politics at play in the hearts and minds of our ethnographic subjects. When the migrants we have interviewed express ambivalence, it is not an ambivalence about their loyalty to the United States but a kind of *double ambivalence* about their experiences on both sides of the U.S.-Mexican border. Far from being "doubly loyal to their nation of origin," the politically engaged migrants in our studies express a strongly felt allegiance to both Mexico and the United States. Yet, at times the migrants are doubly ambivalent about *each* nation, and about the modes of political participation on both sides of the border.

The very situatedness of our transnational subjects tends to provoke mixed feelings, depending on the circumstances at hand—for instance, when the migrants become actively involved in state and local political campaigns in the United States and express satisfaction with the economic opportunities afforded by their adopted country, while decrying the continuing cultural and political significance of racial and ethnic discrimination in the United States. Alternatively, when participating in diaspora politics in Mexico, our interview subjects have become embedded in economic and community development "partnerships" with Mexican state and local government officials, while continuing to decry an overall political culture they see as dominated by a corrupt political class. "Loyalty," in short, is never unalloyed and always contingent. It is expressed or withheld by acting subjects, depending on historically specific circumstances.

A key aspect of each of our extended case studies has been a phenomenological quest to discern the different ways Mexican migrants understand, experience, and try to act on their feelings and beliefs about "dual loyalty," being "here and there," and becoming, or not becoming, "transnational citizens." Consider, for example, our study of Andrés Bermúdez, which involved extended ethnographic interviews with the Tomato King over a three-year period. These open-ended conversations revealed considerable ambivalence concerning his hopes, fears, and dreams, far more so than the public persona we observed on the campaign trail. Between the two elections, when Bermúdez had returned to Winters, California, to continue running his businesses, and before the electoral rules had been changed, he discussed at length what might happen if he were to give up his political persona and focus on getting migrants to stop sending remittances back to Mexico and channel their resources instead into improving Mexican American neighborhoods and educational opportunities in California.

In all of our interviews, Bermúdez regularly distinguished between "Andrés Bermúdez's" personal views and the constructed mythological narrative of "the Tomato King." After serving a year in office in Jerez, Bermúdez had begun to express this contradictory sense of selfhood publicly. To symbolize his call for political openness and transparency in Jerez, in delivering the public address on the anniversary of his inauguration, Bermúdez appeared in a white dress suit instead of his usual black cowboy hat and ranchero outfit. The thrust of his message was that, after his term was up, he might well return to California and work toward helping his native community without having to deal directly with local party politics and a political culture he has consistently represented as corrupt and lacking in transparency (Rodríguez 2005).

This has been a recurrent theme in all of our conversations with Bermúdez, who has often made a clear distinction between the people of Jerez and the ruling political class. In hinting at a possible return to the United States, he demonstrates his wavering between making a clean break with Mexico and continuing to engage in a transnational opportunity structure from his base in northern California. In the "clean break" scenario, he has spoken about dedicating his energies to the educational, economic, and political advancement of Mexicans and Mexican Americans in the United States (interviews with Andrés Bermúdez, Davis, California, March 15, 2002, and November 1, 2002). In those moments when his political and economic imagination is more thoroughly transnational, Bermúdez has envisioned how actions he might take in the United States, such as organizing Zacatecas-themed marketing outlets in U.S. cities where migrants are concentrated, could be directed toward the benefit of the peoples and communities of Zacatecas (interview with Andrés Bermúdez, Jerez, Zacatecas, August 15, 2005).

In the end, the Tomato King chose neither of these two "exit" paths, opting instead to jump scales within the Mexican political arena. Less than two years into his term, Bermúdez resigned the mayoral post in Jerez to run for federal deputy in the July 2006 elections. That campaign proved successful and was the PAN's only victory within Zacatecas's five federal electoral districts. Although he did not make good on his threats to abandon Mexican party politics altogether, Bermúdez's fluidly binational persona offered him important symbolic capital in his bid for a seat in the legislature. By credibly representing the threat that migrants might enact a full-scale exit from the Mexican political scene in response to the continuing control exerted by the traditional political class, Bermúdez's gestures toward a return to the United States both mobilized support from his grassroots base and weakened the veracity of the political attacks coming from his opponents.

Not unlike Bermúdez, the protagonist of our earlier story of translocal politics, Ángel Calderón, also has enunciated a "Plan B" if things don't work out to his satisfaction in Guanajuato. The theme of Calderón's imagined political agenda in Napa and throughout California is ethnic empowerment of Mexican migrants, particularly farmworkers, in the state that depends so much on their labor. While remaining active in community development politics in El Timbinal despite his break with the Panista regime in Guanajuato, Calderón has begun to act increasingly on the basis of this hoped-for political agenda in California in modes of political engagement that underline the simultaneity of transnational life.

How has this second face of transnational citizenship emerged? Recall that Calderón and his fellow migrants from El Timbinal were initially involved in self-organized community improvement projects in their native village such as rebuilding the town plaza and improving the local school facilities. In the mid-1990s they were persuaded to join a "public-private" partnership with Panista state officials from Guanajuato in which the migrants financed the building of a textile factory (maquiladora) in their hometown. Over time, these wider connections, initially forged during the gubernatorial administration of Vicente Fox in Guanajuato, gave the migrants access to local political circles in Napa. For example, using his transnational connections, Calderón coordinated several cultural events including an exhibition of Guanajuato art treasures at the Napa Valley Museum in 2000. These public events were accompanied by performances by musicians and appearances by political elites from Guanajuato, including that state's newly elected governor, Romero Hicks. Local politicians and community leaders from Napa were invited to participate in these events, which received extensive favorable local press coverage. The visits and events simultaneously promoted pride in Guanajuato and gave Calderón and his migrant network a legitimacy in Napa that they had previously lacked. Members of the network then began to take full advantage of their newly acquired access and legitimacy (see Nichols 2000).

In the following ethnographic exchange Ángel Calderón describes his migrant network's interactions with leaders of political and civic affairs in Napa even before his break with Hicks and Oliva.

> SMITH: How do you envision the fact that the Hispanic population has grown 106 percent from 1990 to 2000 here in Napa? These are numbers, but they may become votes if people get naturalized or become citizens. Are you aware of this situation?
>
> CALDERÓN: Yes, we have been participating in the political life of Napa in the last two years. I know several Mexican Mexican or Mexican American guys in top positions—for example, in Napa College, in the Chamber of Commerce, in newspapers, in the courts. I know some people, Guillén and Cerrosi, Manuel Trejo, Olguín, Mary Salcedo, John García. They are occupying city [council] seats, running for mayor, and working for the County of Napa. We are organizing something these days to push José Guillén. He is a good person. He was working at the Superior Court.
>
> Some years ago there was no one with a Hispanic last name running for public positions. Today, or in the last elections, these Hispanic politicians were in every Mexican *reunión*. They even showed up at private parties. They invited me to their political meetings and asked for my support. And they invite us to both Republican and Democratic meetings. Last year we had a big *reunión* in Santa Rosa and all of the candidates were there, shaking hands and making themselves noticeable. This year, after the elections, we were joking that none of them came to our meeting. (interview with Ángel Calderón, Napa, California, May 9, 2001)

Ángel Calderón and his fellow migrants have begun to use their political access and legitimacy on the U.S. side of the border by becoming engaged in issue-oriented campaigns to advance the economic and social interests of Mexican migrants at the regional level in California. As the relationship between the migrant investors and the Hicks-Oliva administration soured in late 2001 and their maquila was forced to close, the migrants shifted more of their attention from state policy and politics in Guanajuato to the new political opportunity structure that had opened up for them in Napa. For example, in a recent round of local elections in Napa, Calderón worked hard both individually and through his migrant network as part of a broad-based campaign to successfully pass a local ballot initiative providing for the rezoning of donated farmland in Napa County, on which new county-financed farmworker housing is to be built. The ballot initiative passed with 70 percent support from Napa County voters, enabling Napa County to build the badly needed migrant-farmworker housing.

Ángel Calderón's active citizen participation in Napa, California, now parallels his extraterritorial citizenship in El Timbinal and Guanajuato. He and his network are now well positioned to play an ongoing role in ethnic and issue-oriented politics in Napa and throughout California while continuing to promote community development projects in El Timbinal independently of the Panista state's neoliberal policy initiatives. The guanajuatense migrants are far more active citizens of local and regional political life in the United States as well as in Mexico than nationalists such as Samuel Huntington could imagine. Their activist modes of cross-border political engagement bear no resemblance to either the Guanajuato regional state's quiescent model of "double gratitude" discussed in chapter 3 or to the related postnationalist musings of Appadurai about transnational migrants' putative "double loyalty" to their countries of origin.

Transnational Citizenship in the Receiving Context

This theoretical point is vividly illustrated in the portions of our research devoted to understanding the political practices of the leaders of the Zacatecan Federation of Hometown Associations of Southern California on both sides of the U.S.-Mexican border. The FCZSC, as we have seen, has clearly been a key player in many aspects of Zacatecan political life. In the remainder of this chapter we will describe and analyze the second face of their transnational citizenship. The central questions driving this facet of our inquiry are: What have been the modes of political engagement of the leaders of the FCZSC in U.S. politics? How have their lived experiences in U.S. politics affected these political subjects' personal and political identities? Shedding light on the other face of transnational citizenship requires envisioning the multilayered connections linking sites and actors at different spatial scales, thereby also linking individual and group-based local, regional, and national political agendas within and across borders. Our net has had to be cast ever wider sociospatially to comprehend the scope of the

FCZSC and the political practices and multilayered identities of its key leaders.

We have found that in some instances the effective engagement of the leaders of the FCZSC in state and local politics in Zacatecas has had spillover effects, contributing to their active political engagement in many aspects of U.S. political life. These have included urban electoral politics in Los Angeles and other cities in southern California; ethnic and issue-oriented state politics in California; and even national congressional and presidential politics in the United States. In other instances (e.g., an HTA leader who is a trade union activist in Los Angeles and one of the few female FCZSC leaders, whose story we tell below) participation in grassroots politics in Los Angeles *preceded* their involvement in hometown and home-state politics in Mexico. In still other instances such as that of Manuel de la Cruz, as we shall see, Mexican and U.S. political engagement have been pursued simultaneously.

Not surprisingly, therefore, when our questions concerning their personal sense of national and/or transnational identity and belonging were put to leaders of the FCZSC, the answers elicited have been all over the map, including such responses as: "I am a Mexican."—"I am truly binational." "In both countries I experience the presence of absence."—"I am a feminist activist from East L.A. who loves my home village and will do all that I can to ensure its survival." As these politically engaged Zacatecan migrants begin to tell us their life stories, the undifferentiated view of "the" Mexican migrant proffered by Samuel Huntington disappears altogether, replaced by a wide range of voices in which other modes of identity formation than either "Mexican" or "American" begin to be heard. Many of those we have interviewed love their region and naturalistic representations of it far more than they express love either for their country of origin or destination. Others identify with the extended family that is part of their childhood memories, even as migration and transnational living have transformed the very structure of extended family life. Others forge a political identity by deploring the corruption they attribute to all of Mexico's major political parties, while investing their energies in efforts to change the Mexican political system. Still others insist they are both Mexican and American and see no need to choose between either before engaging in political life on either side of the border.

Even the FCZSC leader Felipe Cabral, who has most consistently described himself to us as having a "Mexican" identity, has expressed clearly positive feelings toward the United States, describing the United States in his presidential letter to FCZSC members in 2005 as "this generous country where we have found welfare and development for our families." In this same letter Cabral offers the Federation's thanks to its institutional partners—the

Rockefeller Foundation; the Mexican federal, state, and municipal governments; as well as First Data Corporation, the parent company of Western Union, one of the world's largest remittance service providers. Because of this binational collaboration, he concludes that "we—*los* zacatecanos," have become "world pioneers" in transnational community development "with the signing of the first 4×1 agreement in Washington, D.C. on October 12th of this year" (Felipe Cabral, FCZSC presidential letter, November 12, 2005).

Questions of identity politics among leaders of the FCZSC, as this example illustrates, are quite complex and varied. We chose to start our search for more patterned regularities by asking the migrants to talk about their political practices rather than immediately homing in on the identities these may or may not express. Issues of identity nonetheless emerged organically in the course of our conversations. We found that leaders of the FCZSC and of the Frente Cívico Zacatecano, one of two political offshoots of the Zacatecan HTAs in Los Angeles, have been active at all levels of U.S. society and politics. The voices drawn from our ethnographies provide a sense of these different modes of political engagement in U.S. politics often missing from the study of Mexican migrant associations, whose leaders are most often studied in terms of their involvement in homeland, home-state, and hometown politics in Mexico. In the chorus of voices that follow, transnational politics begins to reveal its Janus face.

Consider the following case of simultaneous, multipositional political subjectivity. On June 25, 2004, we interviewed the migrant leader Manuel de la Cruz, who has been a past president of the FCZSC, and who, as we have seen in the previous chapter, was elected the first migrant representative of the PRD to the Zacatecan Congress. This interview took place in the state capitol of Zacatecas a week before he was elected to the state legislature. Then still uncertain about his future, de la Cruz reflected on his earlier experience in 2002 of being stripped of a seat in the federal Chamber of Deputies for retaining his U.S. citizenship. Entertaining the possibility that he might encounter a similar roadblock to assuming office in Zacatecas, he enunciated his own U.S.-centered Plan B:

DE LA CRUZ: If, in the worst of all cases, Manuel de la Cruz—pay attention here—weren't to make it to the Congress—you haven't asked me that, but maybe you have it written down there to ask me, "What's going to happen with Manuel de la Cruz if he doesn't make it?" [*laughs*]. . . . If that were to happen . . . I have a Plan B—agreed upon with the organization . . . I am a member of the OME, of the IME, of a number of organizations across the whole U.S. and of a number of Chambers of Commerce, of businesspeople, and they've said to me, "Come on back already, Manuel, it's not worth continuing to fight. They don't want us migrants." I want to continue to struggle on until the last step.

BAKKER: Has the OME given up the battle for Mexico already and dedicated itself to issues facing Mexican immigrants in the U.S., or what?

DE LA CRUZ: Organización de Mexicanos en el Extranjero, no. Many of them are currently members of the PRI. But they're still working, and I am the treasurer of the OME . . . and they're in standby, just waiting to see what happens. Because our Plan B, of us migrants in the U.S., if we don't get this, if they don't provide us this opening in Mexico. . . . I would be going back to the United States where we already have a Chamber of Commerce and Zacatecan businesspeople to provide the resources and for us to build alliances with the young people. Taking them to the best universities in the U.S. and looking for political positions for them. So that Mexicans can take their position in the United States, because we will have seen that Mexico doesn't believe in its migrants, and we will focus ourselves 100 percent on the United States. That's the other step. (interview with Manuel de la Cruz, Zacatecas, Zacatecas, June 25, 2004)

Other parts of our interview with Manuel de la Cruz provide an extensive take on migrant involvement in U.S. presidential politics and also reveal some of the multilayered feelings of political identification experienced by an actor simultaneously engaged in political life in two countries:

DE LA CRUZ: But I have always been very well accepted in the entire [U.S.] government. I was with Bill Clinton a couple of times when he came to Los Angeles. We supported Al Gore. We didn't support Bush! . . . Everyone in my family is an American citizen. My wife voted for the first time in the election between Al Gore and Bush. She cried and cried when Bush won. Because it was the first time that she voted and she would say, "How is it possible that he beat us?" . . . And in these days we're realizing that all of that money that Bill Clinton had put aside in reserves, Bush spends it in a single damn month. And he puts us back in the hole. So, well, my interests are over there [in the U.S.] and the only thing that is here is my wish that Mexico progress.

BAKKER: We have entered into one of the areas that most interests us, which is transnational citizenship. You actively exercise citizenship in both countries, right?

DE LA CRUZ: Of course. Sure. My children are there, my houses are there, everything is there, and here is where my heart is at [*laughs*]. What can you do? What can I do? (interview with Manuel de la Cruz, June 25, 2004, Zacatecas, Zacatecas)

The next voice we hear is that of Francisco Javier González, president of the Frente Cívico Zacatecano, an explicitly binational political organization of Zacatecan migrants in southern California. Francisco speaks as the official spokesperson for his organization rather than as an individual U.S. citizen. This contrasts to some degree with the FCZSC, because the latter is an officially chartered nonprofit organization under U.S. law and is thus legally precluded from taking partisan positions, as a collective organization, in U.S. politics. Some FCZSC leaders have interpreted this limitation rather strictly, insisting that in talking about their activities in U.S. politics, they are speaking as individual citizen activists, rather than as official representatives of the Federation. This sense of constraint by U.S. law is one reason some leaders of the Federation told us they sought to create the FCZ as an explicitly political organization in the first place.

The FCZ, whose activities in Zacatecan politics we discussed in chapter 6, also plays an active role in many aspects of U.S. politics. Francisco González succinctly described this other face of political engagement. He noted that the Frente is regularly engaged in electoral politics in the United States, describing at length their support for the victorious Democrats Jesse Loaera (the mayor of Norwalk), Representatives Loretta Sanchez and Grace Napolitano, state Assemblymember Lou Correa, and Republican Lee Vaca for county sheriff. González told us that the FCZ also had supported Lieutenant Governor Cruz Bustamante, a Democrat who ran unsuccessfully against Arnold Schwarzenegger in the 2004 recall election. He then turned to the Frente's involvement in U.S. presidential politics:

> I'm going to tell you about what happened with Al Gore. We went to receive him at the airport; we had a big banner: Frente Cívico Zacatecano. . . . We were right in front with our Frente Cívico Zacatecano [banner]. When he got off of the airplane he started shaking hands and he goes back and forth, back and forth. . . . And so he stopped and he said, "I know about you guys already. I know you guys are Frente Cívico Zacatecano." And he started speaking Spanish. He said, "*Me da mucho gusto muchachos y gracias por apoyarme*" [I am very pleased and grateful for your support]. He shakes my hand and he gave me a hug. Al Gore. I carry that experience with me. (interview with Francisco Javier González, Norwalk, California, November 13, 2003)

Guadalupe Gómez is another key migrant leader and past president of the FCZSC who has been very active politically on both sides of the border. Gómez described himself to us as a "truly binational" person. Each year it is customary for the Federation president to write an open letter to club members at the beginning of a booklet distributed at the organization's annual convention celebrating the Day of the Zacatecano in Los Angeles. Gómez wrote his 2002 open letter in English and underlined his political efforts in the United States:

> I was also invited by the White House to be in an event with our President of the United States, George W. Bush in Washington D.C. on October 11th,

2002. In this trip I also visited the U.S. Congress. I met with our beloved Congresswoman, Grace Napolitano and Nancy Pelosi, the highest ranking Democrat in the House of Representatives. . . . We discussed issues such as legalization, health and education, which are very important to our people. But most importantly, we opened up a line of communication that will enable us to work together to solve the problems we are facing in our society.

In the same letter Gómez tied his political activities in California to his concern for community development in Mexico, noting that "thanks to Assemblyman Marco Antonio Firebaugh, from the 5th District, the Program 3×1 was presented in our California State Legislature and the Senate with the objective of getting the California Government to participate in the development of the Mexican communities with the most migration to the north." The photographs included in the Federation's 2002 publication included an image of members wearing Federation T-shirts while participating in a protest demonstration calling attention to the large number of Mexican border crossers who have died in the Arizona desert while trying to enter the United States. Another photo showed Federation members carrying a large FCZSC banner while participating in a street march in Central Los Angeles demanding social justice for immigrants. In still another photograph, Guadalupe Gómez is standing in front of the U.S. flag, surrounded by two U.S. Marines, while participating in a ceremonial event at the White House.

In his letter to paisanos the following year, dated November 15, 2003, Gómez noted that when he became president of the FCZSC, "we divided our focus on both sides of the border" and "began participating in civic activities" in the United States. Among the activities Gómez emphasized were the Federation's establishment of a scholarship fund for Mexican American youth; participation in an initiative to obtain California driver's licenses for undocumented Mexican migrants; involvement in a get-out-the-vote drive; various efforts to expand citizenship among migrants; and political lobbying of U.S. federal government agencies to establish a legalization program for undocumented migrants.

In an interview with Gómez conducted shortly after he ended his term as president, we asked him to reflect on his personal sense of identity as a political leader who had achieved visibility and success on both sides of the U.S.-Mexican border. Here is how he described his gradual transformation into a transnational citizen:

GÓMEZ: When I first came here, I used to ask myself when I used to go back, I didn't know where I was from! I said, "What am I doing?" I used to ask myself, "What am I doing here? What am I doing here in the United States; this is not where I'm from . . . Why? Why am I here?" . . . And when I went back, I also felt strange over there. "What am I doing here?" you know, "Where am I from?" You struggle to find your identity. But as you grow older, you see things and you realize that "Hey, wait a minute. I know where I am from, but I know that I am here . . . that I set roots here and I feel comfortable here." Now I'm thinking, "I am transnational! I am a binational person." . . . And truly a binational one, because I am one of the luckiest persons in the world that can live two cultures. I do!

SMITH: Do you think that that takes time, just like it did in your case?

GÓMEZ: Last year, when I went to Congress and I had a meeting with Nancy Pelosi . . . a lot of things went through my mind. I couldn't believe I had a Congresswoman, the top Democratic leader in the House. And we were talking about issues! [*laughs*]. I was thinking about when I was milking cows in Zacatecas. I was thinking about those moments . . . and I was showing my people's concerns, "We're concerned about education. We're concerned about health care. We're concerned about the clinics that are closing in Los Angeles." I was the voice of my people there in Congress! (interview with Guadalupe Gómez, Santa Ana, California, May 14, 2004)

Martha Jiménez is the next FCZSC leader we will meet. Jiménez is simultaneously the public relations officer of the FCZSC, the president of her hometown club in the Zacatecan village of Las Animas, and a program coordinator for the Los Angeles office of the Mexican American Legal Defense and Education Fund (MALDEF), a major Latino interest group in the United States. Jiménez has been a longtime community activist in Los Angeles. She played a key role in the 2005 mayoral campaign of Antonio Villaraigosa, the first Mexican American to be elected mayor of Los Angeles. She has extensive experience in the nonprofit sector, community organizing, and voter registration activities among Mexican Americans. Her résumé emphasizes her English and Spanish language proficiency and her seven years of grassroots experience in the FCZSC. It also mentions her "proven ability to fundraise at the local and transnational level."

At the very outset of our interview with her on March 25, 2005, Martha Jiménez introduced a host of issues that required Mexican migrants to become engaged in U.S. politics. She began by calling for a binational policy initiative, involving U.S. as well as Mexican government officials, to stem the tide of unnecessary deaths of Mexican migrants in the Arizona desert. She continued by calling on HTAs and their federations to form coalitions with U.S.-based Latino, pan-ethnic, and immigrants' rights organizations to promote issues of common interest such as the expansion of U.S. citizenship among migrants and improved access by minorities to higher education:

JIMÉNEZ: The Mexican hometown associations need to learn how to work on broad coalitions. They need to work with other Latino or immigrant organizations and not speak just to [place of origin] because that doesn't take us very far. So the Federación Zacatecana has started doing that by having some of their board members take an active role in different organizations.

SMITH: That are more Latino and less . . .

JIMÉNEZ: Yes, yes, such as the Coalition for Humane Immigrant Rights [CHIRLA]. We are working with CHIRLA, and every time that there is a press conference to address the immigration issues, the driver's licenses, access to higher education, we have a say. But we are not only people that show up to press conferences, we work the agenda, we talk about what is the best approach.

SMITH: You put ideas out there?

JIMÉNEZ: Yes. We are not tokens for anyone. We have to negotiate and be strong advocates for the community. The other organization is the National Association of Latino Elected and Appointed Officials (NALEAO). It has been my duty since seven years ago to insure that we provide resources not only to our community but to other people from other nationalities, regardless of race, color, or national origin. So through the NALEAO Citizenship Forum/Coalition workshops we have been able to work very closely with all the elected officials at the national level by cosponsoring the workshops. People come on a determined date and they get to do their whole process of filling out their N-400 Naturalization Form. And there have been times where we have had up to five hundred people come in. And the members from our federación have also become empowered [as have] other members of other federations. (interview with Martha Jiménez, Los Angeles, March 25, 2005)

Jiménez has made it her mission to take concerted steps to tap into some of the political energy and social capital she has found in Mexican hometown associations and channel it into the formation of more broadly based political coalitions in U.S. cities promoting issues such as the acquisition of U.S. citizenship, minority group empowerment, and the advancement of immigrants' and human rights. Even though our conversation focused largely on more inclusive pan-Latino coalitions, it is clear from her comments concerning the Federation's activities in promoting immigrants' rights that the coalitions she has in mind extend more broadly to encompass non-Latino immigrants as well. In fact, the Federation has already coalesced with new Asian and South and Central American immigrants in Los Angeles, as well as trade unions, in an organization called the International Coalition to promote legalization and civil rights for all of America's new minority groups (interview with Guadalupe Rodríguez, Los Angeles, March 25, 2005).

Later in our conversation, Jiménez provided a riveting example of the Federation joining the Los Angeles Coalition for Humane Immigrant Rights in a protest demonstration against President Bush's proposed guest-worker program, which is viewed by coalition members as little more than the old bracero program in a new guise:

> You want to know how we organized when President Bush said that he was going to create this Bracero program. It was the zacatecanos that said, "No, we have to tell him that we can't do that." It was the zacatecanos and CHIRLA; we organized a press conference in the federal building in downtown L.A. And I work also with a coalition of braceros–I happen to know probably a thousand braceros in Los Angeles. So we said: "Okay, President Bush is saying today that he wants to reform immigration and that the way to do it is through a bracero program. No! We have to prove to him that he is wrong." So we organized a press conference, we brought media from all over, the bilingual media, we sent press releases all over and my father was chosen as a spokesperson. And my father said, "President Bush, usted no sabe lo que está haciendo. Yo fui un bracero; mis colegas han sido braceros [President Bush, you don't know what you are doing. I was a bracero; my friends were braceros]. What you have to do is create a program that brings the people out of the shadows. They need to be regularized; they have been here for years. We cannot accept your bracero program version for the new century." It got sent all the way to Mexico because we kept getting phone calls when they televised it. (interview with Martha Jiménez, Los Angeles, March 25, 2005)

In other parts of our conversation, Jiménez spoke extensively about her local lobbying activities on behalf of the residents of her East Los Angeles neighborhood of City Terrace, describing her frequent visits to the office of L.A. Supervisor Gloria Molina to discuss neighborhood problems and address neighborhood needs. She claimed that other zacatecanos who are Federation members "do the same thing," particularly showing political clout in local electoral politics in Los Angeles. These revelations about Jiménez's passionate engagement in Latino politics in Los Angeles, prior to her involvement in HTA politics, prompted the following interview exchanges, in which we asked her to describe the personal trajectory of her political activism and the roots of her transnational political identity:

> SMITH: One of the things that we have seen is a lot of people who have had their first and only experience of politics and leadership at the grassroots level in Mexico and then they . . . become active here, but your story seems different. You learned your politics in Los Angeles.
>
> JIMÉNEZ: The American way [*laughs*].
>
> SMITH: And then you found the Federation. So this process of binational influence works both ways.
>
> JIMÉNEZ: I have been an activist ever since I was a child. It's the example that was set for me back in México; my grandparents were leaders in their

communities. I saw them building schools, churches, paving the streets, making the first water *pozo* [well]. I saw the first teachers. So, I come from a strong background in that respect. And here in the States, well, I grew up in this neighborhood in City Terrace and I was learning to speak English as a child when I came from México–I was eleven years old. So at the church I used to see a lot of civic movement taking place, and I would go and sit in on the meetings with the mayor of Los Angeles or people that come and inform. And ever since I was little I used to say, "I want to be the voice of City Terrace," and so it just happens that we are working on empowering, not only La Federación, but also this community.

Sᴍɪᴛʜ: We want to know how your activities have affected your sense of who you are. Because you're active here, you're active there. You form coalitions here, there, and then across the border. . . . How does that affect how you feel about your political identity?

Jɪᴍᴇ́ɴᴇᴢ: Having a dual citizenship makes you have a way of looking at the world differently. And I just don't see myself detached from México, because México is inside my heart; I cannot detach myself. (interview with Martha Jiménez, Los Angeles, March 25, 2005)

In pursuit of her multistranded yet deeply transnational vision of dual citizenship Martha Jiménez recently accepted an administrative leadership position with the Mexican American Legal Defense and Education Fund to coordinate efforts to channel the social capital of the leaders of migrant HTAs in greater Los Angeles from eight Mexican states (Jalisco, Michoacán, Nayarit, Sinaloa, Colima, Guanajuato, Yucatan, as well as Zacatecas) systematically into the building of broad coalitions to advance the interests of Mexican American communities. MALDEF's national project, which Jiménez heads in southern California, is supported by several philanthropic foundations including the Rockefeller Foundation, the California Community Foundation, the Hass Fund, and Western Union/First Data Fund. It constitutes a far-reaching effort by this alliance to broaden the local and regional focus of the HTAs and to reconstitute HTA leaders' political vision, creating new political subjects capable of acting–and willing to act–politically, both "here" and "there." To achieve this goal MALDEF recently launched the Immigrant Leadership Program for Responsible Educational Development. This program seeks to enhance the leadership, "capacity building," advocacy, legal, technical, financial, and public policy skills of 180 selected HTA leaders in southern California. These leaders will participate in a fourteen-week series of workshops and lectures "presented by top presenters ranging from elected officials, attorneys, professors, community organizers, U.S./Mexican government representatives, hometown association leaders, philanthropy representatives, etc." (Mexican American Legal Defense and Education Fund 2005)

As envisioned by MALDEF and the donor community, "participants will learn about their rights" in the United States, particularly the processes of gaining citizenship, working with community organizations, and otherwise participating in U.S. democratic political life. As Martha Jiménez explained to us (interview, Los Angeles, March 24, 2005), it is also hoped that through these efforts a broader kind of transnational political consciousness will come to replace the narrower local and regional diaspora consciousness that still characterizes many HTA leaders in southern California and throughout the United States.

Transnational Citizenship: Defending Duality

What conclusions about the second face of transnational citizenship can be drawn from these ethnographic encounters? Ángel Calderón's political experiences in Napa illustrate that social and political capital accumulated in one country can be transferred to another over time. The political practices and identities of the leaders of the FCZSC we have just described more richly illustrate this second face of transnational citizenship. Key leaders of the FCZSC have become active in the past decade at all levels of U.S. society and politics. One of their leaders, Guadalupe Gómez, has successfully expanded the FCZSC's engagement with the U.S. face of transnational citizenship. With transnational leadership provided by Martha Jiménez, an alliance of private philanthropic foundations and MALDEF is seeking to broaden, deepen, and institutionalize this sort of political engagement even further. The alliance hopes to transform these activists into skilled advocates for Mexican immigrants in U.S. cities. The goal is to take people who have a proven track record of community improvement in their Mexican places of origin and equip them with the legal, technical, and political knowledge to become effective voices for Mexican Americans at the grassroots level in the United States, while maintaining the power they have acquired at the transnational level. The full range of transnational political connections and targets of the Federation and its political offshoots is depicted visually in map 4.

Time will tell whether this more comprehensive and affirmative vision of dual identity and dual citizenship will fully materialize. In this regard, it is worth recalling our earlier observation that rather than being "doubly loyal" to their nation of origin, the migrants we have studied clearly express dual allegiance to both countries. Yet this duality is conditional and contingent. Depending on the questions posed, the migrants express dual ambivalence about life in each nation and about the modes of political participation on both sides of the border in which they are engaged. On balance, however, because they often act politically on the basis of what

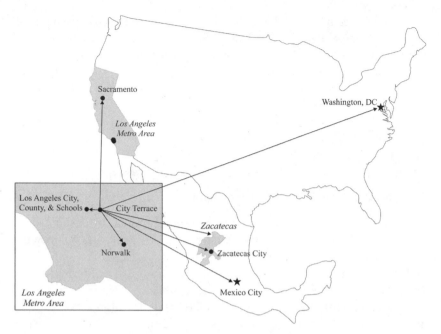

Map 4. The binational spaces of Zacatecan migrant political engagement

they *don't* like in each country, they continue to act politically, both "here" and "there," and do so with a growing sense of transnational political efficacy.

This point is well illustrated in the following lengthy exchange with Guadalupe Rodríguez, an FCZSC vice-president whose principal sphere of operation within the Federation is oriented toward political activism in the United States:

> BAKKER: We'd like to understand the feelings of someone who develops what we call a transnational or binational identity, a person who actively participates in two societies. . . . Some people in the United States argue that the work that an organization like the Federation does is dangerous for the United States, because it robs this country of migrants' efforts and dedication, of immigrants that should be dedicated to the United States. . . . It takes away those efforts because they are dedicated to Mexico, toward improving their communities of origin. . . . Or are you somehow able to create a balance and do both things: participate in Mexico as well as the United States?
>
> RODRÍGUEZ: I think that they are wrong. Why? For example, if we analyze what the Federation is spending in order to create a federation, right there it is contributing, already, to the growth of this country. The events that

are organized are massive events where, even if they don't believe it—I'm not sure who thinks in that way—the Federation is even creating jobs. Being a federation, being united to help out our co-nationals, our people, is automatically contributing to the welfare, it is contributing to create jobs in the Unión Americana.

Hundreds and thousands of residents in different parts of the United States are now becoming citizens. Who are the people that are defending the United States? You are going to see that a large number of them are Latinos, they're Mexican. They are risking their lives for you, for him and for me. . . . I mean, they don't give us credit for that. And they don't want to see that. . . . And I am fighting and I have been fighting all of the time. But more than that, not only that they become citizens, that they get registered, but that they go to vote! . . . What for? So that in reality the work that we're doing gets recognized. That our people here be recognized, their work, the effort that they're making, and that those who don't recognize it, that they recognize the power that the Latino has here with the Unión Americana and that he is contributing. (interview with Guadalupe Rodríguez, Los Angeles, March 25. 2005)

In the final analysis, sentiments such as this profoundly challenge Arjun Appadurai's romantic imagining of a "post-national" moment of emancipation occasioned by the disjuncture of nation and state by migration and media flows. Likewise, Samuel Huntington's notion of cultural capital as a historical legacy of socialization to the values of Anglo-Protestantism is far removed from the actual lived experiences by which cultural, social, and political capital are being acquired, invested in, deployed, and spent by transnational Mexican migrants in California. Huntington's grand narrative ignores the actual practices and identities by which new modes of citizenship on both sides of the U.S.-Mexican border are coming into being.

8 The Boundaries of Citizenship

Transnational Power Revisited

> What do we claim when we claim that we understand the semiotic
> means by which . . . persons are defined to one another? That we
> know words or that we know minds? In answering this question, it
> is necessary . . . to notice the characteristic intellectual movement,
> the inward conceptual rhythm . . . namely, a continuous dialectical
> tacking between the most local of local detail and the most global of
> global structure in such a way as to bring them into simultaneous
> view. . . . Hopping back and forth between the whole conceived
> through the parts that actualize it and the parts conceived through
> the whole that motivates them, we seek to turn them, by a sort of
> intellectual perpetual motion, into explications of one another.
>
> CLIFFORD GEERTZ, *Local Knowledge*

The stories of migrant political transnationalism we have profiled in this book offer intriguing insights into enduring debates regarding identity, belonging, and citizenship in this era of large-scale, cross-border migrations. What do the border-crossing political engagements of our ethnographic subjects have to say regarding the theoretical antinomies of immigrant incorporation and transnational connections that have dominated the migration research field in recent years? Do the transnational political practices and identities adopted by our research subjects constitute a final nail in the coffin of those earlier conceptions that envisioned citizenship and political community as tightly circumscribed within the territorial boundaries of the nation-state? Is the contemporary experience of transnational migration in the context of neoliberal globalization providing the conditions for simultaneous political engagement in multiple nation-states? Or are we in need of a more nuanced account of the limits and possibilities for a migrant politics of simultaneity? What is the play of agencies in the construction and enactment of transnational citizenship across the U.S.-Mexico divide? What are the implications for democratic theory and practice of the inclusions and exclusions entailed in these new forms of migrant political transnationalism? Finally, what is the staying power of U.S.-Mexican migrant political transnationalism?

Certainly the particular form of "transnational citizenship" exercised by our ethnographic subjects is far removed from the images of "postnational" or "global" citizenship envisioned by some international relations scholars. Nor is this form of dual engagement captured in the projected fears of long-distance nationalism and divided loyalties contained within some recent scholarship on the impact of global migration on national identity formation in the United States (Anderson 1998; Huntington 2004b). The former seeks to erase the power of nation-states as taken-for-granted containers of citizenship status and political identity, whereas the latter holds onto a vision of nation-states as the exclusive and morally most appropriate site for the attribution and formation of citizenship and political subjectivity. Our ethnographic subjects, while recognizing the continuing significance of nation-states, are far more flexible in negotiating the practices of citizenship across borders. They help to shed light on the changing nature of citizenship and political practice in what has been termed the "age of migration" (Castles and Miller 2003) and the increasingly extraterritorial extension and global reach of nation-states.

We began this political ethnography of transnational citizenship by invoking George Marcus's call for "an ethnography of complex connections" that itself becomes "the means of producing a narrative that is both micro and macro, and neither one particularly" (1989, 24). We identified four distinct contexts to be kept constantly in mind as our ethnographic subjects narrated their stories: the *historical context* of the particular interstate relations, the conditions affecting migrant reception and exit, and the state policies that have shaped migration and citizenship between the United States and Mexico; the *political-economic context* (now called neoliberal globalization), which has ushered in an historically contradictory form of North American economic integration facilitating expanded capital mobility while seeking to restrict labor mobility across the border; the *sociocultural context* of migrant recruitment, histories, and narratives, and the changing gender and class relations within both countries, which strongly affect the timing and geography of migratory patterns; and the prevailing *institutional context* that our ethnographic subjects must accommodate to or resist, as they attempt to politically construct new spaces for practicing citizenship across borders. These reciprocal contexts constitute the opportunities and constraints experienced by our ethnographic subjects, situate them in particular power-knowledge venues, and affect their transnational practices in the interconnected locations in which they are orchestrating their lives. We hope that the stories we have told have succeeded in melding context and social action into seamless narratives operating at the conjuncture of structure and agency. This final chapter explicates the interplay of structure and agency, context and social action in the political lives of our ethnographic subjects.

Narratives of Migration History, Political Culture, and Political Action

All of the extended case studies narrated in this book have been set in a wider historical context of over a century of state-mediated Mexican labor migration to the United States that has institutionalized niches for el migrante at the bottom reaches of U.S. labor markets in many sectors, and most prominently in the agricultural sector. This context is reflected in the initial work experiences of Ángel Calderón and his fellow guanajuatense migrants from El Timbinal narrated in chapter 3. It is also reflected in the personal trajectory of Andrés Bermúdez, the Tomato King, whose legend of migrant achievement starts with the millionaire entrepreneur beginning his first journey across the U.S.-Mexican border in the trunk of a car. Bermúdez initially worked at the low end of the service sector in southern California and in 1974 moved into the agricultural sector at a farm labor camp in Winters, in northern California. There he gradually moved up the economic ladder to become a highly successful tomato grower, farm-labor contractor, and inventor of a tomato-transplanting machine. Similarly, the Zacatecan Federation leader Lupe Gómez's migration narrative began with picking beans as a child in the fields of Zacatecas and moved through farm work in California as a teenager. His sense of the arduous and dead-end nature of this occupational trajectory prompted him to attend a California community college in Los Angeles where he studied accounting and business administration. This enabled him to move on to an eventually successful career preparing taxes in the predominantly Latino city of Santa Ana in Orange County, near Los Angeles. It is transnational upward-mobility narratives such as those expressed by Calderón, Bermúdez, and Gómez that have given many of our key players the status advantages to become successful political actors in their respective transnational social spaces.

In this book we also have tried to pay close attention to the wider political culture and institutional context in which transnational political struggles are being played out. Popular resentment of Mexican political party institutions and the prevailing political culture was a prominent part of all of our narratives. Skepticism about the traditional clientelist role of Mexican political parties was found in the translocality of Napa–El Timbinal, as well as in Andrés Bermúdez's and the Zacatecan Federation leaders' shared emphasis on the need to transform Mexican politics by eradicating corruption. Such transformational aspirations only make sense in the context of the emergence of wider pressures to change the contemporary institutional context of political party politics in Mexico. These popular pressures bore fruit when Vicente Fox of the opposition PAN defeated the ruling PRI candidate in the 2000 presidential election by campaigning successfully as the "candidate of change." Fox's election substantially opened up the previously closed PRI-dominated political system, but his victory has not yet significantly changed it. Fox's overtures to Mexican migrants to join his struggle for change and his celebration of them as national "heroes" further served to legitimate migrant participation in Mexican political life.

When seeking office at the local municipal level in Jerez, the Tomato King took advantage of this wider political context of migrant political reincorporation. That context offered him some significant opportunities to promote change. The increasing importance of migrants in official state discourses and policy making, at all three scales of government, benefited Bermúdez because his political opponents, cognizant of the fundamental economic role of migrants in the local economy, were deterred from using his status as a migrant to overtly challenge his right to participate politically. Indeed, the PAN's opportunistic recruitment of the Tomato King in his second run for mayor in Jerez and his more recent candidacy for the Mexican Chamber of Deputies demonstrate the growing legitimacy of el migrante in Mexican political discourse and practice. The passage of the Ley Migrante in Zacatecas, which institutionalized migrant political inclusion, is a second major example of the political fruits of the migrant-as-hero narrative. This changed discursive positionality of el migrante helped transform the political permissions and constraints of the prevailing institutional framework for elections. When we move from the level of political discourse to the level of political action, the migrants have demonstrated a clear capacity to reposition their practices at multiple political scales. This jumping of scales highlights the capacities of actors to restructure the contextual constraints and opportunities in which they are emplaced. It also highlights the complex scalar dynamics involved in the making of transnational citizenship.

The Multiple Scales of Transnational Politics

Our extended case studies demonstrate the limitations of a purely translocal understanding of the political dynamics at work in the study of migrant political transnationalism. This is perhaps most clear in our analysis of the multiple electoral coronations of the Tomato King. Several intersecting scales of politics, from local to transnational, came together in our narrative of the Tomato King. The timing and character of the self-presentation of El Rey del Tomate fit remarkably well with the multiscalar political contexts in which his campaign was embedded. These contexts spanned both sides of the U.S.-Mexican border. On the Mexican side, they included a changing political opportunity structure in Zacatecas in which the Mexican government's policy offensive toward the reincorporation and political mobilization of migrants activated the aspirations of a wide range of migrant community leaders. They provided material and symbolic support for the pioneering candidacies of the Tomato King. This was combined with growing local grassroots activism in Jerez. This activism was fostered by a shift from a PRI-led governing coalition at the state level to a PRD administration that owed much of its success to its incorporation of U.S.-based migrant activists, as we have shown in chapter 6. This new political opportunity structure in the Mexican political arena also opened up a new space for engaged participation by public intellectuals from the University of Zacatecas, who became crucial policy and political advisers to the migrant candidacies of the Tomato King.

The transnational character of Bermúdez's persona was clearly essential to his success. His status as a transmigrant made him a political "outsider," a benefit in this political context given the electorate's generalized mistrust of politicians, as he was not seen as corrupted by political structures operating at the national and local scale. His "outsider" status also gained him the political support of aspiring transnational political activists in other U.S. cities, such as Chicago and Houston, who hoped that the Tomato King's precedent-setting success in Jerez would open up opportunities for them to become reengaged in electoral politics in other Mexican cities such as Guadalajara and even Mexico City. (Bermúdez interview, March 15, 2002.)

Yet, given the long history of transmigration in Jerez, Bermúdez was at the same time able to be seen by voters at the municipal scale as a transmigrant "insider," as "one of us." The fact that his success was gained in the United States was important because it left him less susceptible to accusations that his wealth had been generated through corrupt or illicit means than if he had gone from rags to riches within Mexico. Bermúdez carried these general themes back to the translocal scale, thereby gaining significant support for his campaign. The translocal economic clout he could project as a major employer and contractor of farmworkers in the United States enabled him to claim that he could provide up to three hundred temporary visas to fellow Jerezanos (Mena 2001), offering them the possibility of tapping into the income-generating capacity of the U.S. economy and engaging in transnational social reproduction. He thus condensed popular longings for greater local economic opportunities with wider calls for governmental efficiency and transparency, mirroring the discourse of neoliberal globalization.

The Contradictions of Migrant Electoral Politics

This repositioning of migrants as legitimate political actors in Mexico's slowly emerging democratic politics and the migrant's capacity to jump scales and blur established boundaries of political practice are not, however, guarantees of political transformation. The multiscalar politics of migrant political activists has contradictory elements that may constrain the strategic alternatives of migrant political candidates. The cultural and geographical mobility of migrant activists does not mean that they are free-floating subjects, unconstrained by the particular power-knowledge venues through which they move. Instead, they must organize and orchestrate their practices within such venues. One of these power-knowledge venues is the prevailing political culture that we have been discussing, one which migrants are seeking to transform.

For example, we have found that potential election-day supporters of migrant candidates such as the Tomato King respond to traditional as well as changing dimensions of political culture. In the Jerez elections voters expected to see the fruits of effective patron-client relations even as they responded to appeals for "change." This helps to explain the sensed obligation of the Tomato King's campaign team to deploy some of the traditional campaign tactics of the PRI regime they sought to finally overthrow. This led them to offer free meals and raffle off domestic appliances at campaign rallies to attract support. Ironically, such moves, far from offering a whole-scale democratic transformation, serve to culturally reproduce the same structures they aimed to politically transform. This contradiction highlights the continuing embeddedness of electoral politics within prevailing cultural structures and the need for migrant activists and their allies to overcome the practices of clientelism if they are ever to effect the political transformation they so desire.

This is not to say that migrant activists are unaware of such contradictions. In a number of ways our migrant activists have begun to challenge the persisting structures and practices of the clientelist political culture that they profoundly mistrust. Ángel Calderón, for example, the migrant leader from Guanajuato who collaborated with Fox and his policies when he was governor, was unwilling to extend that collaborative spirit to Fox's PAN gubernatorial successor. In part this was because the successor, Romero Hicks, showed little follow-through in carrying out Fox's policy directions or responding to past beneficiaries of these policies after the election cycle. The new party elites in Guanajuato were far less attentive to Calderón's local concerns and needs than Fox had been. This is a typical feature of the prevailing political culture in Mexico that migrants are seeking to change, as new victors in elections reward their own supporters by redistributing positions of power and patronage while widespread poverty remains unaddressed.

In the case of the Zacatecan Federation leadership, autonomista activists such as Lupe Gómez and Francisco Javier González have been even more skeptical than Calderón and his fellow guanajuatenses. The autonomistas have expressed little faith that Fox as president or any other opposition party politicians among the existing political class in Mexico were capable of successfully transforming Mexico's corrupt, clientelist, and authoritarian political culture. Instead, they have argued forcefully that Mexico will only change if its migrants return from the United States and make the political system change by ushering in a new way of doing things, without corruption. Bermúdez repeatedly expressed this same view to us, proclaiming his absolute mistrust of all politicians and consistently claiming that the only way in which Mexico was going to "progress" was if successful migrants from the United States returned to Mexico and replaced today's politicians. Even the loyalista federation activist Manuel de la Cruz expressed similar mistrust for the "vile corruption" he sought to eradicate by bringing in "American" political practices of transparency, efficiency, and accountability.

This ideological dimension of migrant leaders' "Americanization" discourse tends to present an overly romantic view of U.S. political culture as entirely open and transparent, while ignoring evidence of corruption, exclusion, and biased political participation in U.S. political life (see, for example, Manza and Uggen 2006; Smith and Tarallo 1995; Connolly 1969). Although this celebratory representation of their newfound political culture in the United States echoed deeply held aspirations for political change in Mexico and also partially reflected their own upward economic mobility and increasing influence in U.S. politics, it is a potentially risky political strategy to deploy in Mexico, given that nation's historically antagonistic relationship with the United States and the importance to the nationalist project of the opposition to foreign, and especially U.S., meddling in national affairs. While numerous scholars have correctly noted that Mexican national officials have made an abrupt break with this traditional antagonism by adopting a policy of *acercamiento* (rapprochement) (Guarnizo 1998; R. Smith 1998) and have supported deepening neoliberal integration with the United States, it is not entirely clear that such a policy change has been effective in erasing long-held popular nationalist sentiments at the grassroots level. Although nationalist antagonism toward the United States may be weaker in states like Guanajuato and Zacatecas with long histories of U.S.-bound labor migration, we have seen the continuing significance of nationalist opposition in the debates over migrant political rights, even in Zacatecas where those rights have come the farthest.

The Political Agents of Neoliberalism

Turning to the political-economic context of neoliberalism, another layer of contextual opportunities and constraints is revealed. In three of our extended case studies—the social construction of translocal factory ownership witnessed in Napa–El Timbinal, the multidimensional networks of power intertwined in the transnational coalition politics of the Tomato King, and the emerging developmental model of "productive investment" being pursued by the Zacatecan Federation—the discourses and practices of migrant activists have been influenced by and inflected with the prevailing international political-economic practices of neoliberalism. Neoliberalism, however, is not a pre-given structural feature of an object called "the global economy." Rather, neoliberalism is a socially and politically produced project promoted by the ruling elites of the world's leading nation-states and the supranational institutions they have created to promote that project. To succeed in shaping the world, this project needs collaborative agents operating on the ground within the specific nation-states that collectively make up the international economic system. In particular societies these agents may be state officials, private actors in civil society, or both.

In our case from Guanajuato the central agents promoting the neoliberal project were state party officials from the conservative PAN. These transnational actors reached across the U.S.-Mexican border to lure the state's transnational migrants from Napa–El Timbinal and other translocalities into the neoliberal project as players at the bottom reaches of a global commodity chain by rechanneling these migrants' collective remittances. What had once been projects to improve everyday social life in their communities of origin were converted into an investment scheme that made migrant donors into the local capitalist owners of subcontracting textile factories. In the case of El Timbinal, this transnational maquila went bankrupt in the wake of the economic downturn and disruption of U.S.-Mexican geopolitical relations in the aftermath of the events of September 11, 2001. An unintended effect of these developments was the alienation of the migrants from the neoliberal project and a shift in their role back to the two local poles of their translocality, as providers of community betterment projects in El Timbinal and engaged local citizens in urban politics in Napa, California.

In the case of the election of the Tomato King in Jerez there were two principal agents of neoliberalism in civil society. The first was the Tomato

King himself, whose campaign discourse touted return migrant entrepreneurialism as a solution to the widespread poverty of his city and state and whose specific policy agenda proposed incentives to attract transnational migrant entrepreneurs back to their places of origin as well as to promote global investment in the locality of Jerez. In his first campaign, for example, Bermúdez claimed to have attracted Taiwanese and Japanese investors who would create jobs in Jerez (Grover 2001). Ironically, this promise never materialized because the labor force necessary for industrial work in Jerez as a global production site either had already left for the United States or were unwilling to abandon their traditional agriculturally based survival strategies to take up factory work. The second agent of neoliberalism in this case was the leadership of the Federation of Zacatecan hometown clubs in Los Angeles, who supported the Tomato King in part because they themselves were largely entrepreneurial small-business owners and transnational political activists who might gain new opportunities for investment and political influence in Mexico as a longer-term result of a Bermúdez victory.

In the case of the transnational practice of "migrant-led development" in Zacatecas that we analyzed in chapter 4, assessing the significance of neoliberalism as a structural context for migrant and state-centered agency is even more complex. Institutionally, the phenomenon of neoliberal investment by migrant leaders must be understood collectively, in terms of emergent transnational policy networks, and not just individually. For their part, state-centered actors in Zacatecas have consciously sought partners for joint "productive investment" projects from migrant entrepreneurs as well as from global development agencies. The key leaders of the Zacatecan Federation of Hometown Associations have willingly entered into a collaborative relationship not only with agents of the Zacatecan regional state but also with the global development community, another institutional agent of neoliberalism. Their partners in this global development industry include private foundations such as the Rockefeller Foundation and supranational development organizations such as the Inter-American Development Bank. Through this kind of three-sided institutional networking, the importance of "social investment" (e.g., infrastructure and school improvements) by the clubs has been deemphasized in favor of the promotion of collective remittances for "productive investment." The hometown clubs have begun to shift their projects in a neoliberal direction in a transnational "partnership" with the regional state and the so-called donor community. For reasons spelled out below, this neoliberal offensive is unlikely to provide a solution to the endemic poverty in the cities and rural regions of Mexico that is a principal cause of the long history of transnational migration across the border underlying all of our narrative stories. This is perhaps the "widest whole" within which micro-macro narratives of U.S.-Mexican political transnationalism need to be understood.

The Pitfalls of the Turn to "Productive Investment"

What can be said about the economic development model of migrant-led productive investment so highly touted by state-centered actors and the donor community that underlies the Mi Comunidad maquiladora initiative in Guanajuato and the new direction being pursued by the Zacatecan Federation and some of its club leaders? The most obvious problem with this approach is its targeting. Rather than focusing on the resources and comparative advantages of particular localities in Mexico that might become the target of investment by migrants, the states of Guanajuato and Zacatecas have chosen to link economic development goals to a limited range of places where migrants have already formed transnational connections with their communities of origin. These places tend to be rural, isolated, and economically stagnant localities with limited transportation and communication infrastructure, although they do have a long community tradition of migration and an established history of migrant engagement in hometown community improvement projects. As such, these localities may serve as ideal sites for encouraging migrant-funded investment projects, but these projects are unlikely to generate significant economic growth and development or to stem the tide of migration for several reasons.

With respect to sustained economic development, as we have seen in the case of the maquiladora in El Timbinal, profits available to migrant factory owners are limited within the subcontracting niche of the global textile industry and are reduced even further due to the poor roads connecting these villages to major urban distribution and marketing centers. Furthermore, as we have shown in chapter 3 and as noted by others (Iskander 2005), the low wages offered in this sector are insufficient to attract a steady labor force without sacrificing profits.

In fairness, the regional state officials designing the Mi Comunidad program in Guanajuato did recognize the limitation of the global subcontracting system and sought to locate their maquilas more favorably within that system. In their initial designs, planners envisioned the migrant-funded maquilas as self-sufficient enterprises making and branding their own textile products under the leadership of a regional university-based textile-design center. Yet, because of the political logic of patronage politics, these plans, originally conceived during the gubernatorial administration of Vicente Fox, never materialized under that of his successor, Romero Hicks. As should be apparent from this discussion, political forces, geographical opportunities and constraints, institutionalized production networks and systems, as well as local labor relations all work to mediate the effects of market mechanisms. In short, it takes more than the infusion of migrant capital to make a viable and economically sustainable village.

Even if sustained economic development were achievable in some migrant-sending villages, this success would be quite unlikely to stem the tide of future migration from such villages. This is in part because the migration process is a cultural as well as an economic phenomenon. It has long been recognized that Mexican migration to the United States has become a local way of life, a rite of passage for young people coming of age in sending communities (Mines 1981; Massey et al. 1987; M. P. Smith 2003a, 2003b). Other studies suggest that if policymakers wish to stem the tide of migration they should target their policies toward communities that have not yet established migration as a way of life (Cornelius 1990; Alarcón 1995). Such communities, lacking a long tradition of migration, would be more likely to benefit from job-creating investment and to retain their local population by creating new local employment opportunities.

An understanding of the cultural element of migration does not seem to enter into the consciousness of political elites and policymakers interested in promoting migrant-led investment projects. This lack of attention to the cultural dynamics of migration is a logical flaw in the targeting of localities for investment. It may be logical, *politically*, to tap into preexisting migrant networks with an established history of translocal community action. But it is precisely in these communities where migration has become a cultural expectation and a taken-for-granted way of being in the world that is unlikely to be easily erased simply by creating local job opportunities.

Moreover, the status incentives that are part of the state's political offensive add a social-psychological dimension to these cultural understandings. The very practices of the state that enhance the social and political status of migrants in order to reincorporate them into the "global Mexican nation" and rechannel the flow of their remittances toward productive investment, as we have illustrated in earlier chapters, provides a strong psychological incentive to migrate rather than to stay behind and take advantage of whatever newly created jobs may materialize. The representation of migrants as heroes in official discourse, the construction of statues honoring their migration, and the empowerment of migrants within important political spheres all work to reinforce migration and make evident that migration is a reliable route to upward economic and social mobility and political access and power.

Moving the politics of representation to a broader scale, the "remittances-to-development discourse" of the international donor community appears to be the latest in a long line of technological quick fixes for problems of global poverty and "underdevelopment." Migrant remitters as subjects of development and agents of change have become the successors to the small farmers, women, and environmentalists of earlier discourses on "rural development," "women in development," and "sustainable development" (Escobar 1995, 154–211). The migrant remitter is represented as a crucial agent of change and development in official discourses on the development impact of migrant remittances, such as the COESPO report in Guanajuato and the Inter-American Development Bank remittances program. In Guanajuato, the migrant is envisioned as an entrepreneur and his wife as a vital "remittance manager." Despite the abundant state policies targeted toward supporting the "transnational family," that family is represented largely as a self-sufficient economic unit vital to the operation of free markets. In similar fashion, the neoliberal globalization discourses of the IADB tout the growing aggregate amounts of migrant remittances and see them as a way to transform financial markets if remittance providers and recipients are moved into the formal banking sector. The IADB's vision of "financial democracy" is to remedy the fact that only 10 percent of remittance recipients "have access to" bank accounts and other financial services, and thereby link remittances more closely to the logic of markets (Multilateral Investment Fund 2005).

For all of its limitations, the COESPO report at least envisages migrants and the other members of their transnational families as potential agents of economic change. In contrast, the IADB discourse invests banking institutions and the market structure itself with collective agency. In this vision it is not the migrant entrepreneur that directs investment flows but the infusion of the "lost billions" of migrant remittances into the formal system of global financial flows that will produce economic development and channel capital toward its most efficient purposes. Ironically, as we have shown in chapter 4, the actual practices of the regional state and the donor community have little to do with this utopian vision of the market as the driving force in economic development. Instead, both institutional actors have engaged in collaborative partnerships with collective migrant organizations seeking to mobilize these migrants' social capital and rechannel the social investments they have made in their communities of origin toward productive business enterprise. Both the state and donor community in effect are participating in the *political* production of economic organization rather than simply planting the seeds of market growth and sitting back to watch it work its magic.

Imagining Alternatives to Neoliberalism

The fluid play of agencies contained in these collaborative partnerships lies in stark contrast to the agency-less imagery contained not only within the neoliberal development discourse of global development agencies but also within more progressive critiques of development discourse that anticipate the social production of an "anti-politics machine" as a structural consequence of such discourses (Ferguson 1990). Such representations of the depoliticizing effects of development discourse limit, if not discount entirely, the social imaginary of the targets of development.

There is a growing awareness of the social imaginary as an important dimension of "cognitive agency" found in transnational networks and practices (Appadurai 1990; Mahler and Pessar 2001). In our extended case studies the migrant leaders we have interviewed are perfectly capable of imagining something different. Rather than being trapped within the hegemonic logic of the "free market," our migrant leaders valorize other goals and agencies in the process of economic development. The social imaginary of the migrant leaders from Zacatecas often highlighted the crucial role of the state in creating and maintaining markets, producing infrastructure, and even setting prices that would allow for the reproduction of campesino livelihoods. In another way of imagining alternative possibilities, the migrant leaders from Guanajuato clearly value the social status they have achieved as benefactors in their sending community more than the profits derived from their role as capitalist investors in the El Timbinal maquiladora project. These leaders were fully aware that their energies had been directed away from the types of social investment projects they most valued and which were the source of their transnational social status and community power. Hence, they were skeptical partners in these transnational public-private "partnerships" rather than ideologically mystified devotees of the transformative powers of the "free" market.

There are, of course, limits to the impacts of the social imaginary as a transformative agency. Imagination is a cognitive process that needs to be materialized in the actual practices of social and political actors before it can have any practical real world effects. The alternatives envisioned by migrant actors can clearly lead to alternative practices. In the Guanajuato case, migrant leaders exercised an exit option, when they disengaged from their partnership with the regional state to turn back to their self-organized community development projects in Mexico and their incipient engagement in political and community development activities in Napa. The Zacatecan leadership has chosen instead to exercise a voice option, by remaining engaged in public-private partnerships. Indeed this leadership group has accepted the largesse of the donor community as a means to accelerate and expand its moves toward productive investment, even though this might entail the erosion of their heretofore successful social investment agenda. (For a theoretical articulation of these alternative forms of agency, see Hirschman 1970; see also, Smith, Tarallo, and Kagiwada 1991.)

The play of the Zacatecan migrants' voice in the productive investment partnership remains an open question. If their alternative vision of migrant-led development is to be put into practice it will obviously require a much more substantive role for the state than is now available within the dominant discourse. Although this possibility might seem remote under the neoliberal partnership as it is now configured, if migrant leaders are able to reconfigure state politics in Zacatecas and elevate more of their number to key political and policy-making positions—an ambition clearly imagined by certain migrant leaders—they may be more likely to redefine the role of state and market along the lines they have imagined. Thus, the issue of the democratization of Mexican political life becomes a central problematic in this equation. Whether and how migrants might reconfigure regional politics in Zacatecas and other sending states raises intriguing questions regarding the meaning of migrant political empowerment and the nature of the Mexican democratic opening.

Democratic Inclusion: Elite Succession or Democratization?

In the extended case studies we have narrated throughout this book, are we seeing the emergence of transnational social movements seeking to expand migrants' partial membership in the "global" Mexican nation? Or are these new transnational political actors simply seeking, for their own benefit, to open up elite spaces within local and regional power blocs? In other words, are we seeing the transformation or the reproduction of existing structures of inequality? Or perhaps these developments are more complex and nuanced in their implications, requiring us to move beyond such a binary framework. In addressing these possibilities it is crucial to ask: Who stands to benefit from the migrants' emergent transnational socioeconomic and political practices?

Much of the literature exploring migrant transnational political practices has noted that the transmigrants that maintain the most active transnational ties and interests in politics tend to represent an emergent transnational elite (Itzigsohn 2000; Guarnizo 1997, 2001). Members of this new elite tend to be better educated and/or economically secure migrants; they are usually entrepreneurs who are long-time U.S. residents, often naturalized citizens, and who are overwhelmingly male (Guarnizo, Portes, and Haller 2003; Fitzgerald 2000). These transnational political actors are said to be uninterested in transforming the unequal power structures and social hierarchies in their countries or communities of origin. Instead, they seek their own personal incorporation at the top of such structures and hierarchies (Guarnizo 1997, 2001).

In terms of their actual on-the-ground political practices we have found that the migrant political activists profiled in this book have tended to operate through the traditional channels of political power distribution in Mexico. Some of these leaders have been affiliated with established homeland political parties in immigrant communities. Others have maintained a nonpartisan stance while promoting public policies to expand spaces for migrant candidacies and their official incorporation into political elite status. When allowed by law, still others have sought political office, claiming to represent migrant interests. Prominent examples from our Zacatecan case would include, respectively, the leaders of Zacatecanos PRImero and the Frente Cívico who campaigned actively for the passage of the Ley Migrante, and Andrés Bermúdez and Manuel de la Cruz, both of whom benefited from that very law.

In contrast to this reproductionist perspective, a more transformational approach has been enunciated in some of the political transnationalism literature. This approach envisions an emerging transnational citizenry contributing to the democratic transformation of their communities and countries of origin. From this perspective, migrants' experiences in the United States have given them a glimpse of the democratic possibilities available in the "developed world," and they want to transmit those possibilities to their homeland. Accordingly, these migrants are represented as seeking to bring more democracy, less corruption, and increased respect for civil and human rights to the homeland political system (Portes 1999; Guarnizo, Portes, and Haller 2003). They describe their experiences within the political system in the United States to friends and family and help them to begin imagining an alternative political system (Levitt 2001b). They utilize their increased economic clout not for personal gain but to create spaces for popular political participation (Laguerre 1999).

We have found that our transnational political activists have indeed been highly critical of the efforts of ruling political elites, blaming them for the poverty and economic instability driving many to migrate. Candidates such as the Tomato King have made an explicit link between development and democracy, attributing the failure of development in migrants' communities of origin to the engrained corruption embedded in government institutions and bureaucracies slowly emerging from undemocratic rule. They believe that underdevelopment is explained as much by the corruption of government officials and institutions as by structural features of the world capitalist economy. This same critical stance has been expressed by key leaders of the Zacatecan Federation, sometimes even by those loyalista leaders who continued to collaborate with the Monreal administration. In this book we have thus found substantial evidence supporting both of these perspectives.

The important point is that we should not be surprised by this duality because the transnational actors we have interviewed are multipositional subjects. The reality of their lived experience on both sides of the U.S.-Mexican border has produced a highly contingent subject positionality. Our principal transnational political actors are engaged in an ever-changing, dialectical internal struggle over their personal and political identities in which conflicts between inclusion and transformation, elite succession and democratization, participation in homeland and U.S. immigrant politics are not generally viewed in either/or terms. The complex and contingent political identities we have uncovered in this book suggest that any attempt to generalize out of social and historical context about the nature and significance of migrant political transnationalism is problematic.

Politics is an inherently multidimensional and continually shifting process that is unavoidably fraught with contradictions. In the final analysis, politics, whether local, national, or transnational, is a process of becoming rather than a state of being. Although the presence of elites as players in the process of mass democratic politics is unavoidable, the nature of their relationships with mass publics ranges from authoritarian control to democratic accountability and is historically and contextually contingent rather than structurally given. Accordingly, rather than seeking fixed generalizations about the character and significance of migrants' transnational political practices at the present historical juncture, it is more fruitful to focus analysis on the continuing interplay between states, elites, interest groups, social movements, and mass publics in specific sites of politics, as we have done in this book, to map the local, national, and transnational political spaces where social and political relations are being negotiated, constructed, and reconstituted. Focusing on the contextually specific locations or spaces where these political ties are constantly *in the making* promises to yield much more than context-free classificatory schemes in assessing the democratic possibilities of transnational political practices.

Democratic Exclusion: Gender, Class, and New Political Subjectivities

Class and gender relations are key dimensions of the sociocultural context in which new forms of transnational citizenship are being formed. When we assess these power relations, we must inevitably confront questions of exclusion from as well as inclusion in newly emerging spaces of political participation and representation. Who is excluded from the representations and practices of the Mexican state and the migrant activist community in opening up new spaces for el migrante? What differences do these exclusions make for the construction of Mexico's new transnational democratic order? Where are the new spaces for women and ordinary nonelite migrants in the new democratic opening for "migrant" political participation?

A voluminous body of academic literature has developed over the last three decades to bring together the study of gender and migration. Pierrette Hondagneu-Sotelo (2003) has nicely articulated three distinct stages through which this literature has evolved: (1) an early stage that sought to rectify a near total absence of empirical research on the presence of women in international migration flows; (2) an intermediary stage that challenged the prevailing research strategy, which viewed international migration as a "household survival strategy" in which the household was viewed as a unitary social actor, rather than as an arena of conflict, contestation, and inequality between men and women, parents and children, nuclear and extended family obligations, and so forth; (3) and a third stage that emphasizes the centrality of gender in structuring migration, "permeat[ing] a variety of practices, identities and institutions implicated in [migration]" (Hondagneu-Sotelo 2003, 9).

At the same time that migration studies were being opened up to issues of gender and power, the literature on transnationalism within which we have situated this book emerged to powerfully challenge the "methodological nationalism" (Wimmer and Glick Schiller 2002) of mainstream migration research. Yet, as others have shown (Mahler 1999; Goldring 2001a, 2001b; Pessar and Mahler 2003), the transnational optic also has been slow to incorporate questions of gender into its prevailing research agenda. Recently, however, ethnographers have begun to move the study of gender from the periphery to the core of transnational studies (Mahler and Pessar 2006). Nonetheless, the growing body of research on political transnationalism is still largely focused on the political reincorporation of male migrants into homeland, home-state, and hometown political structures and processes (Guarnizo 1998; R. Smith 2003b; Bakker and Smith 2003; but Goldring 2001a, 2001b, 2003 offers an important exception).

The relationship between gender, power, and emerging transnational citizenship regimes was not initially central to the research problematic driving this book. Nonetheless, the research process itself moved us to interrogate this relationship at several critical junctures in our narratives. We were struck by official state representations of el migrante and "his" family, such as in Guanajuato's COESPO report, that showed a complete lack of awareness of the presence of women in the phenomenon of U.S.-bound migration other than as stay-at-homes in sending communities. At a more immediate level, some of the female HTA leaders we interviewed spoke about their continuing exclusion from significant positions of power and their modes of resistance to this within the Los Angeles Federation of Zacatecan Hometown Associations. This lived reality of the gendered construction of citizenship and power within migrant hometown associations was brought home vividly to us in the midst of one ethnographic interview with a female HTA leader. Our conversation was punctuated by a series of impassioned denunciations of the *machista* practices prevailing within the Federation. As if to validate these claims, a male Federation leader interrupted the rhythm of our interview to tell our interview subject to make a pot of coffee for a pending meeting. In an act of "everyday resistance," our interview subject not only refused to comply with his demand but also told us after he had left that not even her own father would dare to speak to her in such an imperial tone, barking orders rather than asking favors. Thus, our research has shown us that gender matters at all levels, from the production of state policies to the mesolevel of organizational practice to the microlevel of everyday domination and resistance.

How are these gendered exclusions played out in the central theme of our book—the making of citizenship across borders? Structural biases against women, such as the taken-for-granted assumption of migration as an exclusively male phenomenon, became ideologized in state policy documents and discourses that made heroes out of male migrants, while ignoring female migration altogether as a social phenomenon. This effect is nowhere more clear than in the exclusive use of *el* migrante—an explicitly male-coded representation—in state policy documents, like the COESPO report and the Mi Comunidad program in Guanajuato. In such formulations, the male migrant is not only a symbol of absence and loss (Byrnes 2003) but becomes inscribed with nearly magical social resources that must be recaptured and which, thus, underlie the very logic of migrant reincorporation policies. The male-headed household is taken as a unitary subject, and state policies are specifically designed to reinforce that particular type of household formation. Nowhere in these state-policy formulations is any space created for female migrants as potential agents in the reproduction or transformation of their home communities. Female agency is absent from official discourse, except in the form of the wives and mothers left behind who are represented, both in the language of state policy and in statues that glorify the male migrant, as simple appendages of adventurous transnational male breadwinners.

Not all the efforts to reincorporate migrants into Mexican political and economic development have been as explicitly and exclusively gendered as the Guanajuato political offensive. The representations of the migrant in the Ley Migrante reforms in Zacatecas, for example, are more universalistic and gender-neutral. Those constitutional reforms have extended certain rights of citizenship to any Zacatecan migrant who continues to own property and fulfills a number of bureaucratic requirements with respect to taxation and voter registration. Yet, as feminist scholars of citizenship (e.g., Seidman 1999; Lister 2001) have correctly argued, the very universalism underlying discourses on citizenship ignores the myriad ways in which citizenship is differentially experienced by men and women. As in the case of citizenship in the nation-state, so also in the new social spaces and institutional domains of transnational citizenship, undifferentiated categories of citizens tend to ignore the continuing significance of patriarchal social relations, which generate differential resources for the practice of citizenship such as women's available time, household and care-giving responsibilities, and limited access to a historically male-dominated public sphere. Thus, even the presumably gender-neutral policies of migrant reincorporation into the transnational Zacatecan public sphere, by failing to address gender hierarchies and inequalities, work to reproduce or even reinforce exclusionary social relations.

In sum, whether taking the form of state policies that either represent el migrante as an explicitly male subject or democratic reforms that treat all migrant citizens as equal, patriarchal social structures are inscribed in state policies and political practices. This is not to say that patriarchy is entirely determinative and uncontested. Quite the contrary, we have witnessed on numerous occasions the contestation of this prevailing social structure and the struggle for more inclusive forms of citizenship empowerment across borders. Despite the barriers to women's empowerment, we have interviewed a woman who has become a migrant maquila owner, others who became presidents of their HTAs, and one woman who went from being the L.A. Federation's Señorita Zacatecas to becoming president of the breakaway Orange County Federation, in which position she coordinated the philanthropic activities of several Zacatecan HTAs. Moreover, not only have women been able to enter into leadership positions, some have also sought to change the political culture of migrant politics. For example, one of our most active female migrant leaders has routinely and openly dedicated her energies to resisting patriarchal domination of everyday politics within the Zacatecan Federation.

Another potential new social actor that has been excluded from both the theoretical inscription of the collective migrant as an emerging social subject and from the practices of expanded voting rights is the ordinary migrant who does not belong to the privileged groupings of migrant reincorporation policies, such as the hometown associations that are engaged in community betterment projects in their communities of origin. Recall from our discussion of the Ley Migrante reforms in chapter 6 that, far from offering an opening of the political sphere to the participation and representation of the full range of Zacatecan migrants, the Ley Migrante proposed to open up that space for a much more delimited category of new political participants, the "collective migrant," namely that group of HTA leaders engaged from abroad in social and community activities in Zacatecas (Moctezuma Longoria 2003b). The final version of the bill went beyond this narrow delimitation, recognizing any migrant's "simultaneous and binational residency" for the purpose of holding all offices except for governor if he or she could demonstrate, at least six months prior to an election, that they possessed a home in the state as well as a registered taxpayer ID card, a federal census ID number, and a voter credential card. Yet even here, the eligibility criteria would clearly exclude a large proportion of the Zacatecan population resident in the United States, particularly those social classes that lacked the resources to maintain home ownership in the state.

Likewise, the other requirements for obtaining recognition as a binational citizen also require the material resources and legal status to move freely back and forth across the U.S.-Mexico border. These material and legal resources are also unevenly distributed by class and tend to exclude the large proportion of migrants who are both poor and undocumented. These same social-class barriers to political recognition and participation, as we have shown in chapter 6, are also a prominent feature of the procedure established for registration and voting from abroad in Mexican presidential elections. In sum, the new politics of inclusion in the global Mexican nation are also a politics of exclusion.

The Two Faces of Migrant Political Transnationalism

Many of the migrant activists whose stories have been narrated in the previous chapters have successfully articulated a transnational political practice, engaging in both the "homeland" politics of Mexico and the ethnic politics of the United States, sometimes simultaneously. The cases of Manuel de la Cruz, Guadalupe Gómez, and Martha Jiménez discussed in chapters 6 and 7 are vivid examples of this simultaneous transnational political practice. The politics of simultaneity, however, is not restricted exclusively to this handful of Zacatecan activists. The relative openness of the U.S. political system to interest group politics of all kinds has opened up a space for transnational grassroots political organizations and movements to flourish. This receptive context for group formation in the United States, combined with both the policy incentives of the Mexican state and the political efficacy demonstrated by well-established HTAs and their federations, has led to an exponential growth in the numbers and scope of Mexican migrant HTAs. In 1996 there were 320 HTAs, largely from traditional migrant-sending states (Díaz de Cossío, Orozco, and González 1997). By 2003, the number of HTAs had grown to 623, and their reach extended to twenty-seven of the thirty-one Mexican states. The state of Zacatecas remains one of the leaders in this form of political engagement, with 126 HTAs concentrated largely in major cities such as Chicago and Los Angeles (Rivera-Salgado 2006). In 2005 the membership in Mexican hometown associations in California alone was estimated to be between 250,000 and 500,000 active members (Hecht 2005).

As Carol Zabin and Luis Escala Rabadán (1998) have shown, such HTAs create a lively space for political dialogue and debate that both keeps migrants connected to their communities of origin and helps integrate them into U.S. politics and society. Growing numbers of migrants are drawn into this matrix through the venues created by activist groups such as the Zacatecan Federation and its political spin-off, the Frente Cívico. These developments have brought more and more migrants into simultaneous political engagement with both societies, even if the mass membership in the HTAs may not participate as intensely in cross-border politics as the leading activists we have profiled here.

Their form of simultaneous transnational politics and the modes of transnational citizenship it entails contradict the expectations of some scholars that for political subjects to be "truly transnational" they must entirely set aside national identities (Waldinger and Fitzgerald 2004). The politics of simultaneity we have uncovered also challenges the view, presented by some scholars of U.S. ethnic politics, that diasporic and immigrant politics constitute "alternate social universes" (Jones-Correa 2005). Our ethnographic subjects, and the larger pool of transnationally oriented migrants they represent, view themselves neither as "citizens of the world" nor as forced to choose between mutually exclusive national identities.

In short, a sizable and growing number of today's transnational migrants view homeland engagement as compatible with immigrant incorporation. Such migrants are perfectly capable of acting politically both here and there, transferring political capital freely in both directions. Fully comfortable negotiating a dual political identity as citizens of two nation-states, these migrants live their lives in terms of and/also rather than either/or possibilities. The leading autonomista political activist Lupe Gómez is perhaps the best embodiment of this politics of simultaneity. Gómez has done more than any previous or subsequent FCZSC president to bring the Zacatecan Federation into urban, state, and national politics in the United States and proudly touts his personal communications with President George W. Bush and House Democratic leader (now Speaker of the House) Nancy Pelosi. At the same time, Gómez has seriously considered a future run as a migrant candidate for governor of Zacatecas.

The transnational political trajectory of activist Martha Jiménez offers another compelling example of simultaneous political engagement, demonstrating that migrant transnational politics does not necessarily flow in a unilateral direction, moving from an exclusive homeland orientation to a host-country orientation. Jiménez began her political life as a passionate grassroots activist in the City Terrace section of East Los Angeles. Her political repertoire soon grew to include hometown community development politics in Las Ánimas, Zacatecas. As she put it, she learned politics "the American way" in Los Angeles and then sought to transfer her newfound political skills and energies to democratizing struggles in her "home" state of Zacatecas. Jiménez now seeks to further integrate urban ethnic politics and transnational politics by drawing on her political connections with leading Latino political activists in Los Angeles that want to expand their connections with hometown association leaders. Jiménez's very duality as a transnational citizen activist has uniquely positioned her to tap into the political and social capital of Mexican hometown associations, helping to organize a leadership-training program that seeks to broaden HTA leaders' dual political engagement and institutionalize a politics of simultaneity.

When we move from the individual level of analysis to the mesostructural level where "institutions interact with structural and instrumental processes" (Guarnizo and Smith 1998, 25), another layer of complexity in interrogating the politics of simultaneity is revealed. A mesostructural focus on the FCZSC and its affiliated political groupings such as the Frente Cívico and Zacatecanos PRImero, for example, allows us to see political simultaneity as an organizational reality achieved through something of a transnational division of labor. In these organizations, political roles have been divided so that some members focus on the exigencies of political coalition formation in the United States while others engage in the political arena of Mexico. Thus, even in cases where the politics of simultaneity does not apply at the level of individual political subjectivity, it may nonetheless operate inter- and intra-organizationally. In short, the institutionalization of transnational political relations within and among migrant associations facilitates the emergence of simultaneous political engagement at the mesolevel of organizational practice.

Yet another level of complexity in analyzing the politics of simultaneity is revealed when we view the strategic deployment of the concept "Plan B" by some of our ethnographic subjects. In this symbolic use of politics, activists who are simultaneously engaged in politics on both sides of the U.S.-Mexico divide tend to use the representation of Plan B as a threat of "exit" from the Mexican political system if migrants fail to gain the spaces for "voice," access, and influence to which they think they are entitled. These actors remain interested in political life on both sides of the border but strategically frame their modes of engagement in Mexican and U.S. politics as a set of alternative sequential steps rather than simultaneous political practices.

By this discursive move, Plan B is represented as a full-scale turn to immigrant politics in the United States, a kind of general strike to be invoked if migrant activists are shut out of relevant political spaces in the Mexican homeland. Our interviews with the Tomato King illustrated this strategic deployment when, contemplating a collective migrant withdrawal from Mexican politics after he was stripped of his first electoral victory, he envisioned a migrant turn to politics in the United States, investing money now destined for hometown improvement projects in scholarship funds for Mexican American youth and other means of promoting ethnic empowerment and upward social mobility in the United States.

As a final caveat to our analysis of the politics of simultaneity, we must note that some migrant activists are not regularly engaged in simultaneous political participation. Past FCZSC president Felipe Cabral, for example, is actively engaged in Zacatecan partisan politics from Los Angeles as a leader in the PRI-affiliated migrant political organization Zacatecanos PRImero, but he has expressed little interest in electoral or neighborhood politics in the United States.

Given the complex and variegated political identities and practices of our ethnographic subjects, it is impossible, at the analytical level of the individual, to resolve all of the theoretical tensions between a "homeland" and "host land" political orientation. This is because the migrant activists we have studied do not constitute a single unitary political subject firmly planted at either of these poles. In this sense, we would agree with Peggy Levitt and Nina Glick Schiller that "it is useful to think of the migrant experience as a kind of gauge, which, while anchored, pivots between a new land and a transnational incorporation" (2004, 1011). For some of our research subjects the gauge has centered at the median point of "simultaneity of connection," while others tend to gravitate toward one or the other of the competing poles.

The Staying Power of Migrant Political Transnationalism

What is the staying power and likely future effectiveness of the transnational political practices that we have identified in this book? Our answer to this question depends on three critical contingencies: (1) the barriers and opportunities faced by doubly engaged migrants as they attempt to shape political outcomes in both Mexico and the United States; (2) how natives on both sides of the U.S.-Mexico border respond to the binational activism of the transnational political subject; and (3) the extent to which transnational political activism is reproduced over time, from one generation to the next.

The first of these contingencies depends on the changing institutional context of state policy incentives, political party agendas, and intergroup dynamics that will either promote or impede continuing cross-border mobility and binational political engagement. On the Mexican side of the border, we expect that most of the factors that have helped produce the binational subject will likely continue well into the future. State policy programs and discourses heralding migrants as heroes and encouraging their continuing integration into the political and economic development of Mexico are now well established. They have brought useful resources to Mexico from both migrants and the donor community. These resources are not likely to stem the tide of migration, which has deep cultural as well as economic roots. Yet state actors seeking legitimacy from political actors both inside and outside Mexico can represent them symbolically as constructive efforts to ameliorate the economic conditions that make migration a "necessity." On their part, migrant activists from several other Mexican states have gained enhanced status, legitimacy, and power in processes of state and local governance, similar to the Zacatecan case we have profiled here. Michoacán, for example, now also has a "migrant deputy" in its state legislature representing the PRD party (Shore 2005). This institutionalization of the migrant's place in local, state, and national electoral politics in Mexico can be expected to temper the impact there of political and cultural claims, based on an earlier "territorialized" image of the nation, that represent migrants as being "out of touch" with the needs and desires of "natives," due to their absence from the locality, state, and nation.

There is, however, a potential for a political backlash emanating from political forces in states, regions, and localities in Mexico that do not benefit from the transnational public-private partnerships that have become highly touted models of global development. As the model of HTA-led infrastructure development unevenly distributes benefits to localities with well-established HTAs, other localities, often with equally if not more pressing infrastructure needs and endemic poverty, are neglected. For example, at the local level, in the states of Zacatecas, Jalisco, and Michoacán, as Burgess (2005) has shown, the localities that have benefited from projects funded under the 3×1 program are on average larger, wealthier, and more urban than those that have no projects. Uneven development is thus a potential consequence of migrant-led development projects, even though this unevenness is not yet a reality because of the thus far limited developmental impact of the 3×1 program in the places it has been implemented. The likelihood that such a cleavage might eventually emerge and generate disruptive political conflict is also undermined by the very marginality of the neglected localities.

It must be recognized, of course, that even if the state policy context in Mexico is conducive to and continues to promote cross-border mobility and migrant transnational engagement, the institutional and state policy context in the United States also affects the long-term prospects for Mexican migrant political transnationalism on both sides of the border. As Wayne Cornelius (2001)has shown, the militarization of the U.S-Mexico border, ostensibly meant to limit illegal migration, has important unintended consequences. Most notably, because undocumented migrants now stay in the United States for longer periods of time because of the high costs and risks involved in recrossing the border, these policies have increased the "illegal" migrant population as newly arrived undocumented migrants are added to the large numbers already here. These policies clearly may have a dampening effect on the expansion of transnational engagement as undocumented migrants' ability to physically cross the border is limited, thus undermining their capacity to establish and nurture transnational connections.

Unless and until U.S. immigration policy establishes regularized pathways to citizenship for this large undocumented population, the conditions seem ripe for millions of Mexican migrants to remain undocumented and thus inactive citizens of either nation rather than active transnational citizens of both. This is because, as Guarnizo, Portes, and Haller have found, "it is not the least educated, more marginal, or more recent arrivals who are most prone to retain ties with their home country politics" (2003, 1229) and pursue transnational ties. Rather, transnational engagement, as our study has shown, is largely the domain of migrants who have established an economic foothold in the United States and acquired U.S. citizenship, critical factors enabling migrants to move freely across borders.

Public policies promoting the militarization of the two-thousand-mile-long border separating Mexico and the United States have symbolic as well as material effects. On their surface these policies constitute an unwelcoming context of reception and might thus be expected to discourage engagement in U.S. politics by transnational political subjects. But the very visibility and materiality of the gigantic border fence, the many deaths it has caused to undocumented migrants, and the blocked mobility that it symbolizes have also created an inviting target for mobilizing political protest by grassroots coalitions united around the plight of the undocumented. This is precisely what activist leaders in the FCZSC, such as Martha Jiménez and Guadalupe Rodríguez, have described to us—the construction of broad grassroots coalitions, uniting Mexican and Central American HTAs with U.S.-based Latino, multiethnic, and immigrants' rights organizations and engaging in street-level political resistance to these exclusionary and murderous policies.

Such coalitions are moving beyond reactive resistance to border militarization and toward a more proactive agenda promoting pathways to legalization, educational opportunity, and family reunification. For example,

HTAs in Chicago and Los Angeles were key to forming broad alliances with labor unions, church-based organizations, and other ethnic organizations during the historic wave of immigration protests and rallies that broke out in 2006. Under the banner of immigrant empowerment, the FCZSC recently obtained over ten thousand signatures from individual club members in greater Los Angeles supporting a bill in the California Assembly that would allow undocumented immigrant students access to higher education, in-state tuition, and financial aid (Ramakrishnan and Viramontes 2006, 115).

These new types of grassroots political engagement by transnational activists in U.S.-oriented political coalitions take place within the context of the hotly contested politics of immigration policy currently playing out at all levels of the U.S. government. The demands of the grassroots coalitions we identified above are hardly likely to persuade the more nativist sectors of this debate, such as the armed bands of Minutemen "patrolling" the border in California and Arizona, the followers of populist media personality Lou Dobbs, or the anti-immigrant activists in places such as Hazleton, Pennsylvania, and Escondido, California, who have enacted local legislation requiring landlords to verify the legal status of their tenants.

At the national level, leaders of the two major parties, eyeing the spectacular growth of the Latino community and its growing voting strength, might be more receptive to the demands of these coalitions. On the central question of legalization, the Republican Party is sharply divided and the Democratic Party, while generally supportive, must also respond to internal pressures to do something about "the illegal immigration problem." At the time of this writing, the Democratic Party has retaken control of both houses of Congress and is now in a position to take the lead in fashioning a legislative policy in response to the widespread clamor for "comprehensive immigration reform." The Democratic response is unlikely to be as draconian as last term's immigration bill passed by the Republican-dominated House of Representatives (HR 4437), which focused almost exclusively on border-control measures. While Democratic legislators are likely to propose legislation offering some pathways to legalization and citizenship, they confront the limited capacity of the U.S. political system to broker a solution to its broken immigration policy in the face of a sharply divided polity, now punctuated by the decreasing congressional clout of the Bush administration, which had previously proposed some pathways. In short, although there remains some hope for progress on this issue, in the absence of a clear-cut constituency or political will national immigration policy is more likely to remain broken than to produce the more inclusive solution favored by the transnational immigrants' rights coalition. If so, the blocked mobility experienced by the undocumented is likely to continue in the years ahead and remain a prime target for grassroots mobilization and protest by cross-border political coalitions.

Another way to assess the staying power of transnational political subjectivity is to move from the macro level of the policy and institutional context of the U.S. and Mexican states to the efforts within households, community-based networks, and migrant organizations to transmit and reproduce a sense of transnational identity and an orientation toward transnational political action. The literature on transnationalism and its future has framed the issue of staying power largely in terms of household transmission of transnationalism to the "second generation" (see, for example, Kasinitz et al. 2002). In our view, this way of framing the issue is too restrictive because it posits a radical separation between the public and private spheres as separate and autonomous containers of social life. In drawing attention only to the internal dynamics of "family life," it overlooks the way in which organizational and societal-level factors on both sides of the border interact with household dynamics in efforts to transmit transnational identities and ways of life (for this sort of opening up of the "second generation" concept, see Fouron and Glick Schiller 2002). There is clear evidence that leaders and members of hometown associations are trying to transmit a transnational orientation to their children through their organized roots-forming activities, such as dances, pageants, and *charreadas* (rodeos), and their philanthropic activities, such as educational scholarships and other awards to the children of HTA members, which valorize membership in HTAs (Orozco, González, and Díaz de Cossío 2000). These activities have borne some fruit, as more young people born in the United States are coming to take leadership roles in HTAs and federations across the United States (Moctezuma 2005).

Beyond the interaction of household and organizational factors reproducing patterns of belonging and participation in HTAs, we can expect that, more broadly, transnationalism will have staying power because migration and transnationalism are social, and not simply familial, processes. The economic and cultural contexts shaping both migration and transnationalism are likely to continue, prompting millions of individuals to migrate. We anticipate that many, but by no means all, of these future migrants will follow the pattern of today's migrants and become transnationally engaged. People migrate not as isolated units of consciousness but as members of extended families, sending communities, and receiving places that influence their understandings of what life is all about and where it can be lived. They are emplaced within a transnational social field situated between historically specific regions and localities where a transnational sensibility has taken hold. These situated subjects constitute a substantial pool of new recruits for producing and reproducing transnationalism as a way of life.

The Contingency of Migrant Political Transnationalism

Thinking through our extended case studies of transnational politics theoretically, we have drawn the conclusion that when acting political subjects are emplaced both "here" and "there" in transnational networks and projects, the identities they experience and the facets of selfhood they orchestrate depend considerably on the contingencies of time and circumstance. Identities and social actions predicated on those identities change over time, as human agents interpret timing and contingent circumstances differently in the multiple venues and political spaces in which they are capable of acting. Transnational migrants, like everyone else, occupy multiple social locations and are subject to the inner tensions and conflicts derived from their multipositionality. Their lived experience engenders capacities and repertoires for social practice in geographic and social locations that cross borders, but how they will act and when are products of historical contingency. The contingency of migrant political transnationalism has clear implications for democratic theory and practice. There is no uniform and inexorable process of reproduction or transformation of existing regimes of social inequality. The results of transnational political practice are always a complex combination of historical timing, contingency, and human agency.

In the face of ungrounded, if not essentialist, theoretical speculation on immigrant nonassimilation, such as that found in the writings of Huntington and Appadurai, a growing number of anthropological and sociological case studies of global migration have begun to document the political practices of dual citizens (Goldring 1998; R. Smith 1998; Guarnizo 1998; Levitt 2001b; Martínez Saldaña 2002; Moctezuma 2003b; Østergaard-Nielsen 2003b). Yet, ironically, because these studies have been concerned largely with the political (re)engagement of migrants with their sending states and societies, which we have called the first face of transnational citizenship, their very documentation of homeland, home-state, and hometown political engagement by migrants can be too readily (mis)read as providing additional grist for the mill of essentialist arguments predicting the absence or decline of affiliation by immigrants with their receiving nation-states and societies. For this reason we chose to address the discourse on dual loyalty and national identity formation by also focusing our analytical lens on the second face of transnational citizenship—migrant political practices in the receiving context.

All of our extended case studies, to a greater or lesser degree, underline the simultaneity of transnational political experience. Our findings regarding the second face of transnational citizenship stand in sharp contrast to essentialist views of national identity formation that view the nation-state as a kind of naturalized, tightly bounded, cultural container of citizen loyalty and political obligation. These findings demonstrate the limitations of Samuel Huntington's ideologically driven notion of socialization to the values of Anglo-Protestantism as essential to acquiring an "American" identity and to practicing U.S. citizenship. His understanding of how the world works is simply mistaken. His undifferentiated view of national identity formation abstracts the notion of citizenship from the actual contemporary practices of transnational citizens.

In similar fashion, the stories we have narrated stand in stark contrast to Arjun Appadurai's postnationalist expectations concerning the waning power of receiving states and societies in this age of cultural globalization. In all of our extended case studies the politically engaged migrants we profile express, to differing degrees, allegiance to both countries. This sort of dual loyalty is conditional as well as contingent. Rather than being doubly loyal to their nations of origin because of their embeddedness in transnational mediascapes, our Mexican migrant political activists are *doubly ambivalent* toward each nation and about the modes of political participation on both sides of the border in which they have chosen to engage. Our migrants live in real rather than "virtual" neighborhoods and, using both their imaginative and their material resources, they try to improve living conditions in both the real places they came from and those in which they currently live. Their practices underline their social connectedness and

Fig. 9. California march in defense of "the undocumented," San Francisco, 2006. Photo by Pat Smith.

multiple emplacement across borders rather than their emancipation from assimilative social structures.

Our rejection of both the nationalist and postnationalist essentialisms should not lead us to prematurely celebrate the rise of el migrante as a new social subject. As we have shown, both state-centered discourses on the heroic male migrant and migrant-centered discourses touting the virtues of the collective migrant that have legitimated new political spaces for migrant political participation are themselves based on essentialist readings of the migrant experience. These discourses ignore the very real social differences and political divides cutting through the social space of transnational migration and citizenship. The new social subject of el migrante is constructed, as we have shown, on the basis of exclusions, primarily in terms of gender and class. Accordingly, el migrante should not be regarded as a single unitary social actor.

Lest we conclude this book with a pessimistic message of continuing exclusions from emerging spaces of transnational citizenship and democracy, it is important that we return to our key themes of historical contingency and human agency in the formation of social subjectivity. Given the fluidity of both politics and identity formation, the inclusions and exclusions from transnational citizenship we have revealed in this book should not be viewed as etched in stone. What currently constitute competing social identities might instead be envisioned as elements capable of being brought together in more expansive political projects aimed at bringing to fruition alternative imaginaries that contest the hegemony of neoliberal ideology and practice as well as the traditional gender stratification that offer vast swaths of Mexican society few opportunities, making the harrowing trek "*hacia* El Norte" seem preferable to staying put. This is, of course, the central political dilemma of our time, finding the means and the issues to stitch together "chains of equivalence" across multiple differences and antagonisms and, thus, begin forming political coalitions capable of offering new, more radically democratic possibilities. On the U.S. side of the border, the practical possibility of such new configurations is exemplified by the political energy now being expressed by the broad cross-border coalition protesting border militarization and its human costs. It is our hope that the stories and analyses of "actually existing" migrant political transnationalism contained in this book can further contribute to these urgent political tasks.

Appendix

Transnational Ethnography

Methods, Fieldwork, and Subjects

In writing this book we have sought to develop a research methodology that we have termed transnational ethnography. This is an approach to qualitative research that is, in many ways, still a work in progress, evolving to keep pace with the lives of our transnational subjects. We have made this move in an effort to apprehend the changes wrought by processes of globalization over the past three decades that have disrupted any neat correspondence between place and culture. Although traditional ethnography had been a place-based project, focusing attention on one place over time to map the character of "local culture," places have now become less self-contained and more intertwined with other places across the globe. As a result, social relations themselves have become more spatially distanced. The practices of social, economic, and political actors and their networks have forged ever more precise and efficacious translocal connections. The steps we have taken to keep up with these developments have required us to travel to and conduct fieldwork in multiple interconnected places spanning the U.S.-Mexican border. In so doing, we have built on the work of scholars (Marcus and Fischer 1986 [1999]; Burawoy 1991; Hannerz 1998; Burawoy et al. 2000; M. P. Smith 2001, 2005c) who have recognized the need to reterritorialize ethnography to deal with these changing conditions.

Methods

To begin our respatialization of ethnographic practice we decided to further develop a multisited research imaginary first articulated by George Marcus and Michael Fischer (1986). Their strain of ethnographic practice, termed "anthropology as cultural critique," sought to refocus ethnographic inquiry amid rapid global sociocultural and political-economic transformations on what they called the *power-domination-accommodation-resistance* motif. This motif situated the constitution of subjectivity and identity within the fluctuating context of once-taken-for-granted sociospatial boundaries. It provided an intelligible starting point for understanding the complex dynamics by which new subject positions could be seen to emerge in and through, for and against presumably "global" driving forces. Marcus and Fischer stressed the emergence of diverse modes of "local" accommodation or resistance to "global conditions" as a strategy for mapping cultural changes "from below" in a world that seemed to some to be an increasingly homogenized expression of global modernity "from above." This work advanced the study of the hybrid identities emerging from new forms of intercultural contact and communication brought about by global migration but did not shed light on the connections among people and places being enacted by transnational actors, networks, and institutions.

Two decades have now passed since Marcus and Fischer first issued their call for anthropology as cultural critique. Since then, the fieldwork of Michael Burawoy and his collaborators (2000), practicing what they call "global ethnography," has added much to our understanding of the dynamics of these transnational interconnections and provided a sound justification for the sort of extended case studies, relying on ethnography and participant observation in multiple interconnected field sites, that we have reported on in this book. Our research approach also has benefited from our exposure to a substantial body of richly textured ethnographic case studies in migration studies that have focused specifically on transnational migration and the networks and the practices that sustain it. This work, reviewed at the outset of our book, has been uniquely sensitive to the contexts in which transnational migrant networks, practices, and identities have emerged and, thus, underlines the importance of contextualizing transnational ethnographic storytelling.

In this book we have combined our transnational ethnographic research imaginary with a historicized contextual approach to political-economic and social relations. Framing our interviews within the historical, political-economic, sociocultural, and institutional contexts specified in the first two chapters of our book, we have asked our Mexican migrant subjects to construct their understanding of the opportunities and constraints they face in the world(s) in which they live. We then have asked our subjects to talk about the ways in which they appropriate, accommodate to, or resist the forms of power and domination, opportunity and constraint that they experience as they traverse political and cultural borders.

Through this recombinant method of social inquiry we have sought to make sense of the power relations and meaning-making practices of our ethnographic subjects. We have found that the social spaces through which the subjects we have interviewed move and within which they operate to give meaning to "home" are indeed increasingly multilocal and also multiscaled, thus making transnational ethnography and carefully historicized political-economic and social research both necessary and possible. Through this fusion of heretofore distinct, and at times opposed, approaches to social science research we have sought to place the discourses and practices that constitute migrant transnationalism at the very center of social theory and research.

Fieldwork

Our fieldwork was conducted in multiple locales where transnational connections have been forged linking migrants and their social networks to places of power and meaningful social action in California and in the Mexican states of Guanajuato and Zacatecas. Research on the transnational connections linking Guanajuato and California was conducted between 2000 and 2003. Our case studies of transnational connections linking Zacatecas and California were carried out in multiple phases between 2001 and 2005. Consistent with the transnational ethnographic nature of our fieldwork, interviews and extended conversations for each of our extended case studies were conducted in English, Spanish, and, at times, bilingually with key informants whose lives are at the center of our stories. The field research for our cases linking Napa and Los Angeles to places of power and meaning in Guanajuato and Zacatecas, respectively, were funded by grants from UC MEXUS.

Our first extended case study of the Napa–El Timbinal translocality brought us to field sites in the cities of Napa, Calistoga, and San Jose, California, as well as to the village of El Timbinal, Guanajuato, and to Guanajuato, the capital city of the state of Guanajuato. The research was conducted in three stages. An initial round of qualitative field interviews with Ángel Calderón and his compatriots in Napa, California, that form the core of the case study were jointly conducted by Michael Peter Smith and postgraduate researcher Gustavo Galindo in 2000–2001. This stage of the research also included a field trip to San Jose, California, for informal interviewing of Guanajuato's political elites and wider participant-observation research, including conversations with migrants and their families during a two-day *convivio* and inauguration ceremony for five new Casas Guanajuato presidents from northern California, including the Napa president, Ángel Calderón. During the second stage of this research, in spring 2001, Smith and Galindo conducted field research in two principal field sites in Guanajuato: (1) the capital city of the state, Guanajuato, where they interviewed political elites and policymakers from the Partido Acción Nacional (PAN, National Action Party) who dominated Guanajuato's state government and (2) the migrants' natal village of El Timbinal, where the field researchers conducted an extended interview with the male manager of the migrant-financed textile maquiladora and had conversations with a small group of female factory workers and with other community residents, while Patricia Smith photographed and videotaped the surroundings. In the third stage, over the course of the next two years, Smith conducted several follow-up interviews with Calderón at his workplace, a migrant labor camp in Calistoga, California. The level of formality of these interviews ranged from informal conversations to tape-recorded and transcribed ethnographies with Calderón to the videotaping of a meeting he had with visiting officials from the Guanajuato state government. Research consultations also took place with Mexican researchers and a collaborator at the Centro de Investigaciones sobre América del Norte (CISAN, Center for North American Studies) at the Universidad Nacional Autónoma de México (UNAM, National Autonomous University of Mexico) in Mexico City.

Our research for our second extended case study, on the transnational electoral politics of the Tomato King, was conducted at multiple sites in both countries over an extended period from 2002 to 2005. We began in California with a serious of tape-recorded interviews with Andrés Bermúdez in Davis, near his home and business in Winters. These initial ethnographic encounters were carried out in the aftermath of Bermúdez's disqualification from the office of mayor of Jerez in 2001 and before he had decided to run a second time. Our initial interviews with Bermúdez were subsequently enriched by extensive informal conversations and participant observation during a round-trip journey made by Bermúdez and Matt Bakker to a conference on extraterritorial voting rights at the University of Southern California in Los Angeles in 2003.

Several research trips were then made to Jerez, Zacatecas, and its surrounding villages, in 2002, 2004, and 2005, where we engaged in participant observation and conducted tape-recorded interviews with local residents, Bermúdez and his collaborators, and other local political elites. In the summer of 2002, Bakker traveled to Jerez where he spent several weeks conducting research on local interpretations of the Tomato King phenomenon. During this period of field research, Bakker interviewed local political elites, including Bermúdez's rival mayoral candidates from the other two major political parties, the Partido Revolucionario Institucional (PRI, Revolutionary Institutional Party) and the PAN, as well as the mayor and other local elected officials. These elite interviews were supplemented by formal interviews and informal conversations carried out with a wide range of grassroots supporters and opponents of the Tomato King. In addition, Bakker engaged in participant observation at several bermudista movement protest events.

Two years later, during the final weeks of Bermúdez's second run for office in 2004, both authors traveled to Jerez, where we attended campaign events, had conversations with Bermúdez and his supporters, and observed the campaign at the grassroots level. In the final days leading up to this second election a number of additional interviews were conducted with Bermúdez. Given the constraints on Bermúdez's time at the end of the campaign, tape-recorded group interviews were conducted with him by Bakker and members of the Mexican and U.S. press. Bakker also accompanied Bermúdez's campaign staff in their final preparations. In the course of this participant observation, Bakker conducted additional interviews with Bermúdez's campaign coordinator and with the president of the PAN at the municipal level. In the summer of 2005, as the Tomato King was finishing his first year in office, Bakker returned to Jerez and conducted additional interviews with Bermúdez and his principal adviser.

For our other three extended case studies, on the transnational connections being forged between Zacatecas and southern California, we conducted field research on the transnational politics of the leaders of the Federación de Clubes Zacatecanos del Sur de California (FCZSC, Zacatecan Federation of Hometown Associations of Southern California) in various localities in Greater Los Angeles and in Zacatecas in 2003–5. Tape-recorded interviews were conducted with key leaders of the Federation and its spin-off organizations, such as the Frente Cívico Zacatecano (FCZ, Zacatecan Civic Front) and Zacatecanos PRImero, in the cities of Los Angeles, Norwalk, Hawaiian Gardens, Long Beach, and Wilmington, California. This phase of our research also entailed participant observation in November 2003 at the National Convention of Zacatecan Organizations in the United States, held in Los Angeles and Montebello, California, and hosted by the FCZSC. This convention included a business meeting, a conference, and the Federation's yearly banquet crowning its Señorita Zacatecas. During that trip we observed the migrants leaders' interaction with top Zacatecan and Mexican political elites such as Governor Ricardo Monreal; Sergio Soto, the director of the federal 3×1 program; and various municipal presidents. We also participated in formal discussions at conference workshops and had sustained informal conversations with Federation leaders, individual HTA leaders, and migration scholars from both Mexico and the United States who were guests at the various events.

In 2004 we traveled to Zacatecas to deepen our understanding of the transnational politics both *of* and *in* the Federation. We went to the state capital of Zacatecas, where we had lengthy conversations with key public intellectuals from the University of Zacatecas, who have extensively studied migrant political transnationalism in Zacatecas and have been active participants in passage of the Ley Migrante, the transnational bermudista coalition, and the conceptual development of the "collective migrant" as a new social actor in transnational politics. We interviewed public officials on state policies toward migrants and the move toward HTA-driven "productive projects." We also conducted a detailed ethnographic interview with a former FCZSC president just days before he was to be elected as one of the first two "migrant deputies" in the Zacatecas state legislature.

To contextualize our ethnographic material, we gathered a substantial body of documentary data on the historical emergence of public policies in Mexico, Guanajuato, and Zacatecas designed to politically reincorporate migrants into the "global Mexican nation" and reorient their loyalties and identities so that they would contribute to a variety of development projects promoted by Mexican state agencies and the global donor community. Some of the public officials we interviewed provided us with useful documentary materials. Additional materials were gathered from other U.S. and Mexican sources. In Mexico, these sources included the Instituto Nacional de Estadística, Geografía e Informática (INEGI, National Institute of Geography, Statistics and Information), the Coordinadora de Fomento al Comercio Exterior del Estado de Guanajuato (COFOCE, Guanajuato International Trade Commission), the archival resources of the CISAN, the legal decisions of the Mexico's highest electoral court (Tribunal Electoral del Poder Judicial de la Federación, TRIFE), and campaign documents from the Tomato King. In the United States, we gathered documents from key governmental, quasi-governmental, and nongovernmental organizations, such as the U.S. Census Bureau, the Inter-American Development Bank (IADB), the Mexican American Legal Defense and Education Fund (MALDEF), the Pew Hispanic Center, and the Rockefeller Foundation, among others. We also drew on other materials documenting transnational interconnectivity, such as the magazines *Bi-nacional* and *Pa'l Norte* and the materials of the right-to-vote organization, Coalición para los Derechos Políticos de los Mexicanos en el Exterior. Finally, we conducted a comprehensive review of Mexican and U.S. press accounts of the transnational connections being forged by Mexican migrants across the international divide.

The Subjects

The Case of the Napa–El Timbinal Translocality

KEY INFORMANTS

Ángel Calderón, the protagonist of this extended case study, is president of the Casa Guanajuato Club in Napa, California, and has been a leading investor in the migrant-financed maquiladora in El Timbinal under the Mi Comunidad program. In 2000, Calderón, who had previously been a chef at the Silverado Country Club, became manager at the Calistoga Farmworker Center, a migrant labor camp in Calistoga run by the California Human Development Corporation (CHDC), a multi-county social services NGO focusing on the economic advancement of Latinos in California. Calderón has participated in this community development corporation's Jane Ruiz Leadership Training Seminar as a pathway to his engagement in civic and community life in Napa.

Juan Manuel Oliva Ramírez was interviewed twice in 2001, in San Jose, California, and in Guanajuato, Guanajuato, when he served as secretary of state to Juan Carlos Romero Hicks, then governor of Guanajuato. At the time, Oliva was also a PAN senator in the federal legislature. In the July 2006 elections, Oliva was elected governor of Guanajuato.

Ramón Flores was executive director of the Mi Comunidad program at the time of the study. In 2001 he was twice formally interviewed in his office in the capital city of Guanajuato and once informally en route by van to El Timbinal and back. He also was videotaped in Calistoga, California, during a meeting held with Ángel Calderón and Susana Guerra, the successor to Lupita Zamora in June 2002.

OTHER PUBLIC OFFICIALS AND POLITICAL ELITES

Genaro Borrego Estrada, former PRI governor of the state of Zacatecas and current PRI senator in the Mexican Senate. Borrego was interviewed for us in Mexico City in January 2001 by Remedios Gómez Arnau of CISAN.

Guadalupe (Lupita) Zamora Alatorre, general director of the Dirección de Atención a Comunidades Guanajuatenses en el Extranjero (DACGE, Program Attending to Guanajuatense Communities Abroad) and director of the Casa Guanajuato program, meeting conversations in 2001 at San Jose *reunión*.

Susana Guerra, general director of the DACGE in 2002, tape-recorded meeting conversations in Calistoga, California.

Aurora Ramírez Maldonado, assistant director of the Distribution Network for the Centro Interuniversitario del Conocimiento (CIC), a national knowledge network, employment training, and educational certification institution that initially trained maquiladora workers and managers. We conducted a tape-recorded group interview in Guanajuato with her and other CIC staff members involved in training programs.

Staff Assistant to Ramón Flores, executive director of the Mi Comunidad program, informal conversations while traveling between Guanajuato and El Timbinal.

OTHER MIGRANT MAQUILADORA INVESTORS INTERVIEWED

Chavela, restaurant manager and migrant investor.

Martín, heavy equipment welder and migrant investor.

Salvador, welding specialist and migrant investor.

Serafín, winery worker and migrant investor.

Medardo, landscape business owner and migrant investor.

INTERVIEWS IN EL TIMBINAL

Salvador, plant manager, maquiladora factory.

Josephine, maquiladora production worker.

Teresa, maquiladora production worker.

José, general store owner, El Timbinal.

Alejandra, director of El Timbinal Women's Medical Clinic.

OTHER INTERVIEWS AND INFORMAL CONVERSATIONS

Hugo Juárez Carillo, cónsul alterno, Mexican consulate in San Jose, conversation at Casas Guanajuato *reunión*, San Jose.

Sergio E. Casanueva Reguart, Mexican consul, conversation at Casas Guanajuato *reunión*, San Jose.

Sandra L. Nichols, Department of Geography, University of California, Berkeley, interviewed in 2000 in Berkeley, California.

Al Sanchez, president of the Casa Guanajuato Club of San Jose, conversation at the Casa Guanajuato *reunión*, San Jose.

The Case of the Tomato King

KEY INFORMANTS

Andrés Bermúdez Viramontes, the protagonist of this extended case study, migrated to the United States in the trunk of a car in 1974 and eventually became an agricultural grower and farm labor contractor in Winters, California. In 2001, parlaying the social and political capital he had acquired as a "successful" migrant, Bermúdez returned to his natal community of Jerez, Zacatecas, to compete in local mayoral elections under the moniker the "Tomato King." Twice victorious in the mayoral elections in Jerez (in 2001 and 2004), he is now a federal deputy in the Mexican Congress, affiliated with the PAN. Bermúdez was interviewed on numerous occasions between 2002 and 2005 in both California and Zacatecas.

Raymundo Carrillo Ramírez is a local political activist in Jerez and Bermúdez's principal adviser since the Tomato King's first mayoral campaign. He now serves as technical secretary for the Comisión de Población, Fronteras y Asuntos Migratorios in the lower house of the Mexican Congress.

OTHER PUBLIC OFFICIALS AND POLITICAL ELITES

Alma Ávila, PRI candidate for *presidente municipal* in 2001 elections in Jerez, Zacatecas.

Ernesto Escobedo, PAN candidate for *presidente municipal* in 2001 elections in Jerez, Zacatecas.

Rafael Hurtado, PRI *regidor* (municipal representative), Jerez, Zacatecas.

Miguel Moctezuma Longoria, professor at the Universidad Autónoma de Zacatecas (UAZ, Autonomous University of Zacatecas) and Bermúdez adviser.

Pablo Rodríguez, PAN party president, Jerez, Zacatecas.

Ismael Solís Mares, *presidente municipal* from 2001 to 2004, Jerez, Zacatecas.

Ricardo Santoya, administrator of "Jerez: Cuidad Virtual" website, Jerez, Zacatecas.

LOCAL RESIDENTS

Alberto, Bermúdez supporter from El Cargadero, Jerez, Zacatecas.

Enrique, transnational migrant and PAN militant, Jerez, Zacatecas.

Jesús, transnational migrant and PRI militant, Jerez, Zacatecas.

Bermúdez supporters at the Casa de Asistencia Bermudista, Jerez, Zacatecas.

Bermúdez supporters following Primer Informe de Gobierno de Ismael Solís, Jerez, Zacatecas.

Anacleto, return migrant and Partido de la Revolución Democrática (PRD, Party of the Democratic Revolution) militant, Ermita de Guadalupe, Zacatecas.

Federico, chile producer and Bermúdez supporter, Jerez, Zacatecas.

Benjamín, PRI militant, Jerez, Zacatecas.

Francisco, reporter and theater director, Jerez, Zacatecas.

Salvador, physician and bermudista militant, Jerez, Zacatecas.

María, small business owner and Bermúdez supporter, Jerez, Zacatecas.

Ramiro, Bermúdez supporter, Los Haro, Jerez, Zacatecas.

Alejandro, migrant Bermúdez supporter, Jerez, Zacatecas.

The Cases of the Transnational Politics of the Zacatecan Federation

KEY INFORMANTS

Manuel de la Cruz was a founding member of the Frente Cívico Zacatecano and president of the FCZSC from 1992 to 1995. He is former "official representative" of the government of the state of Zacatecas in the United States. Currently, de la Cruz is a "migrant deputy" of the PRD in the Zacatecan state legislature (2004–7).

Guadalupe Gómez is the owner of an accounting and tax preparation business in Santa Ana, California. He was a founding member of the Frente Cívico Zacatecano and president of the Southern California Federation of Zacatecan Hometown Associations (FCZSC) from 2001 to 2003.

Efraín Jiménez is the co-owner of an auto repair business. At the time of our interview, he was projects secretary for the FCZSC, in charge of coordinating the submission and approval of member clubs' social infrastructure and productive investment projects under the 3×1 program. He was also the Federation's director of philanthropy, in charge of coordinating a Rockefeller Foundation grant promoting capacity building and productive investment for Federation leadership.

Martha Jiménez is a neighborhood activist and political organizer in Los Angeles. She was a founding member and president of the HTA: Club Fraternidad Las Ánimas. At the time of our interview she was public relations officer of the FCZSC and coordinator of an HTA leadership program run by MALDEF.

OTHER INTERVIEW SUBJECTS

Robert Barker, director of projects, Secretariat of Economic Development, state of Zacatecas, and director of the Invierte en Zacatecas program.

Felipe Cabral, a commercial and residential real estate broker and notary public in Hawaiian Gardens and president of the FCZSC from 2003 to 2006.

Rigoberto Castañeda, restaurant owner in Wilmington, California, and president of the FCZSC from 1996 to 1998.

Felipe Delgado, owner of a furniture manufacturing business in Los Angeles and a founding member of the Frente Cívico Zacatecano. As a loyalista member of the FCZ, at the time of our interview he served as the "official representative" of the government of the state of Zacatecas in the United States.

Raúl Delgado Wise, director of the graduate program in development studies at the Universidad Autónoma de Zacatecas.

Rodolfo García Zamora, professor at the Universidad Autónoma de Zacatecas.

Erika González, former Señorita Zacatecas and president of the breakaway Orange County Federation of Zacatecan Hometown Associations.

Francisco Javier González, president of the Frente Cívico Zacatecano.

Miguel Moctezuma Longoria, professor at the Universidad Autónoma de Zacatecas.

Guadalupe Rodríguez, first vice president of the FCZSC from 2001 to 2003 and liaison to political and immigrant organizations in the United States.

Irineo Saldívar, project coordinator for the FCZSC in Zacatecas.

References

Alarcón, Rafael. 1988. "El proceso de 'norteñización': Impacto de la migración internacional en Chavinda, Michoacán." In *Movimientos de población en el occidente de México*, edited by T. Calvo and G. López, 337–57. Mexico City: Centre d'Études Mexicaines et Centraméricaines and El Colegio de Michoacán.

——. 1995. "Transnational Communities, Regional Development, and the Future of Mexican Immigration." *Berkeley Planning Journal* 10: 36–54.

Alba, Richard, and Victor Nee. 2003. *Remaking the American Mainstream: Assimilation and Contemporary Migration*. Cambridge: Harvard University Press.

Anderson, Benedict. 1983. *Imagined Communities: Reflections on the Origin and Spread of Nationalism*. New York: Verso.

——. 1994. "Exodus." *Critical Inquiry* 20, no. 2: 314–27.

——. 1998. *The Spectre of Comparisons: Nationalism, Southeast Asia, and the World*. New York: Verso.

Appadurai, Arjun. 1990. "Disjuncture and Difference in the Global Cultural Economy." *Public Culture* 2, no. 2: 1–24.

——. 1991. "Global Ethnoscapes: Notes and Queries for a Transnational Anthropology." In *Reconfiguring Anthropology: Working in the Present*, edited by R. G. Fox, 191–210. Santa Fe, N.M.: School of American Research Press.

——. 1996. *Modernity at Large: Cultural Dimensions of Globalization*. Minneapolis: University of Minnesota Press.

Ayón, David R. 2005. "Mexican Policy and Émigré Communities in the U.S." Background paper presented at the conference "Mexican Migrant Social and Civic Participation in the United States," Woodrow Wilson International Center for Scholars, Washington, D.C., November 4–5.

Bada, Xochitl. 2003. *Mexican Hometown Associations*. Albuquerque: Inter-Hemispheric Resource Center. Available at http://www.irc-online.org/content/1696.

Badillo Moreno, Gonzalo, ed. 2004. *La puerta que llama: El voto de los mexicanos en el extranjero*. Mexico City: Senado de la República.

Bakker, Matt, and Michael Peter Smith. 2003. "El Rey del Tomate: Migrant Political Transnationalism and Democratization in Mexico." *Migraciones Internacionales* 2, no. 1: 59–83.

Banco de México. 2005. "Remittances and Development: The Case of Mexico." Paper presented at "International Forum on Remittances," Washington, D.C., June 28–30.

———. 2007. "Remesas familiares." Available at http://www.banxico.org.mx/SieInternet/consultarDirectorioInternetAction.do?accion=consultarCuadroAnalitico&idCuadro=CA11&sector=1&locale=es.

Basch, Linda, Nina Glick Schiller, and Cristina Szanton Blanc. 1994. *Nations Unbound: Transnational Projects, Postcolonial Predicaments, and Deterritorialized Nation-States.* Langhorne, Penn.: Gordon and Breach.

Becerra, Rebecca. 2001. "El Rey del Tomate acudirá a la ONU." *El Sol de Zacatecas*, September 11.

Binford, Leigh. 2003. "Migrant Remittances and (Under)Development in Mexico." *Critique of Anthropology* 23, no. 3: 305–36.

Block, Fred. 2005. "Introduction to Contradictions of Capitalism as a World System." In *Enriching the Sociological Imagination: How Radical Sociology Changed the Discipline*, edited by R. F. Levine, 283–90. Boulder: Paradigm Publishers.

Bob, Clifford. 2005. *The Marketing of Rebellion: Insurgents, Media, and International Activism.* New York: Cambridge University Press.

Brysk, Alison. 1996. "Turning Weakness into Strength: The Internationalization of Indian Rights." *Latin American Perspectives* 23, no. 2: 38–57.

Burawoy, Michael. 1991. "The Extended Case Method." In *Ethnography Unbound*, edited by M. Burawoy et al., 271–87. Berkeley: University of California Press.

Burawoy, Michael, Joseph A. Blum, Sheba George, Zsuzsa Gille, Teresa Gowan, Lynne Haney, Maren Klawiter, Steve H. Lopez, Seán Ó Riain, and Millie Thayer, eds. 2000. *Global Ethnography: Forces, Connections, and Imaginations in a Postmodern World.* Berkeley: University of California Press.

Burgess, Katrina. 2005. "Migrant Philanthropy and Local Government." In New Patterns for Mexico, edited by B. J. Merz, 99–123. Cambridge, Mass.: Harvard University Press.

Byrnes, Dolores M. 2003. *Driving the State: Families and Public Policy in Central Mexico.* Ithaca: Cornell University Press.

Caglar, Ayse. 2006. "Hometown Associations, the Rescaling of State Spatiality, and Migrant Grassroots Transnationalism." *Global Networks* 6, no. 1: 1–22.

Calderón Chelius, Leticia. 2003. *Votar en la distancia: La extensión de los derechos políticos a migrantes, experiencias comparadas.* Mexico City: Instituto de Investigaciones Dr. José María Luis Mora.

Canales, Alejandro I. 2003. "Mexican Labour Migration to the United States in the Age of Globalisation." *Journal of Ethnic and Migration Studies* 29, no. 4: 741–62.

Cano, Gustavo. 2004. "Urban and Transnational Politics in America: Novus Ordo Seclorum?" *Center for U.S.-Mexican Studies Paper Series.* Available at http://repositories.cdlib.org/usmex/cano_gustavo.

Cano, Gustavo, and Alexandra Délano. 2004. "The Institute of Mexicans Abroad: The Day After . . . after 156 Years." *Center for U.S.-Mexican Studies Paper Series.* Available at http://repositories.cdlib.org/usmex/cano_delano.

Carpizo, Jorge, and Diego Valadés. 1998. *El voto de los mexicanos en el extranjero*. Mexico City: Instituto de Investigaciones Jurídicas, Universidad Nacional Autónoma de México.

Castells, Manuel. 1997. *The Power of Identity*. Malden, Mass.: Blackwell.

Castles, Stephen, and Mark J. Miller. 2003. *The Age of Migration*. 3rd ed. Basingstoke: Palgrave Macmillan.

Cenzatti, Marco. 1992. "From Dualism to Territorial Problematic in Italy: A Restructuring of Industry and Theory." In *After Modernism: Global Restructuring and the Changing Boundaries of City Life*, edited by M. P. Smith, 181–217. New Brunswick, N.J.: Transaction Publishers.

Chacón, Manuel. 2005. "Zacatecas: Puente para indocumentados." *Zacatecas Hoy*. July 22. Available at http://www.zacatecashoy.com/delta/modules/news/article.php?storyid=1558.

Coalición por los Derechos Políticos de los Mexicanos en el Exterior. 2004. "Propuesta ciudadana de iniciativa de ley que reforma diversos artículos y adiciona un libro noveno al Código Federal de Instituciones y Procedimientos Electorales." In *El voto de los mexicanos en el exterior*, edited by G. B. Moreno, 343–68. Michoacán, Mexico: Gobierno del Estado de Michoacán, Coordinación General para la Atención del Migrante Michoacano.

Cohen, Jeffrey, Richard Jones, and Dennis Conway. 2005. "Why Remittances Shouldn't Be Blamed for Rural Underdevelopment in Mexico: A Collective Response to Leigh Binford." *Critique of Anthropology* 25, no. 1: 87–96.

Cohen, Robin, and Shirin M. Rai, eds. 2000. *Global Social Movements*. New Brunswick, N.J.: Athlone Press.

Comisión Estatal de Apoyo Integral a los Migrantes y sus Familias. 2005. "Programa especial de migración 2005–2006." Available at http://www.guanajuato.gob.mx/migrantes/programa/Prog-Migracion%202005-Ver.030205.pdf.

Connolly, William E. 1969. *The Bias of Pluralism*. New York: Atherton Press.

Consejo Estatal de Poblacion Guanajuato (COESPO). 2001. "Propuesta de política de población para atender el fenómento migratorio de Guanajuato." Guanajuato, Guanajuato.

Consejo Nacional de Población (CONAPO). 2006. "44 de cada 100 mexicanos residentes en EEUU son mujeres." Press release 39/06, September 5. Available at http://www.conapo.gob.mx/prensa/2006/392006bol.pdf.

Cornelius, Wayne. 1990. *Labor Migration to the United States: Development Outcomes and Alternatives in Mexican Sending Communities*. Washington, D.C.: Commission for the Study of International Migration and Cooperative Economic Development.

———. 2001. "Death at the Border: Efficacy and Unintended Consequences of U.S. Immigration Control Policy." *Population and Development Review* 27, no. 4: 661–85.

De Genova, Nicholas. 2002. "Migrant 'Illegality' and Deportability in Everyday Life." *Annual Review of Anthropology* 31: 419–47.

Delgado Wise, Raúl, Humberto Márquez Covarrubias, and Héctor Rodríguez Ramírez. 2004. "Organizaciones transnacionales de migrantes y desarrollo regional en Zacatecas." *Migraciones Internacionales* 2, no. 4: 159–182.

DeSipio, Louis. 2006. "Transnational Politics and Civic Engagement: Do Home-Country Political Ties Limit Latino Immigrant Pursuit of U.S. Civic Engagement and

Citizenship." In *Transforming Politics, Transforming America: The Political and Civic Incorporation of Immigrants in the United States*, edited by T. Lee, S. K. Ramakrishnan, and R. Ramírez. Charlottesville: University of Virginia Press.

DeSipio, Louis, Harry Pachon, Rodolfo O. De la Garza, and Jongho Lee. 2003. *Immigrant Politics at Home and Abroad: How Latino Immigrants Engage the Politics of Their Home Communities and the United States*. Claremont, Calif.: Tomás Rivera Policy Institute.

Diamond, Larry. 2000. "What the Democratization of Mexico Means for All the World." *Hoover Digest* 4. Available at http://www.hoover.org/publications/digest/3493556.html.

Díaz de Cossío, Roger, Graciela Orozco, and Esther González. 1997. *Los mexicanos en Estados Unidos*. Mexico City: Sistemas Técnicos de Edición.

Dolhinow, Rebecca. 2005. "Caught in the Middle: The State, NGOs, and the Limits to Grassroots Organizing along the US-Mexico Border." *Antipode* 37, no. 3: 558–80.

Drainville, Andre C. 1998. "The Fetishism of Global Civil Society: Global Governance, Transnational Urbanism, and Sustainable Capitalism in the World Economy." In *Transnationalism from Below*, edited by M. P. Smith and L. E. Guarnizo, 35–63. New Brunswick, N.J.: Transaction.

Dresser, Denise. 1991. *Neopopulist Solutions to Neoliberal Problems: Mexico's National Solidarity Program*. La Jolla: Center for U.S.-Mexican Studies, University of California, San Diego.

Durán, Agustín. 2005. "Piden su credencial en Tijuana." *La Opinión*, December 11, 1A.

Durand, Jorge. 1994. *Más allá de la línea*. Mexico City: Consejo Nacional para la Cultura y las Artes.

Eckstein, Susan. 2001. "Epilogue: Where Have All the Movements Gone? Latin American Social Movements at the New Millennium." In *Power and Popular Protest: Latin American Social Movements*, edited by S. Eckstein, 351–406. Berkeley: University of California Press.

Edelman, Marc. 2000. *Peasants against Globalization: Rural Social Movements in Costa Rica*. Stanford: Stanford University Press.

Escala Rabadán, Luis. 2005. "Derechos humanos y asociaciones de migrantes mexicanos en California." *Migraciones Internacionales* 9: 84–107.

Escobar, Arturo. 1995. *Encountering Development: The Making and Unmaking of the Third World*. Princeton: Princeton University Press.

Esteva, Gustavo, and Madhu S. Prakash. 1998. *Grassroots Postmodernism: Remaking the Soil of Cultures*. London: Zed Books.

Evans, Peter. 2000. "Fighting Marginalization with Transnational Networks: Counter-Hegemonic Globalization." *Contemporary Sociology* 29, no. 1: 230–41.

Falk, Richard. 1999. *Predatory Globalization: A Critique*. Malden, Mass.: Blackwell.

Faret, Laurent. 2004. "Implicarse aquí, con la mirada hacia allá: la organización comunitaria de los Guanajuatenses en los Estados Unidos." In *Clubes de Migrantes Oriundos Mexicanos en los Estados Unidos*, edited by G. Lanly and B. Valenzuela, 225–52. Guadalajara, Mexico: Universidad de Guadalajara.

Ferguson, James. 1990. *The Anti-Politics Machine: Development, Depoliticization, and Bureaucratic Power in Lesotho*. New York: Cambridge University Press.

Fitzgerald, David. 2000. *Negotiating Extra-Territorial Citizenship: Mexican Migration and the Transnational Politics of Community*. La Jolla: Center for Comparative Immigration Studies, University of California, San Diego.

———. 2005. "A Nation of Emigrants? Statecraft, Church-Building, and Nationalism in Mexican Migrant Source Communities." PhD diss., University of California, Los Angeles.

———. 2006. "Inside the Sending State: The Politics of Mexican Emigration Control." *International Migration Review* 40, no. 2: 259–93.

Flores, Juan. 2005. "The Diaspora Strikes Back: Reflections on Cultural Remittances." *NACLA Report on the Americas* 39, no. 3: 21–26.

Fonte, John. 2005. Paper presented at the conference "Dual Allegiance and the Politics of Immigration Reform," Hudson Institute, Washington, D.C., November 30.

Foucault, Michel. 1991. "Governmentality." In *The Foucault Effect: Studies in Governmentality*, edited by G. Burchell, C. Gordon, and P. Miller, 87–104. London: Harvester Wheatsheaf.

Fouron, Georges E., and Nina Glick Schiller. 2002. "The Generation of Identity: Redefining the Second Generation within a Transnational Social Field." In *The Changing Face of Home: The Transnational Lives of the Second Generation*, edited by P. Levitt and M. C. Waters, 168–208. New York: Russell Sage Foundation Press.

Fox, Jonathan. 2003. "Lessons from Mexico-US Civil Society Coalitions." In *Cross-Border Dialogues: Mexico-US Social Movement Networking*, edited by D. Brooks and J. Fox, 341–418. La Jolla: Center for US-Mexican Studies University of California, San Diego.

Fox, Vicente. 2000. "Discurso en la cena anual de MALDEF." Available at http://www.vicentefox.org.mx/noticias160.htm.

Frente Cívico Zacatecano. 2003. "Ley Migrante." Press release, January 2.

García-Acevedo, María Rosa. 2003. "Politics across Borders: Mexico's Policies toward Mexicans in the United States." *Journal of the Southwest* 45: 533–55.

García y Griego, Larry Manuel. 1988. "The Bracero Policy Experiment: U.S.-Mexican Responses to Mexican Labor Migration, 1942–1955." PhD diss., University of California, Los Angeles.

García Zamora, Rodolfo. 2002. "Los proyectos productivos de migrantes en Mexico hoy." Paper presented at "Second Colloquium on International Migration: Mexico-California," University of California, Berkeley, March 28–30.

———. 2003. "Migración internacional, remesas e impacos regionales." In *Migración, remesas y desarrollo local*, edited by R. G. Zamora, 13–34. Zacatecas, Mexico: Doctorado en Estudios del Desarrollo, Universidad Autónoma de Zacatecas.

Geertz, Clifford. 1983. *Local Knowledge: Further Essays in Interpretive Anthropology*. New York: Basic Books.

Geyer, Georgie Anne. 2005. "Few Mexican 'Transnationals' Voting in Upcoming Elections." Universal Press Syndicate, December 8.

Glick Schiller, Nina, and Georges Fouron. 1998. "Transnational Lives and National Identities: The Identity Politics of Haitian Immigrants." In *Transnationalism from Below*, edited by M. P. Smith and L. E. Guarnizo, 130–63. New Brunswick, N.J.: Transaction.

Goldring, Luin. 1996. "Blurring Borders: Constructing Transnational Community in the Process of Mexico-US Migration." *Research in Community Sociology* 6: 69–104.

——. 1998. "The Power of Status in Transnational Social Fields." In *Transnationalism from Below*, edited by M. P. Smith and L. E. Guarnizo, 165–95. New Brunswick, N.J.: Transaction.

——. 2001a. "Disaggregating Transnational Social Spaces: Gender, Place, and Citizenship in Mexico-US Transnational Spaces." In *New Transnational Social Spaces: International Migration and Transnational Companies in the Early Twenty-first Century*, edited by L. Pries, 59–76. New York: Routledge.

——. 2001b. "The Gender and Geography of Citizenship in Mexico-U.S. Transnational Spaces." *Identities: Global Studies in Culture and Power* 7: 501–37.

——. 2002. "The Mexican State and Transnational Organizations: Negotiating the Boundaries of Membership and Participation." *Latin American Research Review* 37, no. 3: 55–99.

——. 2003. "Gender, Status, and the State in Transnational Spaces: The Gendering of Political Participation and Mexican Hometown Associations." In *Gender and U.S. Immigration: Contemporary Trends*, edited by P. Hondagneu-Sotelo, 341–58. Berkeley: University of California Press.

——. 2004. "Family and Collective Remittances to Mexico: A Multi-dimensional Typology." *Development and Change* 35, no. 4: 799–840.

Gómez, Guadalupe. 2001. "Planes y proyectos de desarrollo emprendidos por los clubes zacatecanos en los EE.UU." Paper presented at "Mexico's National Forum on Immigration," Los Angeles, California, July 13.

Gómez Arnau, Remedios, and Paz Trigueros. 1999. "Comunidades transnacionales e iniciativas para fortalecer las relaciones con las comunidades mexicanas en los Estados Unidos." In *Migración México-Estados Unidos: Opciones de política*. Mexico City: Secretaría de Gobernación, Secretaría de Relaciones Exteriores y Consejo Nacional de Población.

González, Carmen. 2002. "Quieren candidatear a Lupe Gómez." *Imagen*, December 30.

——. 2003. "Acusan de traidor a Andrés Bermúdez." *Imagen*, January 10.

Gonzalez Amador, Roberto. 2005. "Seguir la actual política económica, sugiere Estados Unidos." *La Jornada*, December 16.

González Gutiérrez, Carlos. 1995. "La organización de los inmigrantes mexicanos en Los Ángeles: La lealtad de los oriundos." *Revista Mexicana de Política Exterior* 46: 59–101.

——. 1999. "Fostering Identities: Mexico's Relations with Its Diaspora." *Journal of American History* 86, no. 2: 545–67.

——. 2003. "Las relaciones de México con su diáspora: En busca de una política de estado." In *En la frontera del imperio*, edited by R. Fernández de Castro, 165–75. Mexico City: Ariel.

Group of Eight. 2004. "Fact Sheet: Applying the Power of Entrepreneurship to the Eradication of Poverty." Paper presented at "Sea Island Summit," Sea Island, Georgia, June 9.

Grover, Marcie. 2001. "A Man with Two Countries." *Reporter*, July 12.

Guarnizo, Luis Eduardo. 1997. "The Emergence of a Transnational Social Formation and the Mirage of Return Migration among Dominican Transmigrants." *Identities: Global Studies in Culture and Power* 4, no. 2: 281–322.

——. 1998. "The Rise of Transnational Social Formations: Mexican and Dominican State Responses to Transnational Migration." *Political Power and Social Theory* 12: 45–94.

——. 2001. "On the Political Participation of Transnational Migrants: Old Practices and New Trends." In *E Pluribus Unum? Contemporary and Historical Perspectives on Immigrant Political Incorporation*, edited by G. Gerstle and J. Mollenkopf, 213–63. New York: Russell Sage Foundation.

——. 2003. "The Economics of Transnational Living." *International Migration Review* 37, no. 3: 666–99.

Guarnizo, Luis Eduardo, Alejandro Portes, and William Haller. 2003. "Assimilation and Transnationalism: Determinants of Transnational Political Action among Contemporary Migrants." *American Journal of Sociology* 108: 1211–48.

Guarnizo, Luis Eduardo, and Michael Peter Smith. 1998. "The Locations of Transnationalism." In *Transnationalism from Below*, edited by M. P. Smith and L. E. Guarnizo, 3–34. New Brunswick, N.J.: Transaction.

Hannerz, Ulf. 1998. "Transnational Research." In *Handbook of Methods in Cultural Anthropology*, edited by H. R. Bernard, 235–56. Walnut Creek, Calif.: Altamira Press.

Harvey, Neil. 2001. "Globalisation and Resistance in Post–Cold War Mexico: Difference, Citizenship and Biodiversity Conflicts in Chiapas." *Third World Quarterly* 22, no. 6: 1045–61.

Hecht, Peter. 2005. "A Drive for Clout: Community Groups Representing Mexican Immigrants Form a Confederation to Influence Public Policy in California." *Sacramento Bee*, August 29, A1.

Held, David. 1991. "Democracy, the Nation-State, and the Global System." *Economy and Society* 20, no. 2: 138–72.

Held, David A., Anthony G. McGrew, David Goldblatt, and Jonathan Perraton, eds. 1999. *Global Transformations: Politics, Economics, and Culture*. Stanford: Stanford University Press.

Hendricks, Tyche. 2006. "Mexicans Abroad Prepare for July Election." *San Francisco Chronicle*, January 15, A2.

Hernández, María del Refugio. 2002. "Operará Bermúdez la campaña presidencial de Monreal en EU." *Imagen*, December 29.

Hernández-Coss, Raúl. 2005. *The U.S.-Mexico Remittance Corridor: Lessons on Shifting from Informal to Formal Transfer Systems*. Washington, D.C.: World Bank.

Hirschman, Albert O. 1970. *Exit, Voice, and Loyalty: Responses to Decline in Firms, Organizations, and States*. Cambridge: Harvard University Press.

Hondagneu-Sotelo, Pierrette. 2003. "Gender and Immigration: A Retrospective and Introduction." In *Gender and U.S. Immigration: Contemporary Trends*, edited by P. Hondagneu-Sotelo, 3–19. Berkeley: University of California Press.

Hua, Vanessa. 2002. "Family Values." *San Francisco Chronicle*, September 22, G3.

Huntington, Samuel P. 2004a. "The Hispanic Challenge." *Foreign Policy* (March–April): 30–45.

——. 2004b. *Who Are We? The Challenge to America's National Identity*. New York: Simon and Schuster.

Imagen. 2002. "Anuncia gobierno programa 'Invierte en México.' " *Imagen*, July 7.

Imaz, Cecilia. 2006. *La nación mexicana transfronteras: Impactos sociopolíticos en México de la emigración a Estados Unidos.* Mexico City: Universidad Nacional Autónoma de México.

Instituto Federal Electoral. 1998. *Informe final de la Comision de Especialistas que estudia las modalidades del voto de los mexicanos en el extranjero.* Mexico City: Instituto Federal Electoral.

———. 2006a. "Estadístico por país de residencia de los ciudadanos inscritos en la LNERE." Mexico City: Instituto Federal Electoral.

———. 2006b. "Informe de los resultados de la votación emitida por los mexicanos residentes en el extranjero." Mexico City: Instituto Federal Electoral.

Inter-American Dialogue. 2005. "Press Advisory: Launch of Mexico 4×1 Program." October 12.

Iskander, Natasha. 2005. "Social Learning as a Productive Project: Zacatecas and Guanajuato's Cautionary Tales." Paper presented at "International Conference on Migration, Remittances and the Economic Development of Sending Countries," Marrakech, Morocco, February 23–25.

Itzigsohn, José. 2000. "Immigration and the Boundaries of Citizenship: The Institutions of Immigrants' Political Transnationalism." *International Migration Review* 34, no. 4: 1126–54.

Itzigsohn, José, Carlos Dore Cabral, Esther Hernández Medina, and Obed Vázquez. 1999. "Mapping Dominican Transnationalism: Narrow and Broad Transnational Practices." *Ethnic and Racial Studies* 22, no. 2: 316–39.

Itzigsohn, José, and Silvia Giorguli-Saucedo. 2005. "Incorporation, Transnationalism, and Gender: Immigrant Incorporation and Transnational Participation as Gendered Processes." *International Migration Review* 39, no. 4: 895–920.

Jiménez, Efraín. 2004. "Presentación en Holanda." Paper presented at the conference "The Role of Migrants and Their Remittances in Development," Noordwijk, The Netherlands, November 19–20.

Jones, Richard C. 1995. *Ambivalent Journey: U.S. Migration and Economic Mobility in North-Central Mexico.* Tucson: University of Arizona Press.

Jones-Correa, Michael. 2005. "Mexican Migrants and Their Relation to U.S. Civil Society." Paper presented at the conference "Mexican Migrant Social and Civic Participation in the United States," Woodrow Wilson International Center for Scholars, Washington, D.C, November 4–5.

Kakutani, Michiko. 2004. "An Identity Crisis for Norman Rockwell America." *New York Times*, May 28, B27.

Kaldor, Mary. 2003. *Global Civil Society: An Answer to War.* Malden, Mass.: Blackwell.

Kasinitz, Philip, Mary C. Waters, John M. Mollenkopf, and Merih Anil. 2002. "Transnationalism and the Children of Immigrants in Contemporary New York." In *The Changing Face of Home: The Transnational Lives of the Second Generation*, edited by P. Levitt and M. C. Waters, 96–122. New York: Russell Sage Foundation Press.

Kearney, Michael. 1991. "Borders and Boundaries of State and Self at the End of Empire." *Journal of Historical Sociology* 4, no. 1: 52–74.

———. 1995a. "The Effects of Global Culture, Economy, and Migration on Mixtec Identity in Oaxacalifornia." In *The Bubbling Cauldron*, edited by M. P. Smith and J. R. Feagin, 226–42. Minneapolis: University of Minnesota Press.

———. 1995b. "The Local and the Global: The Anthropology of Globalization and Transnationalism." *Annual Review of Anthropology* 24: 547–66.

Keck, Margeret E., and Kathryn Sikkink. 1998. *Activists beyond Borders: Advocacy Networks in International Politics*. Ithaca: Cornell University Press.

Khagram, Sanjeev, James V. Riker, and Kathryn Sikkink. 2002. "From Santiago to Seattle: Transnational Advocacy Groups Restructuring World Politics." In *Restructuring World Politics: Transnational Social Movements, Networks, and Norms*, edited by S. Khagram, J. V. Riker, and K. Sikkink, 3–23. Minneapolis: University of Minnesota Press.

Kraul, Chris. 2004. "Hopes of Office Lure Migrants Home." *Los Angeles Times*, July 4, A3.

Laguerre, Michel S. 1999. "State, Diaspora, and Transnational Politics: Haiti Reconceptualized." *Millennium* 28, no. 3: 633–51.

La Jornada. 2003. "La 'cuota migrante' para el gobernador." *La Jornada*, March 23.

Landolt, Patricia, and Luin Goldring. 2006. "Activist Dialogues and the Production of Refugee Political Transnationalism: Chileans, Colombians, and Non-Migrant Civil Society in Canada." Paper presented at "Segundo Coloquio Internacional sobre Migración y Desarrollo: Migración, Transnacionalismo y Transformación Social," Cocoyoc, Morelos, Mexico, October 26–28.

Lanly, Guillaume, and M. Basilia Valenzuela Varela. 2004. *Clubes de migrantes oriundos mexicanos en los Estados Unidos: La política transnacional de la nueva sociedad civil migrante*. Zapopan, Jalisco, Mexico: Universidad de Guadalajara, Centro Universitario de Ciencias Económico Administrativas.

Levitt, Peggy. 2001a. "Transnational Migration: Taking Stock and Future Directions." *Global Networks* 1, no. 3: 195–216.

———. 2001b. *The Transnational Villagers*. Berkeley: University of California Press.

———. 2004. "Transnational Migrants: When Home Means More Than One Country." *Migration Information Source*, October 1.

Levitt, Peggy, and Nina Glick Schiller. 2004. "Conceptualizing Simultaneity: A Transnational Social Field Perspective on Society." *International Migration Review* 38, no. 3: 1002–39.

Lipschutz, Ronnie. 1992. "Reconstructing World Politics: The Emergence of Global Civil Society." *Millennium* 21, no. 3: 389–420.

Lister, Ruth. 2001. "Citizenship and Gender." In *The Blackwell Companion to Political Sociology*, edited by K. Nash and A. Scott, 323–32. Oxford: Blackwell.

López Dóriga, Joaquín. 2001. "Juan Hernández es uno de esos personajes . . ." Available at http://www.radioformula.com.mx/Programas/LopezDoriga/articulos.asp?ID=6266.

López Monjardín, Adriana. 2003. "Las élites políticas mexicanas: A 'sacar raja' de la guerra." *Rebeldía* 5: 22–28.

Lozano Ascencio, Fernando. 2004a. "Current Trends in Migrants' Remittances in Latin America and the Caribbean: An Evaluation of the Social and Economic Importance." Paper presented at the conference "Migrants' Remittances: An Alternative for Latin America and the Caribbean?" Caracas, Venezuela, July 26–27.

———. 2004b. "Tendencias recientes de las remesas de los migrantes mexicanos en Estados Unidos." Working Paper No. 99. La Jolla: Center for Comparative Immigration Studies, University of California, San Diego.

Lozano Ascencio, Fernando, and Fidel Olivera Lozano. 2005. "Impacto económico de la remesas en México: Un balance necesario." Paper presented at the conference "Problemas y desafíos de la migración y el desarrollo en América," Cuernavaca, Mexico, April 7–9.

Mahler, Sarah J. 1998. "Theoretical and Empirical Contributions toward a Research Agenda for Transnationalism." In *Transnationalism from Below*, edited by M. P. Smith and L. E. Guarnizo, 64–100. New Brunswick, N.J.: Transaction.

———. 1999. "Engendering Transnational Migration—A Case Study of Salvadorans." *American Behavioral Scientist* 42, no. 4: 690–719.

Mahler, Sarah J., and Patricia R. Pessar. 2001. "Gendered Geographies of Power: Analyzing Gender across Transnational Spaces." *Identities* 7, no. 4: 441–59.

———. 2006. "Gender Matters: Ethnographers Bring Gender from the Periphery toward the Core of Migration Studies." *International Migration Review* 40, no. 1: 27–63.

Manza, Jeff, and Christopher Uggen. 2006. *Locked Out: Felon Disenfranchisement and American Democracy*. New York: Oxford University Press.

Marcelli, Enrico A., and Wayne A. Cornelius. 2005. "Immigrant Voting in Home-Country Elections: Potential Consequences of Extending the Franchise to Expatriate Mexicans Residing in the United States." *Mexican Studies/Estudios Mexicanos* 21, no. 2: 429–60.

Marcus, George E. 1989. "Imagining the Whole: Ethnography's Contemporary Efforts to Situate Itself." *Critique of Anthropology* 9, no. 3: 7–30.

Marcus, George E., and Michael M. J. Fisher. 1986 [1999]. *Anthropology as Cultural Critique: An Experimental Moment in the Human Sciences*. Chicago, Ill.: University of Chicago Press.

Martinez Saldaña, Jesús. 1998. "In Search of Our Lost Citizenship: Mexican Immigrants, the Right to Vote, and the Transition to Democracy in Mexico." Working Paper No. 20. Santa Cruz: Chicano/Latino Research Center, University of California, Santa Cruz.

———. 1999. "Prólogo." In *Los mexicanos y el voto sin fronteras*, edited by R. R. Pineda. Chicago: Salsedo Press.

———. 2002. "Participación política migrante: Praxis cotidiana de ciudadanos excluidos." In *La dimensión política de la migración mexicana*, edited by L. Calderón Chelius and J. Martínez Saldaña, 159–330. Mexico City: Instituto de Investigaciones Dr. José Luis Mora.

———. 2003a. "Los Olvidados Become Heroes: The Evolution of Mexico's Policies towards Citizens Abroad." In *International Migration and Sending Countries: Perceptions, Policies and Transnational Relations*, edited by E. Østergaard-Nielsen, 33–56. New York: Palgrave Macmillan.

———. 2003b. "Reclamando el poder: Los ciudadanos en el exterior y su impacto en la política mexicana." *Migraciones Internacionales* 2, no. 2: 96–120.

Massey, Douglas. 2004. "Review of Samuel P. Huntington *Who Are We?*" *Population and Development Review* 30, no. 3: 543–48.

Massey, Douglas, Rafael Alarcón, Jorge Durand, and Humberto González. 1987. *Return to Aztlan: The Social Process of International Migration from Western Mexico*. Berkeley: University of California Press.

Massey, Douglas S., and Emilio Parado. 1998. "International Migration and Business Formation in Mexico." *Social Science Quarterly* 79, no. 1: 1–20.

McMichael, Philip. 2000. *Development and Social Change: A Global Perspective*. 2nd ed. Thousand Oaks, Calif.: Pine Forge Press.

Mena, Jennifer. 2001. "3 Men, 2 Nations, 1 Dream." *Los Angeles Times*, June 30, A1.

Menand, Louis. 2004. "Patriot Games: The New Nativism of Samuel P. Huntington." *New Yorker*, May 17.

Mestries, Francis. 1998. "Tradición migratoria y organización comunitaria: El caso de Zacatecas." In *Población, desarrollo y globalización*, edited by R. M. Zenteno, 165–85. Tijuana: Sociedad Mexicana de Demografía; El Colegio de la Frontera Norte.

Mexican American Legal Defense and Education Fund. 2005. "Hometown Association Leadership Program Overview." Policy document provided to the authors. Los Angeles:MALDEF.

Middlebrook, Kevin J., ed. 2001. *Party Politics and the Struggle for Democracy in Mexico: National and State-Level Analyses of the Partido Acción Nacional*. La Jolla: Center for US-Mexican Studies, University of California, San Diego.

Mines, Richard. 1981. *Developing a Community Tradition of Migration to the United States: A Field Study in Rural Zacatecas, Mexico, and California Settlement Areas*. La Jolla: Program in United States-Mexican Studies, University of California, San Diego.

Moctezuma Longoria, Miguel. 2002a. "Los migrantes mexicanos en los Estados Unidos y la inversión productiva en México." *Migraciones Internacionales* 1, no. 3: 149–62.

———. 2002b. "La participación política de los migrantes mexicanos: La experiencia de Zacatecas." Paper presented at "Second Colloquium on International Migration: Mexico-California," University of California, Berkeley, March 29.

———. 2003a. "The Migrant Club El Remolino: A Bi-national Community Experience." In *Confronting Globalization: Economic Integration and Popular Resistance in Mexico*, edited by T. A. Wise, H. Salazar, and L. Carlsen, 195–210. Bloomfield, Conn.: Kumarian Press.

———. 2003b. "La voz de los actores: Ley migrante y Zacatecas." *Migración y Desarrollo* 1. Available at http://meme.phpwebhosting.com/~migracion/modules/ve1/Lavozdelosactores2.pdf.

———. 2004. "Construcción extraterritorial de la ciudadanía sustantiva y Ley Migrante de Zacatecas." In *La puerta que llama: El voto de los mexicanos en el extranjero*, edited by G. B. Moreno, 279–96. Mexico City: Senado de la República.

———. 2005. "Morfología y desarrollo de las asociaciones de migrantes mexicanos en Estados Unidos: Un sujeto social y político extraterritorial." *Migracion y Desarrollo* 5. Available at http://meme.phpwebhosting.com/~migracion/modules/ve5/3.pdf.

———. N.d. "Membresia, ciudadania y participación política de los mexicanos en el extranjero." Unpublished manuscript.

Mouffe, Chantal. 1988. "Radical Democracy: Modern or Postmodern?" In *Universal Abandon? The Politics of Postmodernism*, edited by A. Ross, 31–45. Minneapolis: University of Minnesota Press.

Multilateral Investment Fund. 2005. "Remittances 2004: Transforming Labor Markets and Promoting Financial Democracy." Paper presented at the conference "Sending Money Home: The 2004 Map of Remittance Flows to Latin America," New York, March 24.

Nevins, Joseph. 2002. *Operation Gatekeeper: The Rise of the "Illegal Alien" and the Making of the U.S.-Mexico Boundary*. New York: Routledge.

Nichols, Sandra. 2000. "Mexican Immigration and Transnational Networks in Napa, California." Paper presented at "Workshop on Immigration and the Changing Face of Rural California," University of California, Davis, October 5–6.

Olesen, Thomas. 2005. *International Zapatismo: The Social Construction of Solidarity in the Age of Globalization*. London: Zed Books.

Ong, Aihwa. 1999. *Flexible Citizenship: The Cultural Logics of Transnationality*. Durham: Duke University Press.

Ong, Aihwa, and Donald Macon Nonini, eds. 1997. *Ungrounded Empires: The Cultural Politics of Modern Chinese Transnationalism*. New York: Routledge.

Orozco, Graciela, Esther González, and Roger Díaz de Cossío. 2000. *Las organizaciones mexicano-americanas, hispanas y mexicanas en Estados Unidos*. Mexico City: Centro de Estudios Migratorios y Fundación Solidaridad Mexicano Americana.

Orozco, Manuel. 2000. "Latino Hometown Associations as Agents of Development in Latin America." *AD/TRPI Working Paper*. Washington, D.C.: Inter-American Dialogue.

Østergaard-Nielsen, Eva, ed. 2003a. *International Migration and Sending Countries: Perceptions, Policies, and Transnational Relations*. New York: Palgrave Macmillan.

——. 2003b. "The Politics of Migrants' Transnational Political Practices." *International Migration Review* 37, no. 3: 760–86.

Partnership for Prosperity. 2002. "Report to President Vicente Fox and President George W. Bush: Creating Prosperity through Partnership." Monterrey, Mexico, March 22.

Peck, Jamie, and Adam Tickell. 2002. "Neoliberalizing Space." *Antipode* 34, no. 3: 380–404.

Peschard, Jacqueline. 2005. "El voto de los mexicanos en el extranjero." *Datamex: Análisis de Coyuntura Mensual sobre México* 6, no. 3: 1–4.

Pessar, Patricia R., and Sarah J. Mahler. 2003. "Transnational Migration: Bringing Gender In." *International Migration Review* 37, no. 3: 812–46.

Petras, James. 1997. "Imperialism and NGOs in Latin America." *Monthly Review* 49, no. 7: 10–33.

Pew Hispanic Center. 2005. "Survey of Mexican Migrants: Attitudes about Voting in Mexican Elections and Ties to Mexico." Washington, D.C.: Pew Hispanic Center.

——. 2006. "Survey of Mexicans Living in the U.S. on Absentee Voting in Mexican Elections." Washington, D.C.: Pew Hispanic Center.

Piper, Nicola, and Anders Uhlin. 2003. *Transnational Activism in Asia: Problems of Power and Democracy*. New York: Routledge.

Polanyi, Karl. 2001. *The Great Transformation: The Political and Economic Origins of Our Time*. Boston: Beacon.

Portes, Alejandro. 1996a. "Global Villagers: The Rise of Transnational Communities." *American Prospect* 2: 74–77.

———. 1996b. "Transnational Communities: Their Emergence and Significance in the Contemporary World System." Working Paper Series No. 16. Baltimore: Program in Comparative and International Development, Department of Sociology, Johns Hopkins University.

———. 1997. "Neoliberalism and the Sociology of Development: Emerging Trends and Unanticipated Facts." *Population and Development Review* 23, no. 2: 229–59.

———. 1998. "Globalization from Below: The Rise of Transnational Communities." Working Paper WPTC 98–01. Oxford: Transnational Communities Programme, University of Oxford.

———. 1999. "Conclusion: Towards a New World—the Origins and Effects of Transnational Activity." *Ethnic and Racial Studies* 22, no. 2: 463–77.

Portes, Alejandro, Luis Eduardo Guarnizo, and Patricia Landolt. 1999. "The Study of Transnationalism: Pitfalls and Promise of an Emergent Research Field." *Ethnic and Racial Studies* 22, no. 2: 217–35.

Quiñones, Sam. 1999. "Mexico Emigrants Spin a Bold Idea." *San Francisco Examiner*, June 20, A1.

———. 2001. "Political Punch from Abroad." *San Francisco Chronicle*, April 29, A14.

———. 2002. "Home, Tense Home: Turbulent Times in Local Zacatecan Clubs." *L.A. Weekly*, March 6.

Radcliffe, Sarah. 2005. "Neoliberalism as We Knew It, But Not in Conditions of Its Own Choosing: A Commentary." *Environment and Planning* A, no. 37: 323–29.

Ramikrishnan, Karthrick S., and Celia Viramontes. 2006. "Civic Inequalities: Immigrant Volunteerism and Community Organizations in California." Report of the Public Policy Institute of California. Available at http://www.ppic.org/content/pubs/report/R_706KRR.pdf.

Rivera-Salgado, Gaspar. 1999. "Binational Organizations of Mexican Migrants in the United States." *Social Justice* 26, no. 3: 27–38.

———. 2000. "Transnational Political Strategies: The Case of Mexican Indigenous Migrants." In *Immigration Research for a New Century*, edited by N. Foner, R. Rumbault, and S. Gold, 134–56. New York: Russell Sage Foundation.

———. 2006. "Mexican Migrant Organizations." In *Invisible No More: Mexican Migrant Civic Participation in the United States*, edited by X. Bada, J. Fox, and A. Selee, 5–8. Washington, D.C.: Woodrow Wilson International Center for Scholars.

Rivera-Salgado, Gaspar, Xochitl Bada, and Luis Escala Rabadán. 2005. "Mexican Migrant Civic and Political Participation in the U.S." Paper presented at the conference "Mexican Migrant Social and Civic Participation in the United States," Woodrow Wilson International Center for Scholars, Washington, D.C., November 4–5.

Rivera-Salgado, Gaspar, and Luis Escala Rabadán. 2004. "Collective Identity and Organizational Strategies among Indigenous and Mestizo Mexican Migrants." In *Indigenous Mexican Migrants in the United States*, edited by J. Fox and G. Rivera-Salgado, 145–78. La Jolla: Center for U.S.-Mexican Studies and Center for Comparative Immigration Studies, University of California, San Diego.

Rockefeller Foundation. 2003. "2003 Rockefeller Foundation Annual Report: Expanding Opportunity." New York: Rockefeller Foundation.

Rodriguez, Olga R. 2005. "Rough Going: Migrant Mayor Finds Obstacles in Mexican Town." *Davis Enterprise*, September 19, A1.

Rodríguez Oceguera, Primitivo. 2005. "¿Así se ganó el voto!" *MX Sin Fronteras* 20: 14–20.

Rodríguez Ramírez, Héctor. 2004. "Migración, remesas y pobreza en Zacatecas." Available at http://www.mty.itesm.mx/egap/centros/caep/imagenes/MigracionZacatecas.pdf.

Ross Pineda, Raúl. 1999. *Los mexicanos y el voto sin fronteras*. Chicago: Salsedo Press.

Sachs, Wolfgang, ed. 1992. *The Development Dictionary: A Guide to Knowledge as Power*. London: Zed Books.

Santamaría Gómez, Arturo. 2003. "Politics without Borders or Postmodern Nationality: Mexican Immigration to the United States." *Latin American Perspectives* 30, no. 2: 274–94.

Sassen, Saskia. 1988. *The Mobility of Labor and Capital*. Cambridge: Cambridge University Press.

Schein, Louisa. 1998a. "Forged Transnationality and Oppositional Cosmopolitanism." In *Transnationalism from Below*, edited by M. P. Smith and L. E. Guarnizo, 291–313. New Brunswick, N.J.: Transaction.

———. 1998b. "Importing Miao Brethren to Hmong America: A Not So Stateless Transnationalism." In *Cosmopolitics: Thinking and Feeling beyond the Nation*, edited by P. Cheah and B. Robbins, 163–91. Minneapolis: University of Minnesota Press.

Schild, Verónica. 1998. "Market Citizenship and the 'New Democracies': The Ambiguous Legacies of Contemporary Chilean Women's Movements." *Social Politics: International Studies in Gender, State and Society* 5, no. 2: 232–49.

Seidman, Gay. 1999. "Gendered Citizenship: South Africa's Democratic Transition and the Construction of a Gendered State." *Gender and Society* 13, no. 3: 287–307.

Sherman, Rachel. 1999. "From State Introversion to State Extension in Mexico: Modes of Emigrant Incorporation, 1900–1997." *Theory and Society* 28: 835–878.

Shore, Elena. 2005. "Mexican State Gains First Representative for California Migrants." *Pacific News Service*, January 14. Available at http://news.pacificnews.org/news/view_article.html?article_id=b6f072ea68cb8a253ca98648ab8541d9.

Smith, Michael Peter. 1994. "Can You Imagine? Transnational Migration and the Globalization of Grassroots Politics." *Social Text* 39: 15–33.

———. 1999. "Transnationalism and the City." In *The Urban Moment: Cosmopolitan Essays on the Late-20th-Century City*, edited by R. A. Beauregard and S. Body-Gendrot, 119–39. Thousand Oaks, Calif.: Sage Publications.

———. 2001. *Transnational Urbanism: Locating Globalization*. Malden, Mass.: Blackwell.

———. 2003a. "The Social Construction of Transnational Citizenship." *Journal of International Law and Policy* 9: 105–25.

———. 2003b. "Transnationalism, the State, and the Extraterritorial Citizen." *Politics and Society* 31, no. 4: 467–502.

———. 2005a. "From Context to Text and Back Again: The Uses of Transnational Urbanism." *City & Society* 17, no. 1: 81–92.

———. 2005b. "Power in Place/Places of Power: Contextualizing Transnational Research." *City & Society* 17, no. 1: 5–34.

———. 2005c. "Transnational Urbanism Revisited." *Journal of Ethnic and Migration Studies* 31, no. 2: 235–44.

Smith, Michael Peter, and Luis Eduardo Guarnizo, eds. 1998. *Transnationalism from Below: Comparative Urban and Community Research*. Vol. 6. New Brunswick, N.J.: Transaction.

Smith, Michael Peter, and Bernadette Tarallo. 1995. "Proposition 187: Global Trend or Local Narrative? Explaining Anti-Immigrant Politics in California, Arizona, and Texas." *International Journal of Urban and Regional Research* 19, no. 4: 664–76.

Smith, Michael Peter, Bernadette Tarallo, and George Kagiwada. 1991. "Coloring California—New Asian Immigrant Households, Social Networks and the Local State." *International Journal of Urban and Regional Research* 15, no. 2: 250–68.

Smith, Robert C. 1995. "Los Ausentes Siempre Presentes: The Imagining, Making, and Politics of a Transnational Community between Ticuani, Puebla, Mexico, and New York City." PhD diss., Columbia University, New York.

———. 1998. "Transnational Localities: Community, Technology, and the Politics of Membership within the Context of Mexico and U.S. Migration." In *Transnationalism from Below*, edited by M. P. Smith and L. E. Guarnizo, 196–238. New Brunswick, N.J.: Transaction.

———. 2001. "Local-Level Transnational Life in Rattwik, Sweden, and Ticuani, Mexico: An Essay in Historical Retrieval." In *New Transnational Social Spaces: International Migration and Transnational Companies in the Early Twenty-first Century*, edited by L. Pries, 37–58. New York: Routledge.

———. 2003a. "Diasporic Memberships in Historical Perspective: Comparative Insights from the Mexican, Italian and Polish Cases." *International Migration Review* 37, no. 3: 724–60.

———. 2003b. "Migrant Membership as an Instituted Process: Transnationalization, the State, and the Extra-territorial Conduct of Mexican Politics." *International Migration Review* 37, no. 2: 297–343.

———. 2005. *Mexican New York: Transnational Lives of New Immigrants*. Berkeley: University of California Press.

Soysal, Yasemin N. 1994. *Limits of Citizenship: Migrants and Postnational Membership in Europe*. Chicago: University of Chicago Press.

Spencer, Neville. 2001. "Mexico's New Government: How Much Is New?" *Venceremos* 468, February 28, 64.

Sullivan, Kevin. 2001. "Mexico Reverses Triumphant Return of 'Tomato King'." *Washington Post*, September 11, A18.

Tarrow, Sidney. 1998. *Power in Movement: Social Movements and Contentious Politics*. 2nd ed. Cambridge: Cambridge University Press.

———. 2005. *The New Transnational Activism*. New York: Cambridge University Press.

Terry, Donald F., and Steven R. Wilson, eds. 2005. *Beyond Small Change: Making Migrant Remittances Count*. Washington, D.C.: Inter-American Development Bank.

Thelen, David. 2000. "How Natural Are National and Transnational Citizenship?" *Indiana Journal of Global Legal Studies* 7: 549.

Tiechart, Joshua. 1981. "A Town Divided: Economic Stratification and Social Relations in a Mexican Migrant Community." *Social Problems* 29, no. 4: 411–23.

Torres, Federico. 2001. "Migrants' Capital for Small-Scale Infrastructure and Small Enterprise Development in Mexico." Document prepared for the World Bank. Available at http://www1.worldbank.org/wbiep/decentralization/laclib/remittances.pdf.

Tribunal Electoral del Poder Judicial de la Federación. 2001. *Juicio de Revisión Constitucional Electoral: Expediente SUP-JRC-170/2001*. Mexico City: Tribunal Electoral del Poder Judicial de la Federación.

Vacio, Ana María. 2001. " 'El Rey del Tomate': Buscaré a Fox." *El Sol de Zacatecas*, September 10.

Waldinger, Roger, and David Fitzgerald. 2004. "Transnationalism in Question." *American Journal of Sociology* 109, no. 5: 1177–95.

Wapner, Paul. 1995. "Politics beyond the State: Environmental Activism and World Civic Politics." *World Politics* 47: 311–40.

Wimmer, Andreas, and Nina Glick Schiller. 2002. "Methodological Nationalism and Beyond: Nation-State Building, Migration and the Social Sciences." *Global Networks* 2, no. 4: 301–34.

Wolfe, Alan. 2004. "Native Son: Samuel Huntington Defends the Homeland." *Foreign Affairs* (May–June): 120–25.

Woo Morales, Ofelia. 2001. *Las mujeres también nos vamos al Norte*. Guadalajara: Universidad de Guadalajara.

Yaworsky, William. 2005. "At the Whim of the State: Neoliberalism and Nongovernmental Organizations in Guerrero, Mexico." *Mexican Studies/Estudios Mexicanos* 21, no. 2: 403–27.

Zabin, Carol, and Luis Escala Rabadán. 1998. "Mexican Hometown Associations and Mexican Immigrant Political Empowerment in Los Angeles." Report prepared for the Aspen Institute, Nonprofit Sector Research Fund.

Index

Page references in italics denote maps and photographs.